Creative research com

Manchester University Press

Creative research communication

Theory and practice

Clare Wilkinson and Emma Weitkamp

Manchester University Press

Published by Manchester University Press
Altrincham Street, Manchester M1 7JA

www.manchesteruniversitypress.co.uk

British Library Cataloguing-in-Publication Data
A catalogue record for this book is available from the British Library

Library of Congress Cataloging-in-Publication Data applied for

ISBN 978 0 7190 9651 8 paperback

First published 2016

Typeset in Sabon by
Servis Filmsetting Ltd, Stockport, Cheshire
Printed in Great Britain by
Bell & Bain Ltd, Glasgow

Contents

Figures, tables, boxes and case studies

Figures

Tables

Boxes

Case studies

Acknowledgements

Many people have contributed to this volume, directly and indirectly. We would like to thank all those who spoke to us as we developed the case studies and agreed for their work to be included in this book. We would also like to thank all the students we have worked with over the years who have inspired and challenged us in our conceptualisation of the field. Through these challenges, these students have also indirectly highlighted the need for a book such as this that draws together the disparate strands of the field of research communication. We also acknowledge the projects we have drawn on as we developed this text; these projects demonstrate the rich diversity of research communication activities undertaken by academics and practitioners alike.

PART I

Introduction

I

Creative research communication

Internationally, public engagement and communication has become an important aspect of research and policymaking, allowing research establishments, and their researchers, to explore public perspectives on their work as well as providing access to research findings to wider publics. Alongside this, a considerable research communication and public engagement community has emerged, who are interested not only in the design, techniques and methods for research communication and engagement but also approaches to communicating creatively and evaluating the impact of such work. This community encompasses a broad range of disciplines, from practical engagers through to researchers studying how and why such practices emerge, as well as their wider influence and impact. The community is interested in research communication and public engagement activities emerging from a wide range of subject areas, particularly the sciences, but also the social sciences, humanities, mathematics and the arts. Though research communication activities are well established in the United Kingdom, there is extensive work occurring at an international level which warrants attention and sharing beyond national boundaries.

Science communication

Taking the sciences as a starting point, the time since the mid-1980s has seen an increased interest in how best to communicate scientific issues. Science communication, broadly understood to focus on the public communication of scientific subjects to non-experts, was brought to the fore by the highly influential Bodmer Report, titled *The Public Understanding of Science*, in 1985 (The Royal Society 1985), and subsequently the scientific community has been under sustained pressure to undertake public communication and engagement activities. That is not to say that communication did not play an important role before this time; in fact, as will be documented in Chapter 2, the sciences have a long record of attention to the role of communication and education. Nevertheless, the mid-1980s marked a resurgence of effort and thinking where science communication is concerned (Wilkinson, 2010). Scientists were not only encouraged to communicate their work but were provided with funding, training and support to go about this, with an assumption that improved communication would assist in resolving issues associated with poor public understanding. This paralleled work in formal educational contexts which, since the middle of the twentieth century, had sought to improve scientific literacy internationally (Wilkinson, 2010; DeBoer, 2000). However, as many scientists were considering the role of communication in their work for the first time, some approaches were marred by reliance on a theory which became known as the 'deficit model', an assumption that communication follows a straightforward and linear process, whereby the main problem to be solved is public ignorance of scientific issues (Wilkinson *et al.*, 2011a; Irwin, 2009; Trench, 2008). This distorted many complex scientific issues which were emerging at that time; issues that were not simply about understanding, but about motivation, trust, ethics and power, to name but a few of the complexities. Science communication then had two functions:

> Science communication has emerged in recent years as an area of research and practice in its own right. Its origins can be traced to a practical concern with how to disseminate scientific knowledge from specialist communities of scientists to diverse audiences such as policy-makers, journalists and wider publics. However, what started as a set of practical questions about how to communicate science soon bumped up against theoretical questions shared by the field of science and technology studies. (Doubleday, 2009: 26)

Thus by the turn of the millennium, science communication embraced a language of dialogue, context and engagement, alongside a more critical consideration of the role of research communication. No longer would science communication be only about communicating 'one way' (though this was and is still evident in many science communication approaches); instead there was to be room for consultation and participation (Wilkinson *et al.*, 2011a; Rowe and Frewer, 2005). Marked by a whole range of approaches, from dialogue events to online consultations, and citizens juries to consensus conferences, science mirrored trends occurring in many other fields by embracing (at least verbally) a broader agenda for engagement (Davies *et al.*, 2009; Chilvers, 2008; Davies, 2008).

At first many such communication and engagement initiatives were primarily focused on 'STEM' subjects (science, technology, engineering and maths), an acronym which originally emerged in the United States. Over time as the infrastructure for 'science' communication has increased, we have seen an extension of this conversation, with some now proposing a model which includes the arts and design: STEAM (science, technology, engineering and maths, art and design, or science, technology, engineering, art and mathematics, depending where you are based; see http://stemtostcam.org/, http://steam-notstem.com/ as examples). STREAM has also been proposed which would add religion and the arts to the mix, whilst STEMM also incorporates medicine. It is perhaps easy to overlook the role of the social sciences within these acronyms, perhaps on the assumption that they would fall within the 'science' category, but it is important to remember that such disciplines are rarely fully recognised within the typical 'science' communication activities encompassed in STEM agendas and therefore they may warrant an additional reminder.

Aside from an awareness of the acronyms (of which there are also many more iterations), there is the problem of distinguishing disciplines. Bastow *et al.* (2014) estimate there to be a multitude of disciplines that make up the social sciences, arts, humanities, science, technology and engineering – often with no standard international definition or consistency around which groupings feature where – for the purposes of research funding for example. This complex web of disciplines becomes further complicated by subjects, such as geography, that overlap the social sciences, arts and design, as well as STEM subjects (Bastow *et al.*, 2014). In some spaces disciplines will be collaborating, in others competing, and it is a network likely to become ever further complicated by the emergence of increasing multi- and trans-disciplinary working. While this may encourage an extension of science communication approaches to other disciplines and agendas, it is important not to forget that many disciplines are forging their own paths where research communication is concerned, and to recognise the unique features of some subject areas, as well as their commonalities.

The institutionalisation of public engagement

In the context of the United Kingdom, and to an extent Europe, we are currently in a period of initiatives which some have described as 'the institutionalisation of public engagement' (Maile and Griffiths, 2014a:16). Public engagement, loosely framed, involves researchers conversing with, listening to and engaging with non-experts. The institutionalising of this agenda would include initiatives such as the establishment of a

National Coordinating Centre for Public Engagement (NCCPE) in 2007 which sought to liaise with UK universities nationally to support their work with members of the public, as well as the inclusion of public engagement within impact criteria in the national Research Excellence Framework (Maile and Griffiths, 2014a). Public communication and engagement thus has the potential to influence a university both financially and in terms of its research ranking. We would add to these types of structural changes additions to funding criteria, which now promote the inclusion of research communication within research funding applications as 'pathways to impact' and increasingly seek to enable researchers to take ownership of engagement activities, rather than have them conducted by others on their behalf. For instance, a number of schemes that previously supported engagement activities on their own, post research, have now been encapsulated within more traditional research applications as part of dissemination, communication or engagement 'packages'. This means that the researcher must now take a more central role in the communication of their own research. As Maile and Griffiths (2014a:17 emphasis in original) describe, such approaches indicate not only an instrumental perspective of knowledge but also a *'centralised diktat*, rather than voluntary participation' where public engagement is concerned.

There are perhaps reasons why researchers from the arts, social sciences, design and other such disciplines (including the sciences) are wary of such developments. Whereas in the late 1990s it would have been a researcher's own choice and desire to communicate, sometimes in the face of a lack of support at department level, this offered them a certain freedom to use communication techniques of their choice, perhaps relating these to their disciplinary area or on their own terms. New institutional incentives to engage and communicate offer benefits in that researchers may be better recognised or supported in their activities, for instance through promotional criteria, but this may also change the quality, individuality and motivations for communicating publicly. Those researchers who hold communication as something central to their role, carry it out for personal enjoyment or who only see quite tangential benefits, may question the broader drivers and the impact they may have on the actual engagement that takes place. As such, research communication poses questions not only for individual researchers but also for their broader disciplinary homes.

Public disciplines

Beyond the boundaries of what is being encouraged by institutional and policy initiatives, a number of disciplines have been engaging in conversation around their own 'public' standing. Some of these conversations have included the idea of 'public' disciplines such as 'public sociology' and 'public criminology', encouraging professional disciplines to think about how they can engage with publics and stakeholders outside academia, and what responsibilities they have regarding wider public agendas (Loader and Sparks, 2011; Braga *et al.*, 2008; Sprague, 2008; Turner, 2007; Burawoy, 2005). These approaches seek to encourage academics to actively participate in public debates of relevance to their fields, providing their knowledge in more public ways (Burawoy, 2005).

It may seem surprising that certain areas of social science are now debating this type of public role, as it might be assumed that because they explore social issues, social scientists are more likely and able to communicate their work. However, some subjects, like crime and justice, sexuality or religion, can be controversial and, although this might make them particularly newsworthy, researchers may see themselves as needing to keep out of the debate. They can also be issues which have significant personal relevance to people, and some researchers may feel they are walking into a 'hot climate' if they communicate publicly about their research (Loader and Sparks, 2011: 2; Grauerholz and Baker-Sperry, 2007).

Nevertheless, a decade of increased financial and funding pressures across all subject areas has led to a heightened awareness of the need for a discipline to display its social worth, and there have been various discipline-based 'campaigns' which have lobbied for the importance of a particular field. This focus on demonstrating the public relevance of research is not without criticism. In the arts, for example, there is strong opposition from some researchers to what is perceived as an instrumental approach to arts funding, with artists calling for 'art for art's sake' (Belfiore and Bennett, 2008). Concerns particularly arise about funding streams that encourage artists to work with researchers from other disciplines with a view to helping to communicate their research, in what some artists perceive as a handmaiden role (see Chapter 5). Whether you are a social scientist, scientist, artist or engineer, deciding to communicate your work publicly is something that warrants careful consideration and planning on the part of the individual. Your discipline is now more likely to stand behind you, but at the same time individuals can face particular concerns when at the 'forefront' of that communication effort.

Public intellectuals

Aside from pressure to demonstrate the impact of research, there has also been a renewed interest in the role of academics as 'public intellectuals', particularly as public intellectuals are perceived to be in decline (Eliaeson and Kalleberg, 2008; Posner, 2003). Furedi's (2004: 2–3) critique of the role of universities and the level of public discussion they now generate describes a setting where intellectual furore has been marginalised, where art, culture and education are seen as instruments only of practical purpose and 'engines for economic growth'. He identifies this as an accident of the 'new ethos of managerialism that dominates cultural and intellectual life'. Whilst we might assume that calls on intellectuals to take a greater role in public life would naturally align with increased opportunities for research communication, there are some important aspects to bear in mind with regard to Furedi's argument. Crucially, he is critical of the way that knowledge is now frequently operationalised to appear 'ordinary': 'instead of affirming their authority, the cultural elites appear more interested in appearing relevant, accessible and in touch with popular opinion' (Furedi, 2004: 5–6). Intellectuals are therefore increasingly drawn to appear faceless and professionalised, which Furedi argues diminishes the cultural value of their work, their potential to be taken seriously or to be disruptive protagonists. Furedi explores the paradox that we live in a flourishing knowledge society where at the same time knowledge is being packaged in banal and mundane ways for marketing, consumption and transmission, with value placed in its receipt, above its content. Ever-expanding opportunities for life-long learning, formal education attendance and museum and cultural visits, according to Furedi (2004), may neglect their greater purpose and value. 'There is a new breed of university managers, museum and gallery directors, and "knowledge" entrepreneurs who regard the content of culture and ideas with indifference. Their concern is to use culture to achieve an objective that is quite separate from its inner content' (Furedi, 2004: 3). Furedi posits that 'a precondition for expanding genuine public engagement is the provision of standards equivalent to the best that society has to offer' (Furedi, 2004: 23–4). Thus, whilst Furedi (2004: 108) and others call on academics to fulfil the role of public intellectuals (Calhoun, 2009), they also speak against managerial agendas that see research communication from its instrumental perspective alone; 'bite-sized, easily standardized effort that can be easily measured, weighed and served to an infantilized public'.

This book explores ways that academics can begin to take on Furedi's challenge, stepping up to the role of public intellectuals, by participating in the public sphere through discussion of their research. Whether it is through contributing to political discourse or more practically to policymaking through provision of evidence (Chapter 8), participating in public debates and discussions either in person (Chapter 4) or through the media (Chapter 7), there are opportunities for researchers to take on the role of public intellectuals, contributing to society in many different ways beyond the direct benefits that their research may have. By considering the plurality of publics and their diverse needs and interests, it is quite possible to find a communications niche that neither offers up bite-sized chunks of research nor conceptualises the public as lacking the capacity to consider the myriad of issues raised by research, but instead explains and considers thoughtfully the value of research endeavours and their potential benefits to society.

Research online

Compared with when Furedi (2004) was admonishing academics to take on this public role, the opportunities for researchers to participate in the public sphere have changed dramatically, though many of these opportunities may more easily fulfil more simplistic managerial agendas rather than enable academics to take on the role of public intellectual. Twitter could not be a better example of a 'bite-sized effort', given that it requires research to be summarised for the public in 140 characters or less, though academics might use Twitter to promote more substantial blog contributions. Digital and social media have had an impact on researchers' professional practices in a broad variety of ways, from access to the latest literature, to research collaborations across continents and changes in how data can be accessed or manipulated, as well as the introduction of new research methods. The sheer proliferation of available information is perhaps the most obvious ramification for researchers' professional communication; for instance, some estimates suggest that in the field of medicine two new papers are published per minute (Chalkstream Communications, 2014). From a research communication perspective, however, digital and social media have also opened up opportunities to reach stakeholders and publics (see Chapters 6, 7 and 9). It is now straightforward to create a public blog and many researchers are actively using social media, both for professional communication and to make their research more widely available. However, the plethora of opportunities to communicate online brings challenges, in terms both of choosing the best platform and of generating a readership or followers. Managing and maintaining a strong digital profile also takes time, potentially eating into the periods available for other professional activities.

Research communicators

The years since the mid-1980s have therefore encapsulated many changes for researchers at all levels who are interested in communicating their research. Much has been learned in science communication about what does and doesn't work, and why, whilst other disciplines have been reflecting on their own role in research communication processes. From an individual perspective the students of today are more likely to see communication and engagement training featuring in their plans for the future; whilst the growing institutional and policy infrastructure to support and encourage communication and engagement, particularly when applied to research impact, is subtly altering the possible incentives and disincentives for participation. Thus, these are important times for research communication and, rather than respond only to 'diktats' which may diminish research communication to a tickbox exercise, we would see it as a time to embrace opportunities for creative research communication approaches and to prove their worth. This is an era to channel creatively away from metrics or 'one size fits all', and to engage in ways that work for you as an individual researcher in the context of your own disciplinary potential and desires, and that embrace and recognise the ways that people beyond the context of an organisation or university may creatively add to your research process as well as experience benefits of their own. This book seeks to create a space for creativity as one way to encourage the integrity of research communication activity, and to see research communication as an art, a craft or a conversation, as much as a science, a method or an attainment.

What is creativity?

Novel, new and imaginative are words often associated with creativity, which might be defined as the act of generating something inventive. Boden (2004) defines creativity as ideas or artefacts that are new, surprising and valuable. The use of 'valuable' in her definition suggests that for something to be creative it needs to be recognised as having some worth (whether monetary or in another domain, such as usefulness or visual appeal to the creator). Csikszentmihalyi (1996) also highlights that creativity needs to have some value to society. He explored creativity by interviewing exceptional thinkers, those whose contributions to their field are widely recognised, such as Nobel laureates. It is therefore not surprising that his definition draws out the exceptional aspects of creativity, arguing that creative individuals are those whose work is recognised by their peers and whose ideas are widely adopted in their fields (or more generally in society). Thus, Csikszentmihalyi (1996: 25) defines creativity as being 'to bring into existence something genuinely new that is valued enough to be added to culture'.

Most definitions of creativity now include this notion of value, either to society as a whole or to the relevant field of activity. Simply being novel is not sufficient: that novelty must be recognised by others, normally others with expertise in the field or domain. Amabile (1996) highlights the evaluative nature of this definition of creativity and its focus on the creative product or output, rather than on the processes by which such creative artefacts arise or on the people who create them. She also adds a condition to the definition of creativity that focuses on the process through which creative products arise: that they must be generated through heuristic rather than algorithmic processes. As Amabile (1996: 35) puts it, 'heuristic tasks are those not having a clear and readily identifiable path to solution – tasks for which algorithms must be developed'.

Csikszentmihalyi and Amabile, through their focus on novelty and recognition by a peer group, set the expectations of what would be judged to be a creative contribution higher than most research communication projects are likely to aim, particularly as creativity is rarely the primary purpose of research communication. So, in this context it is worth considering other definitions of creativity which might also shed some light on the value of creative communication approaches both to the research communicator and to those participating in the communication projects.

David Gauntlett, in his book *Making is Connecting*, suggests that what he calls 'everyday' creativity is part of what it means to be human, that we as a species inherently find creative acts both interesting and satisfying. 'Going through the thoughtful, physical process of making something – such as a video, a drawing, a decorated box, or a Lego model – an individual is given the opportunity to reflect, and to make their thoughts and feelings or experiences manifest and tangible' (Gauntlett, 2011: 4). Maslow (1970), in his theory of motivation, suggests creativity is part of self-actualisation, and many others have argued for some type of 'personal' creativity (e.g. Richards, 2007; Craft, 2003; Runco, 1996). Boden (2004) argues that everyone is creative to a degree and suggests that what is important to creativity is that the idea is new to the individual (rather than new to society as a whole). Gauntlett terms this 'everyday creativity', which he defines as:

> refer[ring] to a process which brings together at least one active human mind, and the material or digital world, in the activity of making something. The activity has not been done in this way by this person (or these people) before. The process may arouse various emotions, such as excitement and frustration, but most especially a feeling of joy. When witnessing and appreciating the output, people may sense the presence of the maker, and recognise those feelings. (Gauntlett, 2011: 70)

This level of everyday creativity is much more readily achieved, and one which we could aspire to in developing creative approaches to research communication. It focuses on the process of creating and the impacts that this may have on the maker(s) or communicator(s) and allows for the development of communication approaches that are new in a given context. Although the 'participants' don't feature in this definition beyond that they will recognise the feelings of the maker, it does allow for participants to become part of the project creation and to share in the satisfaction of participating in a creative experience.

We might, then, think of creativity as coming in different levels, from that which is widely acknowledged by society (the type of creativity discussed by Csikszentmihalyi) to that which is widely practised by individuals (as outlined by Gauntlett). These different levels can also be applied to research communications: some communication projects are recognised as truly innovative or ground breaking. These are the projects that 'go viral', with similar projects springing up elsewhere in the world or being adapted to new research contexts. Examples might be formats such as FameLab, which has spread widely throughout the world, or citizen science projects such as the Zooniverse projects that mobilise interested citizens to process data (and at the same time learn about the subject area). On a more individual level, there are many examples of creative approaches to communication, including blogs and websites run by individuals or research groups, outreach projects aimed at school children and research taken to unusual venues, such as music festivals. What makes these projects creative is the way that they combine elements of research communication in novel or unexpected ways and/or introduce new and unexpected aspects (such as creating open source instruments that allow communities to research local issues).

Why is creativity important in research communication?

Why would we want to invest the time and energy in coming up with a creative approach to communication rather than trundling out a tried and tested method? Such tried and tested approaches, by the simple fact that they've been done before and their bugs have been ironed out, are fairly low risk and can provide excellent opportunities for public communication and engagement. As research communication has increased it can be challenging to come up with something that is entirely original, and there is certainly nothing wrong with using communication approaches that have been shown to work in the past.

However, research itself is a creative act in the sense that it involves generating and exploring ideas. Most researchers, at times, enter what Csikszentmihalyi (1996) calls 'flow': a state of pleasure and passion associated with complete focus on a task; a sense of clarity that everything is clicking into place. He argues that we should seek 'flow' in more aspects of our everyday lives. Developing a new approach to research communication can generate this same sense of focus and achievement. Put simply, thinking creatively about how to communicate new research can and should be fun. It also allows innovation; your innovative approach to communication could solve a particular problem in research communication (such as how to communicate a particularly difficult concept or how to reach a particular group of people). Moran (2010) suggests that one of the key roles of creativity is to enable society to innovate and change. As she points out, some innovations work well and are widely adopted, others may be less popular or judged less effective and fall by the wayside. Taking a creative approach is, therefore, not without risks.

It also need not be a lone exercise; though we may still think of the creative genius as a solitary individual, much creativity arises through collaborative endeavour (Sonnenburg, 2004). Sonnenburg defines a specific type of system which enables collaborative creativity to emerge, which he calls a 'creaplex' (from the Latin *creare in complex* – to create in collaboration). A creaplex requires a problem around which the collaboration forms. Successful collaborations produce a novel response to this problem – for example, a novel approach to communication. Galaxy Zoo is an example of just such a creative response to a problem – in this case the problem of how to process the one million images produced by the Sloan Digital Sky Survey.

Amabile (1996) identifies a number of factors which can promote or hinder creative processes. Learning techniques that promote heuristic thinking and strategies to play with ideas are seen to be enablers; as are organisational structures that promote independence and recognise creative thinking (but don't necessarily reward it directly), encouraging people to work creatively without feeling they are under surveillance. Barriers to creativity include stress, competition and lack of external support. Edwards (2008) argues that creativity arises when you think differently and he advocates combining approaches from both the arts and sciences to create what he calls 'artscience', a process whereby 'science mixes with art and art with science, and in the process neither merely serves the other' (Edwards, 2008: 41). In this milieu, where innovators move in an artistic and scientific culture, creativity is catalysed. Edwards defines this process of translation:

> Idea translators (1) passionately espouse some idea that they aim to realise in the arts or sciences; (2) study deeply and open themselves to invigorating new experience in science (if trained in the arts) or the arts (if trained in the sciences); (3) struggle against stiff resistance from colleagues and sometimes even their intended audience; (4) repeatedly test and frequently see their original idea evolve in unexpected ways in this

new environment; and (5) throughout it all maintain a determination to arrive at an original artistic or scientific expression. (Edwards, 2008: 21)

Edwards suggests that creativity arises when individuals are passionate about their ideas, but also willing to explore different ways of thinking. This allows them to step out of the usual conceptualisations of the problem and draw on divergent thinking to look at the issue in a new way. It is this willingness to explore the problem from unusual angles, such as considering how artistic interpretations might help to resolve a scientific problem, or vice versa, that enables a truly creative or innovative response to the problem.

Creativity is like play, and like play it can be fun. Taking a creative approach to your research communication will allow you to play around with ideas, test potential approaches and, with practice, it should lead to creative outputs that not only give you pleasure but that allow your audience to recognise and enjoy your inventiveness. Furthermore, you can design projects which offer participants an opportunity to explore and be creative; this can enrich the experience for some participants and offer additional ways to think about the role and value of creativity in research communication. Ultimately, creativity may become a goal of research communication itself as you challenge yourself to try out new and novel approaches, evaluating each against your own criteria of success.

Creative research communication

This book is designed for a variety of readers: public engagement practitioners, policymakers, science communication students and those based in research settings who are seeking to communicate to and engage others with their research. We have tried to keep the writing engaging, straightforward and conversational, catering both for those who are novices to research communication and also for professionals and academics looking for direct, practical and timely advice from the creative contemporary critical international landscape. The book contains short, snappy chapters that are intended to be an easy but thought-provoking read. Each chapter includes key tips and advice, as well as further resources. Case studies provide tangible examples of the ideas in the book. We have attempted to include as many international examples as possible, and have chosen ones for which at least some materials are available in English, so that readers can find out more about them. We have also sought to provide examples across a range of disciplines, as well as drawing on examples from our own work at the University of the West of England, Bristol. In order to avoid the chapters becoming cluttered we have included full web address details only where a website, project or activity would not be easily identifiable through a search engine.

In Part I we continue our introduction to the context of research communication. Chapter 2 explores the role of research communication over approximately four hundred years, taking in the relationship between public and professional communication, the role of museums, galleries, exhibitions and publishing. In Chapter 3, we consider how people can be involved in research communication as audience members or participants, as well as considering key concepts such as audience segmentation and behaviour change.

Part II moves on to consider more practical advice and critical reflection on the means for research communication. In Chapter 4 we examine face-to-face approaches, how the likes of museums, science centres, galleries, festivals and other venues, as well as the research process itself, can provide opportunities to communicate your research in person. The context of the arts is considered in Chapter 5, first exploring the relationship between science and the arts, then exploring audiences for the arts and how the arts can encourage participation and collaborative practice and finishing with some reflections on the specific consideration of impact where the arts are concerned. Chapters 6 and 7 move to online contexts, exploring digital communication and social media, respectively. In Chapter 6, the role of Web 2.0 sets the scene, before exploring how people engage digitally through activities like video, digital storytelling and gaming. Chapter 7 considers both traditional and social media. The chapter offers advice on writing for both types of media as well as examining how researchers can create a digital profile through approaches like blogging, visual communication and social networking. It is worth mentioning at this stage that traditional media are touched on only briefly in this book, largely because there is already a wealth of material available to facilitate researchers' contributions to these media. Chapter 7 does provide pointers to other resources designed to encourage and facilitate researchers' interactions with traditional media, but focuses only on those areas where we perceive that there is a gap in this information. Chapter 8 examines deliberative approaches to research communication, particularly unpicking the context of 'engagement'. As well as considering engagement with members of the public, the chapter includes content on how to engage policymakers with research. Chapter 9 finishes Part II and explores public contributions to research and how the research community can help to enable communities to tackle the social and scientific issues that they face using research methodologies and open source tools. This chapter covers researcher-instigated projects, under the heading citizen science, before moving on to explore community-initiated research and, finally, do-it-yourself (DIY) approaches.

Part III reflects on broader issues that cross all the communication approaches discussed in earlier chapters. In Chapter 10 we examine how research communicators might think about the impact of their communication activities, both how these can be evaluated and what considering research communication as part of research impact may mean for the future. Chapter 11 looks at the issue of ethics, providing practical advice and guidance for research communicators seeking to create activities and projects in an ethical way, as well as debating the need for a greater consideration of ethics within the context of research communication as a field. Chapter 12 provides some final conclusions on how you might share and disseminate the outcomes of your research communication activities, before offering a series of concluding remarks on the book overall.

2

History

Communicating your research can feel like a new discovery. Many of the researchers we meet have found that their passion to engage and to discuss their subject matter has emerged as a mainly solo pursuit, perhaps inspired by a passionate colleague, favourite television programme or an exhibition visit that occurred by chance along the way. This can leave many researchers unaware that the communication of research to others and their engagement with it has been a long-standing issue within research professions. The history of communicating research is rarely elaborated amongst the constraints and busy content of research methodology training.

> H.G. Wells once asked his readers the question, what was the 'greatest influence upon your mental growth, what book, what teacher, what experiences?' Wells then considered how to respond to that question in his own case, admitting that it could be answered in thousands of ways. (Lightman, 2007: 216)

If we consider the quote highlighted by Bernard Lightman above, is there perhaps some resonance with how you might think about the academics, researchers or scientists who have inspired you? They might be a handful of people, or a hundred, but how often has their communication approach been influential in your view of them? Despite the variety of ways that people view researchers who are renowned for communicating their work, it is impossible to ignore that many of the most well-known academics of our time are also widely known to us because they communicate. Be it Stephen Hawking, Noam Chomsky, Mary Beard or Steven Pinker, their communication, as well as their ideas, whether controversial or undisputed, has formed an important part of their research careers. In this chapter we will explore the history of research communication, from research professionalisation to the creation of learned societies and public lectures, the role of museums and exhibitions, covering almost four hundred years of notable research communication activities and setting the scene for developments from the twentieth century onwards which will be covered in the remainder of the book. This chapter will draw to a close at the outset of the twentieth century, at the end of an era when research had shifted from the private to the professionalised, with developments from the twentieth century onwards being explored in the chapters that follow.

Research in public

From the perspective of the busy research settings of the twenty-first century, where attending notable conferences, publishing in academic journals and sharing ideas at networking meetings requires the ready communication of concepts, we might imagine a bygone era of research where such communication was not expected. However, communication has been crucial to the development of academic research, and whilst the examples provided above are circuits which are now somewhat restricted to professional participation, during the enlightenment era (circa the seventeenth century) communication began in a far less isolated way.

The earliest philosophers and natural philosophers, only later to become known as scientists, did not have access to professional circuits of communication; instead, ideas were shared through far more informal mechanisms. Although the earliest academic writings tended to be in Latin, which restricted access to the more-educated population (this ceased to be commonplace by the end of the eighteenth century), this allowed for the sharing of ideas across national boundaries (Knight, 2009). Early modern universities were home to the discussion of certain specific liberal subjects, and so those developing a passion for the exploration of other fields (including the sciences) did not necessarily find a welcome home within such formalised settings. Developing one's research interests was not always reliant on a refined education; instead, the collision of individual passions, interests and hobbies often allowed models to develop which were more akin to personal pursuit and apprenticeship. At that time the public communication of knowledge throughout a number of countries in Europe was as important as locations like libraries, and the private and public arenas for discussion of new research ideas were far from distinct (Stewart, 2008).

Public communication of ideas was particularly noted in France during the seventeenth and eighteenth centuries, where the wider Parisian public sphere of academies, periodicals, cafés and reading societies provided increasing opportunities to learn and share knowledge across all subject matters, including through research lectures which were open to all (Lynn, 2008; Knight, 2006). Such public discussions included literary journals, debating societies, coffee houses and salons, where discussions included emerging scientific research as well as art and literary criticism (Bennett, 1995). Although these social spaces had an essential role in encouraging more professional communication, access to such groups was not yet defined by professional status. 'Penny Universities' from the late seventeenth century, for example, were based in coffee houses, allowing interested individuals to exchange a small sum of money for refreshment, discussion, negotiations and the exchange of ideas, and often included the sharing of news both verbally and through pamphlets and newsletters. If we take the sciences as one starting point, academies were formally established in London, Paris, Florence and Rome during the seventeenth century (Riskin, 2008; Hooper-Greenhill, 1992) and are seen by many as the first significant move towards professional meeting places beyond the university, although communication still tended to be of a more public style. In Britain the initial publications and presentations of the Royal Society (established in 1660) were often formal but relatively accessible, designed for those with a more general interest, and it was not until the middle of the nineteenth century that the society's publications and presentations took on a far more specialised nature (Knight, 2006).

Without a clear profession or its associated salary, 'researchers' or 'practitioners' of the time who did not teach the classical university subjects such as philosophy, Latin and theology focused their efforts on sustaining their research interests through other means. Some could pursue such interests on account of their individual wealth. With the exception of medical and pharmaceutical training, little scientific teaching occurred within universities, and so a number of historically well-known scientists were also medical doctors in order to provide themselves with a teaching income to support their wider interests (Knight, 2006). Those without teaching salaries often used communication almost as a form of self-employment, to supplement their endeavours. This meant that at times the attention of the emerging scientific figures of the eighteenth century was of a rather practical nature, focused on problems to which functional knowledge could be applied, or on new technological developments which had a clear application (Knight, 2009; Stewart, 2008; Knight, 2006). The public lectures and demonstrations of the likes of Benjamin Franklin (1705–90), Thomas Beddoes (1760–1808) and Sir Humphry Davy (1778–1829) often emphasised 'useful' or applied knowledge (Stewart, 2008), as an interested audience was essential in order to support the growing desire to conduct experiments and the associated need to fund the requisite apparatus (Riskin, 2008). Sir Humphry Davy, with the invention of the coal miner's safety lamp, is often cited as providing one of the first examples of applied science, and accordingly his lectures at the Royal Institution in the early nineteenth century, and later through his presidency of the Royal Society, emphasised public benefit and appeal. Davy described the systematic nature of science as 'refined common sense' and his lectures proved so popular that London's Albermarle Street, where the Royal Institution was then and still is located, was made into a one-way street during his evening orations so as to accommodate the resulting congestion (Knight, 2006: 4).

The establishment of bodies such as the Royal Institution in 1799 is often held up as significant to research communication for other reasons. In comparison to the Royal Society, the Royal Institution had more philanthropic aims, with a lecture theatre and laboratory, neither of which the Royal Society offered at that time (Knight, 2006). The design of the lecture theatre mirrored that of the broader London theatre scene, its upper levels allowing for the entrance of those deemed to occupy the lower social classes to be hidden from individuals at the forefront, who often included noble and royal patrons (Bensaude-Vincent and Blondel, 2008; Knight, 2006). As we will discuss later in this chapter, it is difficult to estimate how wide an audience was truly catered for, as rents alone for the central London location required good patronage from the wealthy (Knight, 2009), and speakers still recited to a somewhat passive audience, gated by lecterns and equipment (Broks, 2006). However, in the eighteenth and nineteenth centuries communicating one's research was a method to fund and legitimise research and develop professional standing, and in order to do that the communication of research needed to have public appeal.

Spectacle and leisure

The desire for an interested audience alongside those with semi-professional interests provided an opportunity for spectacle, drama and debate (Stewart, 2008). Here scientific communication in particular came into its own. Experiments and demonstrations were well-rehearsed manifestations of scientific knowledge (Sutton, 1995) rather than a journey through methods or true experimentation, and particular subject matter proved most amenable to the requirement for public drama. In Western Europe during the eighteenth century the use of electricity in public demonstrations had a particular popularity, one which was seen to encourage the development of scientific understanding about it (Sutton, 1995). Electric shocks might be performed, even involving groups of the audience in an era before risk assessment, and allowing for theatrical display alongside important discussion about the causes of electricity (Stewart, 2008). In one case from the mid eighteenth century, noted by Bertucci (2008: 78), a Professor Georg Richmann was struck by lightning in St Petersburg while experimenting with atmospheric electricity, an event dramatically recorded by an artist who had previously intended to document the scientific effects. Similarly the opportunity to observe medical dissections within anatomy theatres was fashionable, despite its not being unusual to witness audience members fainting or becoming unwell (Knight, 2006).

Dramatic and entertaining depictions of research might be deemed to appear dismissive of its significance, but in fact provided a level of credibility to scientific developments of the day, as well as opportunities for the public replication of new scientific principles (Stewart, 2008). Rather than refined or exclusive, many scientific developments had a practical nature which had resonance with the public (Knight, 2006), and visualising knowledge was seen to be important (Stafford, 1994) as new scientific developments emerged. John George Wood's lectures at the Royal Polytechnic Institution (now the University of Westminster), a gallery of practical science established in 1838, were accompanied by improvised drawings of 'battling ants, gigantic whales, and other creatures' (Lightman, 2007: 177). Unrestricted by formal curricula or course designs, the public lecturers of the late eighteenth and early nineteenth centuries had the freedom to select subject matter which was likely to most interest both their own curiosity and the enthusiasms of their audiences (Knight, 2006).

There was therefore selectivity regarding those topics of growing academic interest which were seen to be most suited for public presentation. For example, mathematics was often rejected as being too abstract, with favour being shown to those issues which would be most 'tangible' and 'sensible' for the public to grasp (Riskin, 2008: 46). The importance of utility and appeal to the audience – resulting in income for the speaker and therefore the opportunity to purchase the tools, substances and materials required to remain in practice – meant that audience interests were key to popular speakers, particularly where the emerging sciences were concerned.

> Disseminators of popular science depended on an audience in order to make a living. Thus, they were very cognizant of the wants and needs of their audience and, in order to ensure their livelihood, clearly targeted their courses to specific groups. In this way the public influenced the form and the content of the information presented to them. (Lynn, 2008: 74)

Research developments had a role to play within leisure pursuits, and lecturing had a competitive spirit during this era. Lectures and demonstrations were seen to be desirable activities amongst the growing popularity of the leisure 'industry' where visits to museums, exhibitions and curiosity shops were increasing in cultural desirability and becoming geographically more accessible (Perez, 2008; Worpole, 1991). The popularity of lectures throughout Europe provoked an international trade in apparatus during the eighteenth century and the lines between professional and public were blurred, as 'boundaries between maker, designer, merchant and user were often not precise' (Stewart, 2008: 15). Tools and apparatus that are now seen to be significant symbolisers of the research method were often influenced by their more public orientation (Fukushima, 2005; Schaffer, 2005). Workshops and manufacturers in many European countries (though less popular in the UK, where trade secrets were more closely guarded) made their sites of production visible as a means to market their wares (Knight, 2009) and to add credibility to new inventions, with countries such as France using 'proof ceremonies' to publicly authenticate a new concoction's efficacy (Perez, 2008).

Art exhibitions first emerged in Rome in the late seventeenth century, where the climate and proliferation of paintings for purchase allowed for their sale to collectors, as well as for wider public viewings of materials which were displayed outside churches and dealers' shops (Hudson, 1975). In this sense, like those working within the sciences at that time, artists in southern European cultures were viewed as craftspeople and in a less elitist manner than that common in many other countries at the time. In France and England even toyshops provided some access to the mechanistic designs and instruments of the day (Perez, 2008; Stafford, 1994); thus in this period the worlds of design, artistry and science also intermingled.

However, the popularity of emerging research ideas was not the responsibility of speakers and artists alone; it was also reliant on the writers, readers and editors who began to recognise its significance (Knight, 2006). The focus of communicative efforts around research coincided with European countries being amongst the first to also experience the 'communications revolution' (Lightman, 2007), circa the mid nineteenth century. There was an appetite for travel writing, and the books and journals published on the extensive voyages and explorations of new territories, written in an accessible and readable way, became widely popular (Knight, 2006) as the craving for understanding more about new research ideas, and the information it was generating, emerged across Europe.

Research inclusivity

Increasing communication around research was not a geographically isolated activity, at least in regard to the European continent. In particular, developments in terms of how research was being professionalised and discussed across France, Germany and Great Britain, as well as other countries in Western Europe, spilled over national boundaries, drawing out both competition and complementary activities. Whilst history has tended to focus on the most notable historical examples and figures, it is recognised that there were estimated to be hundreds of practitioners, a number of whom changed their names to fit their current geographical location, who travelled Europe demonstrating experiments and giving lectures (Bensaude-Vincent and Blondel, 2008; Sutton, 1995). One reason why opportunities for scientific communication specifically are thought to have increased in Britain during the eighteenth century was the restricted access to Paris and to the wider continent during the French Revolution, where science had been advancing rapidly (Knight, 2006).

Lectures, demonstrations and talks were not restricted to the capital cities. In Britain, public experimental lectures were noted in cities including Bristol, Glasgow, Liverpool, Manchester and Birmingham (Stewart, 2008). These were evident in organisations including literary and philosophical societies, the Lunar Society (established in 1765), Mechanics Institutes (circa the 1820s) and Athenaeums (in existence from the late eighteenth century) (Knight, 2006). *Naturforscher* in Germany (originally founded in 1822) held the first annual scientific meetings, which toured different locations in a model which continues to be used today by many associations (Knight, 2009). Agricultural shows, which began to emerge in the mid nineteenth century, provided opportunities for new agricultural equipment and techniques to be showcased to those in the rural regions who were most likely to purchase and utilise them. Interestingly, such shows were also frequently accompanied by artistic displays; for instance, one show in the town of Barnstable, England, was accompanied by drawings by the artist Turner (Hudson, 1975).

Communicative efforts did not, then, focus only on cities, as there were important consumers of new knowledge to reach in wider geographical locations. Large towns, as well as rural locations, were the sites of many of the major industrial developments of the era and therefore opportune locations to reach industrial audiences and secure collaboration, with a number of speakers at the time keen to also access the 'working man'. Although it is difficult to grasp how many truly 'working men' attended such activities, it is striking to note that the public setting of communication meant that, in principle, emerging science and technologies were accessible to far broader populations within society than might be assumed.

For skilled workers and artisans, access to science was increasingly possible, due to the reduced costs of publishing, allowing individuals to read more widely rather than intensively; and increasing one's knowledge was often supported by certain paternalistic employers who were keen to encourage their workers in educational pursuits (Knight, 2006). At times this provided some level of political discontent; for example, in France the increasing instruction in, accessibility and discussion of scientific and intellectual ideas was seen to be a significant influence on political revolution in the late eighteenth century: science was the 'prime suspect as the cause of social and moral collapse' (Knight, 2009: 30). Thus there were concerns that increasing academic interests and the associated questioning of religious principles might lead to social unrest, although these proved largely unfounded in some other countries, including Britain.

Like the working man, women were permitted to be present at scientific gatherings, although often appearing to play a more passive role, and their attendance at literary and debating societies was rare. As such, women were often able to pursue greater success within publishing. Mary Somerville (1780–1872), one of the most noted scientific writers of her generation, garnered considerable credibility, publishing her own experimental work as well as more popular readings (Brock, 2006); however, as a woman it was not considered tolerable for her to speak at or read to learned societies (Knight, 2006). Scientific writings of a conversational and dialogic style were popular amongst female and some male readers alike, and women often also played a role in translating scientific texts from their original languages, as well as writing some of the first 'textbooks' of the era (Knight, 2006). Opportunities for publishing opened up broadly during the eighteenth and nineteenth centuries as journals aimed at the interested rather than the specialist reader also emerged, including the *Journal of Natural Philosophy, Chemistry and the Arts* (1797), *The Philosophical Magazine* (1798) and *Annals of Philosophy* (1813). Such publications included reviews, biographies and notes on work in progress and demonstrated the growing appetite to learn more about developments of the day (Knight, 2006). These periodicals also represented a broader range of subjects; natural philosophy, travel, literature and current affairs reflecting an appeal to the less-specialised reader (Crosland, 2001).

Whilst the increasing availability of publications made knowledge more accessible, it also began to create distinctions between those carving out professional careers for themselves and those who were seen to be popularisers, particularly where the emerging scientific community was concerned.

> The second half of the [nineteenth] century was, after all, a period when cultural authority was particularly important to the men of science. They were especially keen on pushing clergymen and women out of science, since both were seen to be strong supporters of the Church and as barriers to the establishment of a self-defining community of experts. (Lightman, 2007: 28)

Consequently, those occupying more religious stances, as well as females, who were increasingly argued not to possess the intellectual qualities required for a research career, came to find a more welcome home amongst the growing publishing community or in more discreet research settings (Lightman, 2007). Female authors shifted from a mothering and conversational tone over the course of the nineteenth century, to a more confident narrative style, with their text titles becoming broader and no longer selected to appeal only to women and children (Lightman, 2007). In some countries where more professional academic models were adopted early on, such as Germany and France, popularisation tended to be an elite activity, which resulted in the creation of formal organisations for the likes of science writers from as early as the 1850s (Crosland, 2001). Thus, whilst communication sought to some degree to be inclusive in terms of location, background and gender, subtle shifts in definition were starting to occur around who produced such materials and for what purpose.

Exhibitions, museums and galleries

With the rising popularity of demonstrations, talks and textual expressions of emerging academic ideas, so too came an increased focus on impressive celebrations of such activities. World fairs and exhibitions, which occurred most regularly from the mid nineteenth century to the outbreak of the First World War, were significant, as they indicated the growing desire amongst large numbers of people to attend and appreciate the science and art of the day (Hudson, 1975). Around the globe, exhibitions began to emerge as symbols of the prestige of nation-states, 'exercises in nationalist diplomacy' anticipating a 'techno-utopian' and 'uncontestable future' (Dietz, 2005: 910). Their architecture suggested dominance, observation and opulent expenditure; for example the 1889 Paris Exhibition was symbolised by the construction of the Eiffel Tower (Bennett, 1995), and exhibitions frequently resulted in the regeneration of specific urban sites (Pearce, 1995).

A significant milestone in these emerging developments in Britain was the Great Exhibition in 1851, seen to be the first truly international festival (Pearce, 1995); a number of other countries aimed to replicate its success. Involving the arts, as well as science and technology, it was embodied in the building of the ostentatious Crystal Palace, which housed the exhibition. Transport to the exhibition was provided via the newly established railways, which permitted the involvement of vast numbers of visitors across social classes – although, notably, working-class visitors were provided with etiquette booklets (Knight, 2006; Bennett, 1995). The exhibition's impressive visitor numbers and prestige influenced a series of subsequent activities, including public lectures to critically discuss that which had been on display and the purchase of a significant estate in Kensington for development as a new cultural centre mirroring that which already existed in Berlin's museum quarter, and later to house the Victoria and Albert Museum, Natural History Museum, Science Museum and Imperial College (Knight, 2009; Knight, 2006).

The nineteenth century epitomised an era of such modern museum building where, guided by the increasing rationalist research agendas, dusty cabinets of curiosities exhibiting rare, unusual or interesting pieces in isolation were catalogued and curated into logical, ordered classifications and collections (Henning, 2006; Bennett, 1995). Collecting had been a desirable and common hobby amongst the independently wealthy and the aristocracy, and access to such collections was previously restricted to those who were similarly privileged and invited for viewings. From a practical perspective, collections had been housed in 'homes', and though some collections were accompanied by labelling, these were still times of illiteracy which made private collections unsuited to unaccompanied public visitors (Hudson, 1975).

The trajectory of development varied across Europe, but the opening up of previously private collections began earlier in many countries than in Britain (Henning, 2006; Findlen, 1994; Hooper-Greenhill, 1992). The Medici Palace in Florence is frequently acknowledged as the originator of European museums in the fifteenth century (Hooper-Greenhill, 1992), and royal and state collections were gradually made accessible to varying degrees in order to symbolise power and prestige, alongside a sense of some acknowledgement regarding their wider public ownership (Bennett, 1995; Hudson, 1975); for instance, in France much art was 'liberated' following the revolution (Déotte, 2004). Broader access was thus particularly important with regard to newly emerging art galleries, where increasingly the collections of individuals came to be housed in state and nationally associated galleries, no longer symbolising the status and wealth of the individual owner on display in grand reception and dining rooms, but that of the nation (Duncan, 2004; Bennett, 1995). From the mid eighteenth century onwards galleries in Vienna, Dusseldorf, Florence and Munich displayed royal art collections alongside more detailed information and chronological ordering for the purpose of collective educational pursuit (Stafford, 1994). The Louvre in Paris (established in 1793), although not the first museum of its kind, was seen to be one of the most influential in symbolising equality of access (Henning, 2006; Duncan, 2004) as well as new formats for artistic displays, as Pearce discusses in the context of changes in artistic display within this era:

> This [classified collections] gave visitors something to learn, a positive possession, rather than just something to appreciate ... the pictures were divided into national schools and art-historical periods. They were put into uniform frames and clearly labelled, another change necessary for public visitors. A walk through the galleries was a walk through art history. (Pearce, 1995: 126–7)

The capacity for public and research uses amongst the newly emerging galleries, museums, zoos and gardens could often lead to debate regarding their role. The move from private to public reflected the growing distinction between amateur and professional (Stafford, 1994), drawing out new dilemmas and problems. For example, civic access during selected hours was permitted at the Royal Botanic Gardens at Kew (founded in 1759) from around the mid nineteenth century, in response to the public taxes that were required for its maintenance, but this was debated in terms of its potential detriment to research needs (Knight, 2006). The Natural History Museum faced similar issues in balancing the requirements of those using the collections for research, conservation and curation with the needs of those visiting as a leisure pursuit (Knight, 2006).

Despite many collections and the resulting museums moving towards a more public ethos, this caused considerable discomfort, particularly amongst their previous custodians, who had frequently drawn small salaries from tours for selected desirable guests (Hudson, 1975), and early museums were particularly wary of the 'masses'. The British Museum (established in 1753) initially permitted groups of fifteen people per day, whose credentials were rigorously checked in advance, a process which could take a matter of months (Bennett, 1995; Hudson, 1975). Whilst the Victoria and Albert Museum (established in 1852) was more accessible to public visitors, attracting high numbers of visitors in the evening (and therefore likely to be working visitors), still some surprise was expressed at the time that problems with angry mobs and public drunkenness did not occur (Bennett, 1995). Startlingly, one outcome of this worry was a particular encouragement to women to attend museums, as it was thought that their presence would be a calming influence on the wider social classes, due to their 'gentleness of manners' (Bennett, 1995: 32).

Galleries and exhibitions experienced similar dilemmas in satisfying the needs of their traditional clientele amid their wider public responsibilities during the opening years of the nineteenth century. The development of mass production of art resulted in increased access and availability (Bennett, 1995) and the first exhibitions of art in Great Britain were noted from the late eighteenth century onwards. These first exhibitions, established by the Society of Arts, were originally funded via catalogue sales and therefore could be freely attended. However, this permitted access to poorer visitors, who were not seen as possessing the decorum to view art appropriately, and this resulted in a ruling that later exhibitions should not have free admittance (Hudson, 1975). Historically, a number of European locations, such as Rome and Athens, had legacies of public art embodied in sculpture, architecture, temples and churches (Pearce, 1995; Hooper-Greenhill, 1992) which, due to their very nature, were always to some degree publicly accessible. The accessibility of art, its nature as open to interpretation at a time when people were being moulded from the 'gullible' oral and visual consumer into the rational and reified reader (Stafford, 1994), required new responsibilities amongst exhibition and gallery designers, and from their outset public galleries and exhibitions of artistic work raised dilemmas around how 'public' they should be. A problem plaguing many of the newly established museums was how to display their vast quantities of holdings (Knight, 2006), amid the new demands for space that became inevitable with increased visitor numbers. The 'great age' of museum collecting and establishment was also seen to embody colonial notions of power, where materials were gathered from numerous source communities (many of which were assumed to be dying out) for the benefit of western institutional authorities and their future generations (Broks, 2006; Peers and Brown, 2003). Thus, whilst newly established museums were potentially opening up access to treasured materials and resources, they were also raising questions of power, equity and ownership.

As newly established museums discovered their identity, subtle changes emerged in their distinction between education and entertainment. Amusement parks began to develop in the United States in the late nineteenth century, more comfortably adopting a home for novelty and leisure pursuit, in contrast to the educational pursuit of the modern museum (Bennett, 1995). Notably in the United States, the history of museums is almost directly the reverse of that in most European countries, whereby public museums originated before widespread private collecting (Hudson, 1975). Thus the 'appetite for the spectacular' came to be delegated to amusement parks, circuses and fairs (Henning, 2006: 24). Nevertheless, the early evolution of more formalised museum settings, as well as lectures and demonstrations, had important roots in an entertaining era, be it with their small trickeries and pleasurable appeal (Stafford, 1994) or with many of the collections in both European and North American museums tracing their roots to collectors who provided objects for circuses, fairs and other menageries (Bennett, 1995). In summary, by the turn of the nineteenth century there were ever-increasing public spaces for the consumption of research ideas, but with that expansion came increased restrictions as to what those experiences should comprise.

Professionalisation

Although increased sites for communication were then popular amongst those without a specialised interest, these sites also performed significant functions in informing those developing increasingly professional research identities, as reflected in the tensions between museums' collections for research and broader public consumption. An invitation to speak at the Royal Institution's somewhat formal 'Friday Evening Discourses' was seen as a prestigious accolade (Knight, 2006) from the nineteenth century onwards, and those growing in professional reputation began to question how such public but increasingly professional groupings might come to influence professional identity. Spending one's time drawing amusement was seen to require an intellectual purpose (Riskin, 2008), and a widening middle class was keen to pursue these new opportunities to develop knowledge (Stafford, 1994), embodying not only a redistribution of access to knowledge but the 'dissemination of the ideals of democracy' (Henning, 2006: 13). As Bennett (1995) highlights, cultural sites including public lectures, art galleries and libraries provided rational drivers for civilising, cultural and social improvements amongst populations in a similar way to those targeted at health. The increased emphasis on 'rational recreations' through the latter part of the nineteenth century, suggesting that the influence of high culture could improve the moral being of those within all levels of society, reflected the enlightenment view that society could be 'perfected' (Stafford, 1994). 'The public museum emerged as one of the campaigns of the state to direct the population into activities which would, without people being aware of it, transform the population into a useful resource for the state' (Hooper-Greenhill, 1992: 168).

Science increased as a national source of pride and prestige, requiring educational investment. The influence of Prussian expansion and the establishment of scientific research within university contexts in Germany in the nineteenth century prompted concern amongst many nations that educational achievements were crucial alongside military capability. Universities as well as polytechnics began to expand their provision in science and engineering, matters which also started to find their way into school syllabuses (Knight, 2009; Knight, 2006). As science and technology increased, other opportunities to apply scientific principles to broader social questions emerged. Responsibilities which had previously fallen to those with religious or charitable intentions increasingly became public, requiring careful data, evidence and theorising, whereby in the late nineteenth century the disciplines of sociology, psychology and social work all emerged, represented by specific associations as well as academic homes within university environments (Bogenschneider and Corbett, 2010).

However, over a period of considerable research expansion, with emerging perspectives and evidence making huge impacts on health, transportation, politics, religion and national confidence, by the late nineteenth century the enthusiasm for new research was not without questioning in some quarters (Knight, 2009). This public questioning is often overlooked, due to the 'nostalgia' for such times (Schaffer, 2005). Parameters began to be applied to certain areas of research. For example, the British Parliament was one of the first to pass an Act on cruelty to animals, in 1876 after public outcry, one of the earliest instances of the legislative regulation of science, acknowledging that research could have less-desirable outcomes alongside its potential for significant advancement (Knight, 2006). In other cases, new advances inevitably highlighted new risks in the process of their refinement. Transportation accidents, for example, were common, creating public concern, and the mass mechanisation of industry led to questions of skill replacement. Such developments were seen to stimulate questioning around new knowledge but also a requirement for knowledge, science and technology to resolve such problems for the future (Knight, 2009; Knight, 2006).

As research areas became more specialised, their language, symbolism and discussions became more refined. As Knight (2006: 7) describes, 'being a "Renaissance man" was no longer possible ... The world had become specialised: people knew more and more about less and less.' The nineteenth century steadily became defined by the replication of similar research methods, mass production, museum, hospital and university practices which were gradually exported across Europe and then around the globe (Agar, 2012). The dominance of European examples within this chapter is reflective of the fact that the process of research professionalisation in Asia, Africa and Latin America followed a later trajectory, from the twentieth century onwards (Krishna, 2014). For instance, associations for science were formed in South Africa (1902), India (1912), Japan (1925) and Argentina (1933) in the early part of the twentieth century. More broadly, increasing numbers of societies and journals emerged that were dedicated to particular research specialisations, and even within these, subjects were further divided and fragmented (Knight, 2009). Thus, increasingly communication was becoming more distinct in its appeal and distinctions between populariser and professional grew in significance.

By the turn of the twentieth century the role of popularising research and the prominence of broad disciplines became seen by some to be below that of a serious researcher – who should instead be focused on the publication and pursuit of original research around specific disciplines in the face of growing political concerns and the pressures of impending world war (Knight, 2006). In terms of publishing, as more research papers became available, the publication style became more terse; they could no longer provide a 'leisurely' read and, coupled with increasing specialisation, the boundaries between popular and professional publication became far more disciplined (Knight, 2006). Researchers were now being called upon to have other skills, including a greater propensity for working collaboratively amongst colleagues and to generate funding as research became more and more expensive (Knight, 2006), restricting opportunities for wider public pursuits. As professional publications became more specialised, other mediatory writing styles began to emerge, for example science fiction (Knight, 2006). Beyond fiction, specialisation called on authors to write not only for non-specialists but also for specialists whose specific interests might align to other specialisations, revealing 'what their fellow experts in other spheres were up to' (Knight, 2009: 83; Lightman, 2007). As Broks (2006: 19–24) describes, 'popular' became an association separate from elite professional practice, 'the contest was about who could participate and on what terms … excluding the public became a defining feature of what it meant to be "scientific"'.

Summary

Science is both the most public and the most private of activities. Since the early modern era, science has laid claim to being knowledge defined by its accessibility. Gone, in principle were the secret formulas of alchemy, knowledge that would be forever hidden from view. Of course, that picture was never quite right. Competitive secrecy, military secrecy – in many ways the actual 'doing' of science never obeyed the simplistic picture of knowledge always on public parade. (Galison *et al.*, 2005: 332)

In the establishment of research as a field of enquiry the role of public communication was highly significant. It could add resonance to ideas and theories, allow one to declare them as one's own, provide income and expenditure, as well as routes for communication with others seeking to shape research careers. Thus popularisation, and its perceived negative qualities – distractions from the 'real work' of researchers (Hüppauf and Weingart, 2008) – were characteristics that began to be witnessed much more significantly from the twentieth century onwards. That is not to say that there were not critical voices as to how communication should occur at this time; in fact the history of academic communication is packed with tales of rivalry, controversy and disagreement, not only around new discoveries, but also about their wider influence and communication. However, communication, regardless of form, and the communal notions associated with many of the institutional settings which came to embody research (Schaffer, 2005), influenced public views and had a place in enlightenment framings of research.

The tensions that emerged on this path of professionalisation within public contexts, reflected in the final sentence of the quote above from Galison *et al.* (2005), include a number of key aspects which are still debated within research communication today.

Firstly, museums and exhibitions from their outset navigated the predicament of exhibiting the curious and ornamental alongside the instructional and rational (Bennett, 1995). Although previously privately viewed collections were increasingly opened up, it was a considerable period of time before considerations around the visitor's experience became more fully recognised, as Hudson explains in the context of museums: 'They measured their success by the number of people who came through the turnstiles. What the people thought about the museums, or whether they were coming for the first or last time was of no particular consequence' (Hudson, 1975: 7).

Consequently, whilst it is difficult to estimate the exact influence such experiences had specifically on individuals, they were invited for a perceived *mutual* benefit. Stafford (1994: 47) argues that 'participatory enactment' was a driving aim of rational recreation, even if it implied that 'material was internalized interactively' – in other words, that participation occurred within the individual, rather than more proactively. Although many of the efforts of this era allowed for a relatively passive participant, the openness to a participatory element is important to recognise, as is the awareness that participants might be there for enjoyment as well as inspiration and knowledge (Sutton, 1995). Stafford (1994: 130) describes that 'all exhibitionism, whether functioning within art or science, possesses this double inclination toward irrationality and rationality', a dilemma we often face as communicators to this day.

Secondly, and linked to the last point, though the influence on audiences, visitors and participants is tricky to decipher, and it is perhaps convenient to romanticise communicative efforts of the time, the influences on the practitioners and researchers who engaged are clearer. They acknowledged that appeal, novelty and entertainment were important factors, alongside information, and in some cases communication was influential in the development of specific ideas, principles, methods and approaches on this basis. Sutton (1995) makes the point that from a modern perspective it is perhaps easy to assume that the amusing, theatrical and impressive displays of knowledge from the eighteenth century were not 'real science', and yet they featured many of the institutions, individuals and inventions of the time which have subsequently come to embody important and significant research developments.

Finally, on reading this short and necessarily selective history of developments within research communication it is easy to note points of resonance. Eilean Hooper-Greenhill (1992) points out that whilst there are, for example, resemblances to current museum practices in the historical trajectories of the field, these should not be exaggerated such as to shroud the considerable developments that have occurred in museum contexts during subsequent centuries. In summary, whilst we see many familiar patterns in research communication throughout history, and in the relationship between private and public, practice and professional, that will be of interest to communicators today, there are also many contemporary and international influences on communication to be explored in the next chapters.

Recommended reading

Hooper-Greenhill, E., *Museums and the Shaping of Knowledge* (London: Routledge, 1992).

Knight, D., *The Making of Modern Science: Science, Technology, Medicine and Modernity 1789–1914* (Cambridge: Polity Press, 2009).

3

Participants

A crucial stage in any science communication activity is consideration of the groups with whom you will be communicating. The potential audiences for research communication are many and varied, including those with personal and professional interests. It is important to remember that people can have varying levels of interaction, from an audience member who is happy to come along and contribute quite passively, to a very active contributor who might be involved in shaping the direction of a research project as a whole. We will consider the variety of people your research communication might be aimed at in this chapter. We will also introduce you to concepts including audience segmentation, behaviour change and 'nudging' and how they are being used. We will consider these from a critical perspective, how they can be a tool to engage some, but potentially discriminate against others, and how they can be of use practically to readers. Finally, we will discuss how certain people can be overlooked in research communication processes, and considerations you might take from this as a research communicator.

Audiences, participants and public/s

When many people first think about communicating their research they can sometimes be motivated by the desire to reach 'the general public'. In fact, in research communication settings, as in many others, it has become uncommon to refer to a singular public; rather, it is recognised that participants in research communication come from a variety of backgrounds, communities, experiences and perspectives, and the idea of one exclusive and singular public is therefore problematic. In the past many researchers and communicators, such as journalists, often thought of other specialists or 'fans' with a particular interest in a discipline when communicating. Now the reach has become far broader, as Susanna Hornig Priest summarises in relation to science:

> The audiences for science consist of a variety of groups: not just scientists but non-scientist citizens, not just schoolchildren but their parents and other family members, not just the 'fans' of science but activists who may adopt a stance opposed to conventional scientific wisdom. Policy-makers and opinion leaders with no pretensions of scientific expertise can make productive use of scientific results, and this is as it should be. (Hornig Priest, 2009: 223)

In this chapter we will primarily focus on reaching people who are non-specialists, who may or may not have an interest in your particular discipline. Those with related professional interests, such as journalists or policymakers, will crop up in later chapters in the context of particular communicative approaches, but let's start now with a word about audiences. Audiences are traditionally depicted as 'receivers', but this reflects the modern use of the term. An audience would originally have comprised small groups of local spectators capable of responding to and interacting with a public display, presentation or performance; it was only the advent of the modern mass media which saw a depiction of a far larger audience, dispersed consumers, often in their private home environment, which cultivated the depiction of audiences as having a relatively passive role (McQuail, 1997).

Though the communication environment has been changing, with increased opportunities for audiences to be more selective in their choices, there are still widespread opportunities for communicating research to a broad audience in a relatively one-way fashion. This can include through channels like the media, certain social and digital contexts, as well as lectures and presentations, and it is entirely appropriate to communicate in what might be seen as a fairly one-directional route for many research communication approaches, particularly those which set out to reach large numbers of people. However, it is also important to bear in mind that traditional notions around communication and its routes are being challenged in the context of changing communication opportunities. In today's information-rich and diverse multimedia world, even someone who might be rather passively engaging with some news content online, for example, may have made a choice to actively seek it out (Hornig Priest, 2009). The concept of audience has become increasingly diverse, and the context of communication in which it sits is progressively multifaceted; 'we keep the familiar word, but the thing [audience] itself is disappearing' (Carpentier *et al.*, 2014a; McQuail, 1997: 2). Jay Rosen (2011) has even coined the phrase 'the people formerly known as the audience' to reflect the increased role that people can have in selecting and determining media production, but this idea that the passive audience has disappeared comes with a cautionary note:

> We [the people] are still perfectly content to listen to our radios while driving, sit passively in the darkness of the local multiplex, watch TV while motionless and glassy-eyed in bed, and read silently to ourselves as we always have. Should we attend the theatre, we are unlikely to storm the stage for purposes of putting on our own production. We feel there is nothing wrong with old style, one-way, top-down media consumption. Big Media pleasures will not be denied us. You provide them, we'll consume them. (Rosen, 2011: np)

Thus, whilst there are now numerous opportunities to shape, determine and contribute to the personal communication and media that we use, there is still the desire to simply receive or consume. Those looking to participate in different ways find increased opportunities to contribute through routes that may not have existed before, for instance by tweeting a journalist, submitting their photographs or videos to a news channel or directly contacting a researcher through their social media presence.

Significantly, in some settings it may then be more appropriate to refer to someone as a participant than as an audience member. This is particularly the case in the context of certain public engagement approaches where people may go beyond listening to or seeking out some form of communication activity, to additionally being directly involved in contributing to it. Later chapters of this book will consider various examples of this, including activities like festival events, immersive experiences or participation in research itself. Participation in a media context is also not unheard of, and can reflect both participation *through* the media, for instance when you might use social media to participate in public debate, and *in* the media, for example when people generate and produce media content (Carpentier *et al.*, 2014b:131). In these examples considering someone as a 'participant' can better reflect their input in that process, to represent them as an active contributor. Whilst to some degree we might see this discussion as a case of semantics, the labelling of those you are communicating with can be important for a variety of reasons, influencing not only people's expectations of the experience but also how you might perceive and plan for their contribution.

So where does this leave our notion of the general public? Whilst research communicators still talk about the wider population, nations or communities, particularly when making comparisons around their size or features, in research communication it is now quite common to pluralise the term to 'public/s', recognising that the general public in any one setting might be quite different in another. This leads some to describe 'public/s' in themselves as coming into existence only when they are labelled, mobilised, framed or categorised (Barnett and Mahony, 2011; Braun and Schultz, 2010; Thorpe and Gregory, 2010; Michael, 2009). There is not one static, general public out there; instead, a public group may be provoked or come into being in response to a particular activity, issue or concern. Though we are always likely to have a fascination with how many people watch, or now download, the latest prime-time TV show or visit the cinema to see the most recent blockbuster film, today's diverse and multifaceted world often requires more flexible approaches to consider how you identify those with whom you are communicating.

Relationships and expertise

As research communicators we may be interested in the people we communicate with for a variety of reasons. A greater understanding of those with whom you are communicating, their wants, needs, attitudes and interests, allows communicators to tailor and develop more sophisticated communication mechanisms, as well as potentially to spot publics with whom there is less communication. For smaller-scale activities, thinking about a fairly specific group for communication might also be a more efficient use of limited time or resources, allowing you to meet the needs of some rather than many.

For others, particularly those based in the types of organisations that support research communication, like those in the media, museums, science centres, galleries and professional associations, there has always been an interest in the types of people they traditionally appeal to and why. This might be part of an accountability mechanism, for instance in the cultural sector evaluating how users' needs are being met by a publicly funded institution. Alternatively, it might be linked to a direct financial motivation, for example, when securing advertising in a media context it is important to know who the audience are and how they are being reached. As communication routes have diversified there has been a growing emphasis on the need to understand both who you are currently reaching and who you are not reaching. This interest may arise for reasons of social inclusion (for example the museums sector is often criticised for appealing to certain types of people) or because traditional audiences may no longer be apparent (illustrated for instance by the changes that have occurred in print and digital news journalism, where many more people are now accessing information online rather than purchasing a daily newspaper).

The relationship between research communication and people is not always smooth. Returning to the museums sector as one setting for research communication, there has been a somewhat contentious history in terms of their relationship with visitors and communities, and museums' central messages for a considerable time related to the authority and instruction of the privileged within society (Bennett, 1995). It is worth remembering that museums which developed in the late nineteenth century, whilst 'intended *for* the people ... were certainly not *of* the people in the sense of displaying any interest in the lives, habits and customs of either the contemporary working classes or the labouring classes of pre-industrial societies' (Bennett, 1995: 109). Though little attention was then paid to certain sectors of society within the countries where the museums were located, this did not extend to those situated in distant communities and settings. Museum collections were widely sourced from colonised communities and foreign lands, with an inbuilt assumption that such communities would 'die out' in future and thus have little need for such resources. '[T]his was a one-way relationship: objects and information about them went from peoples all over the world into museums, which then consolidated knowledge as the basis of curatorial and institutional authority' (Peers and Brown, 2003: 1).

The modern museum sector has, then, become far more conscious of the displacements of its past, engaging in more 'two-way' processes, returning information and artefacts to people (often indigenous, local, immigrant or religious communities), seeking to better consider how museum representations are relevant to, perceived by and influence members of the societies they seek to represent, as Peers and Brown (2003: 1) describe:

> This new approach to research, which also informs curation and display, involves museums and community members working towards building a relationship of trust, often in cases where none has existed before and where there may be a significant legacy of distrust as a result of the dynamics of earlier anthropological and museum research projects.

As Kidd (2012: 74) describes, the cultural sector has been involved in 'a wholesale re-appraisal of the role and status of "users"', resulting in an increase in participatory, co-production and consultation approaches.

Similarly, the relationship between experts and publics within communication settings has altered. As we will discuss in more detail in Chapter 8, there has been an embracing of the language of participation and engagement where public communication is concerned. People as participants can be informed, but equally might be consulted or involved in collaboration (International Association of Public Participation, 2007), with the ability in some cases to affect decision making and outcomes (United Nations, 2011). As a result, many of the policymakers and learned institutions that seek to engage with members of the public around research issues now see an increased role for public views and consultation. In terms of research communication this has been a significant shift away from the idea of the 'deficit model', whereby formerly the perceived deficiencies in people's knowledge around complex research areas created drivers for the receipt of increased information alone (Wilkinson, 2010). Many research communicators now recognise that people have complex relationships with research, based not only on knowledge, but on views, attitudes, beliefs and trust. With evidence, time and a context for engagement, engagement techniques open conversation to provide mutual benefits (John *et al.*, 2011).

In terms of the media environment, new technology and the internet have been one reason, but as Carpentier *et al.* (2014a) point out, not the only reason, why the concept of audiences has altered to recognise a more engaged consumer of information. In the new media context the idea of 'users' has become particularly significant, reflecting a more active 'use' of materials found online. Carpentier *et al.* (2014a) caution that this can imply that passive consumption of communication materials is in some way second best and that studies on how people use digital and social media simply as a focus for their attention are lacking:

> The incessant and rapid changes in media technologies, production practices, content and audience behaviours tend to attract our attention, while a considerable number of stabilities can be found underneath these changes. Even when media participatory technologies and practices are evolving, our desire to exert our right to communicate seems to be very stable. (Carpentier *et al.*, 2014a: 7)

However, it is undeniable that changes in how we use the internet have shaped the way we are able to influence our own communication practices. This changing ethos around how people might be more involved in communication processes has led to some critical probing. The concept of a more engaged participant has led to a variety of questions around the role of expertise, in terms both of the communication method and of the information underpinning it. What of the role of journalists, for example, when people now consume materials created on smartphones, through blogs or shared via social media? And how is expertise recognised if anyone can hold a valid perspective on the latest emerging research areas?

Changes such as citizen journalism and the rise of blogging and social media have led to some concern that the journalistic role, for instance, is being eroded; however, it can be argued that the increase in access to information actually calls for an increase in such mediatory responsibilities, as people require support in dealing with access to so much information (Frost, 2010).

No longer do journalists pass down the word 'from on high', accessing
information that only journalists can reach and offering the distillation
of this wisdom to others. All can now access this information, and all
can take part in the debate. Interactivity and the involvement of readers
and viewers is now all-important. From responses to articles in blogs or
comments and emails sent to TV and radio news programmes, to web
statistics on who is reading what, journalists now have a much clearer
link to readers and viewers than ever before ... There is nothing to stop
anyone being a journalist, but in order to be paid for it, you need to be
able to do it better than most. (Frost, 2010: 2)

The new media environment means journalists have to actively pursue
consumers, attracting their attention through entertainment and excitement, for increasingly short time periods, and this has often reduced
the time available to journalists for research and the presentation of
detailed information (Frost, 2010). However, it has not necessarily led
to a decline in the need for journalists, as might originally have been
expected; rather, it has led to a changing of the journalistic role, whereby
many journalists now 'harvest' or 'curate' news content produced by
others. Importantly, some question whether this is truly journalism
(Bakker, 2014). Their shifting status is calling on journalists to have
more multimedia expertise, as well as flexibility in their employment,
with freelance working and sometimes even low pay or no-pay work
more common in a media environment that has become reliant on multiple income streams beyond advertising and purchasing alone (Bakker,
2014; Franklin, 2014). It is not only the rise of new media that has
created these challenging conditions for journalists; other contributing
factors include the decrease in journalists' autonomy, reduced opportunities for investigative coverage and questioning of the authoritative
position of journalists within society (Lee-Wright *et al.*, 2012). This is
raising new, significant questions about the journalistic role, including, but not limited to, who is a journalist and what implications such
changes will have for the role of the media in democratic engagement
(Franklin, 2014; Lee-Wright *et al.*, 2012).

In similar ways the increasing openness of research expertise, whereby
public participants are now seen to have useful contributions to make,
has led to concerns around the role of the 'expert'. Furedi describes the
decline of traditional authorities and expertises as having implications:
'The flip-side of the erosion of the moral authority of traditional institutions is the growth of deference to other claim-makers. Increasingly
victims are endowed with a moral claim to authority' (Furedi, 2004:
174).

This has been particularly considered in the context of science. Harry
Collins (2014: 15), in his book *Are We All Scientific Experts Now?*,

describes people as having a new sense of empowerment, 'default exper-tise', the 'right to judge – that ordinary citizens feel they possess because science and technology are so fallible'. In Chapter 8 we will explore these concerns in more detail, but for now it is worth noting that there are two important implications of this in the context of the role of participants.

Firstly, some argue that there is a certain 'nostalgia' within academia, particularly where the sciences are concerned, for a time in the past when people were univocally faithful to expertise and the scientific method, a time which has now been replaced by an era of public igno-rance (Schaffer, 2005). This distorts the ways in which people have always questioned the authority of expertise. Secondly, there is the 'problem of extension' whereby some would argue that the concept of expertise has become too extended, calling forth new ways to distin-guish between the value of peoples' differing contributions (Collins and Evans, 2002). Both aspects may lead researchers to assume that people are more sceptical than they perhaps are about research, and more keen to contribute their views. In fact we know that people express multi-ple perspectives and their engagement levels understandably vary for a variety of reasons. This leads us to our next consideration, that of how we may segment the people with whom we are seeking to communicate.

Segmentation

As we have already discussed, your audience or participants may com-prise multiple facets, personalities and backgrounds, or you might be communicating to a rather specific community or group. Communicators think about those they are seeking to reach in different ways, some simply envisage a 'reference person' to address, or use their knowledge of friends, family and personal contacts to build a picture of those with whom they are communicating (McQuail, 1997). Others when design-ing a project or activity might include a period of piloting (see Chapter 10 for more information on piloting an activity) with a select group of those with whom they plan to communicate in order to find out more about their needs, wants or preferences. Alternatively, it might be the case that they would consider some existing categorisations or studies in order to think about a specific group and how best to target them.

Audience segmentation is now a popular approach in a wide variety of fields including marketing, public relations, public services, the arts, culture and heritage sector, charities and campaigning groups, in addition to environmental, science and development communication (Barnett and Mahony, 2011). Segmentation can occur on a variety of criteria, including by demographic factors, attitudes and interests, to name some of the most popular (Bowater and Yeoman, 2013). It involves a process of dividing people up into 'segments' who would be expected to behave or respond to communication in the same or a very similar way; segmentation has advanced rapidly as an approach, due to the increased sophistication of techniques which can be applied to digital data on customers, clients or publics (Barnett and Mahony, 2011). There are a variety of reasons why segmentation has become a popular technique, but key motivations include that it is seen to provide a better understanding of, and response to, public opinion, as well as understanding how people behave and how we might influence that behaviour to change (Barnett and Mahony, 2011). Barnett and Mahony (2011) describe four key approaches to segmentation, which will now be considered in turn.

Firstly, it is common to segment on the basis of *socio-demographic* variables. This is perhaps one of the most common approaches in research communication where there is often a specific focus on groups who have a particular gender, ethnicity or educational background. The focus on gender and ethnicity is perhaps related to the common concern that specific genders and ethnic backgrounds appear to find certain disciplines unappealing, but it is also important to keep in mind that there are all sorts of ways socio-demographic principles can be considered, including on the basis of age, religion, sexuality, disability, culture and socio-economic context (McMaster, 2008).

Secondly, research communicators might be interested in *geo-demographic* contexts. These can sometimes overlap with some of the variables above, like socio-economic background or ethnicity, but geo-demographic factors would allow you to segment on the basis of where someone lives or is based. In research communication a consideration of such groupings might be most obvious in things like university outreach programmes, where particular schools or locations might be targeted to reach pupils from certain socio-economic backgrounds, as one example.

Thirdly, Barnett and Mahony (2011) highlight *behavioural* indicators, which can relate to a wide range of choices and actions a person might take. In research communication this might include things like the media they use, places they would be likely to visit, or their leisure activities. Dependent on the purpose of the research or activity, it might also extend to less day-to-day actions, like health behaviours, political engagement or environmental actions.

Finally, there are *psycho-graphic* variables, perhaps the most sophisticated and challenging way to group people and also the one around which the most care and caution should be taken. Segmentation on these grounds can include a wide range of things, such as a person's values, attitudes, beliefs and motivations (Barnett and Mahony, 2011). It is commonly the case that such groupings might then be explored for their relationships with other types of variables, allowing the communicator to anticipate if those who share particular perspectives, for example, have common socio-demographic features or behavioural choices.

Many organisations now create complex segmentation profiles based on a variety of factors. Box 3.1 comprises some accessible examples, as well as some brief details on the approach they have taken. This includes a selection of examples from both individual segmentation projects at the level of one organisation and those seeking to be utilised by a number of organisations or locations. Eagle *et al.* (2013) provide some further recommendations on considerations that should be taken into account in determining whether a segment is 'viable' to reach, and these are illustrated in Box 3.2.

Box 3.1 **Segmentation models**

ACORN http://acorn.caci.co.uk/
ACORN categorises people by consumer type and can be used at the level of households, postcodes and geographical area. People are grouped into six categories including 'affluent achievers', 'rising prosperity', 'comfortable communities', 'financially stretched', 'urban adversity' and 'not private households', with further distinctions within these overarching groups.

Audience Spectrum http://audiencefinder.org/explanations/audience-spectrum-faqs/
The audience spectrum breaks down attendance, participation and engagement as well as behaviours, attitudes and preferences at arts, museums and heritage organisations. It includes ten segments including 'metroculturals', 'commuterland culturebuffs', 'experience seekers', 'domitory dependables', 'trips and treats', 'home and heritage', 'up our street', 'Facebook families', 'kaleidoscope creativity', and 'heydays'.

Culture Segments http://mhminsight.com/articles/culture-segments-1179
International standard segmentation system for arts, culture and heritage organisations. It comprises eight segments: 'enrichment', 'entertainment', 'expression', 'perspective', 'stimulation', 'affirmation', 'release' and 'essence'.

DEFRA https://gov.uk/government/uploads/system/uploads/attachment_data/file/69277/pb13574-behaviours-report-080110.pdf
The Department for Environment, Food and Rural Affairs clustered people on the basis of their attitudes, beliefs and behaviours ('positive

greens', 'waste watchers', 'concerned consumers', 'sideline supporters', 'cautious participants', 'stalled starters' and 'honestly disengaged'), with a view to increasing peoples willingness to act on the environment.

Global Warming's Six Americas http://environment.yale.edu/climate-communication/files/Six-Americas-September-2012.pdf
Based on nationally representative survey data in the USA, this work carried out by Yale University and George Mason University groups and tracks six audience segments (the 'alarmed', 'concerned', 'cautious', 'disengaged', 'doubtful' and dismissive') on their beliefs, behaviours and views on policy where global warming is concerned.

The Common Cause Handbook http://valuesandframes.org/hand book/
Although not strictly a segmentation model, this handbook explores how people's values might guide their behaviours and attitudes. The guide defines ten groups of human value: 'universalism', 'benevolence', 'tradition', 'conformity', 'security', 'power', 'achievement', 'hedonism', 'stimulation' and 'self-direction'.

Public Attitudes to Science
https://ipsos-mori.com/researchpublications/researcharchive/3357/Publ ic-Attitudes-to-Science-2014.aspx
The Public Attitudes to Science survey, based on people's attitudes to science, scientists and science policy, groups people into six segments: 'confident engagers', 'distrustful engagers', 'late adopters', 'the concerned', 'the indifferent' and 'disengaged sceptics'.

VALS™ http://strategicbusinessinsights.com/vals/
VALS™ (Values, Attitudes and Lifestyles) is a US consumer-focused model which categorises people into eight types based on behaviour. This includes 'innovators', 'thinkers', 'believers', 'achievers', 'strivers', 'experiencers', 'makers' and 'survivors'.

Box 3.2 **Determining whether a segment is workable**

- *Identifiable* characteristics making one segment clear from another.
- *Measurable* attitudes, behaviours or actions that would allow the communication to be evaluated.
- *Accessible* to reach by communication or contact.
- *Substantial* segments of a scale that would warrant tailored communications.
- *Stable* by size, location or other characteristics.
- *Appropriate* to the purpose of the communication activity.

Source: Based on Eagle *et al.* (2013: 172)

From a research communication perspective, the potential to segment people on the basis of their attitudes and views has perhaps been particularly appealing, as it allows communicators to consider the relationship between disciplines and, as Susanna Hornig Priest describes, 'their worldview':

> It is crucial that members of the scientific community understand that not everyone who will scrutinize – and in some cases make use of – their results shares their values or outlook. Scientists and non-scientists are not divided solely on the basis of their education or expertise, but on the centrality of science to their worldview. (Hornig Priest, 2009: 223)

The types of segments we see mobilised in materials like the Public Attitudes to Science groupings allow communicators to think about those who might be most open to research communication efforts as well as those who would be less interested or aware. You might, for example, select to target 'late adopters' – these are people who had less of an interest in science at school, but now have environmental or ethical concerns and an interest to engage more (Ipsos MORI, 2014). Comparable segmentation efforts are occurring in settings such as museums, cultural institutions and science centres. John Falk's Identity Visitors Model, summarised in Box 3.3, similarly applies segmentation techniques to such locations, focusing not on what Falk describes as the capital 'I' identities of visitors (such as gender, race, nationality and so forth) but on the lower case 'i', the more discreet and minor influences

---

Box 3.3 Identity-related categories for cultural institutions

Explorers: Curiosity driven, interest in museum content and learning.

Facilitators: Socially motivated, encouraging experience and learning of others in social group.

Professional/hobbyist: Content relates to their profession/hobby, often looking for specific content.

Experience seekers: Visiting a museum or cultural institution as a destination.

Rechargers: Seeking refuge and recharge from day-to-day life.

Respectful pilgrims: Visit as a sense of duty to those represented by a memorial or cultural institution.

Affinity seekers: Exhibit, museum or cultural institution connects to their personal heritage or identity.

Source: Falk (2011: 147–8)

on our identities such as friendship, family status or our employment, which Falk (2011: 144) argues have a considerable impact on our 'day-to-day decision making, including those involving leisure decisions like visiting a museum'.

A weakness of this type of segmentation approach, as Falk (2011) points out, is that such identities are highly fluid. In this respect Falk (2011: 152) indicates the model to be a theoretical one, not intended to reflect the permanent identities of individuals, but rather to stress that 'what visitors find important in these venues is most frequently tied to visitors' needs and agendas, rather than to the institution's needs and agendas'. Whilst there is, then, the potential for your audiences or participants to benefit from a segmentation approach – for instance, a communication approach might better meet their interests or requirements – there are also potential dangers. In grouping people, making judgements about their intentions or possible outcomes, care needs to be taken that this is appropriate. At a practical level it is important that subtle assumptions or stereotypes do not influence judgements you might be making about a particular group's interests or choices, but segmentation also raises some broader significant questions.

> Segmentation is explicitly *discriminatory*, in the sense that it is oriented by the imperative to divide a population up and to differentially supply different segments. This feature of segmentation methods is relevant for understanding the translation of segmentation in public engagement, where very often the imperative is not to divide in order to discriminate, but to recognize *diversity* in order to enhance inclusiveness. (Barnett and Mahony, 2011: 11; emphasis in original)

Barnett and Mahony (2011) flag critiques of segmentation which suggest that it can be excluding of certain groups of people, appear manipulative and be distasteful to people, should they find out that they have been filtered in this way. To take one example from the Audience Spectrum model included in Box 3.1: 'Facebook families', people in this grouping are described as follows:

> Arts and culture play a very small role in the lives of this younger, cash-strapped group living in suburban and semi-urban areas of high unemployment. They are the least likely to think themselves as arty, while less than a third believe that the arts is important. Nevertheless, they do go out as families: cinema, live music, eating out and pantomime. (The Audience Agency, 2014: np)

Whilst the above description doesn't intend to be derogatory or condescending, reflect on how you might feel if you met the criteria for a group that are 'cash-strapped', living in an area of 'high unemployment' but 'nevertheless' venturing out. Furthermore, implicit in some segmentation approaches is the expectation that 'change' is needed, be it in someone's attitudes, opinions or behaviours. For some research communication settings this may be appropriate and transparent, but for others it may not.

Behaviour change

> While the aim of the segmentation methods is to generate relatively stable images of public attitudes and values, the increasing emphasis on 'motivational' factors indicates that segmentation methods are primarily deployed to 'generate movement': to change people's attitudes, increase public support, alter behaviour, and overcome barriers and impediments. (Barnett and Mahony, 2011: 5)

Some of the criticisms we may make of segmentation approaches relate to their context within a wider framework of social marketing techniques, and in particular those which are seeking to create behaviour change. Social marketing is used in a variety of settings including health, social policy, science and the environment, particularly by government, non-governmental organisations (NGOs) and civil organisations where changes to a person's behaviour are seen to offer individual and/or common benefits (Eagle *et al.*, 2013). Using principles of marketing and promotion, which we are used to encountering in more commercial settings, can create a sense of discomfort when the same principles, effectively 'marketing' a behaviour, are being used for social or educative reasons. However, as Eagle and colleagues (2013) highlight, there may be some consolation in the fact that people respond differently to these messages, just as they do to any advertising or promotional approach. People are not 'coerced' and some will not buy in to the message; 'social marketing is a holistic approach to behaviour change that, depending on the target audience and the cause, may use neither [the message nor the product]' (Eagle *et al.*, 2013: 5). Indeed some social marketing theories encourage more participation amongst users, depicting a model of 'exchange', or using 'networks' of those targeted to co-create materials (Eagle *et al.*, 2013).

One of the difficulties with marketing of this type is that people are unpredictable; they may not respond to information rationally and the reasons we behave in the ways that we do are incredibly complex, thus it is not and will never be an 'exact science', though social marketing builds a picture of user needs to create a more responsive approach (Eagle *et al.*, 2013). Where behaviour change is an expected outcome of your communication approach, then the principles of segmentation used in social marketing might be one way to predict how people are likely to respond. Many research communication activities may not have specific behaviour

change outcomes in mind, but arguably all communication seeks to influence in some way. Behaviour change where research communication
is concerned might include influencing actions such as continuing to
study a subject at A-level, influencing policymaking around health or the
environment, or simply encouraging someone to attend a local event or
museum. If behaviour change is a goal it might also make sense to carefully consider who is most likely to be able to enact that change. Lefebvre
(2013) posits that there are three key questions that should be asked in
determining which target segment/s are most appropriate to engender
change and these are summarised in Box 3.4.

Box 3.4 Determining the target segment

---

1 'Who are the people at the highest risk?' Are there particular priority segments that would benefit from the information you plan to
   communicate?

2 'Who are the people most open to change?' Are there particular priority segments that would be most likely to change their behaviour
   and/or motivate it in others?

3 'Who are the critical-for-success groups?' Are there other stakeholders (peers, media, organisations, policymakers) who can also contribute and influence?

Source: Based on Lefebvre (2013: 129)

Promotion of behaviour change can be very apparent in communication materials. Take for instance some health promotion materials,
which often use startling visual images or statistics around particular
behaviours to capture attention. In other cases social marketing might
be far more subtle in encouraging behaviour change. Particular attention might be paid here to the concept of 'nudge'. Nudge, originally
proposed by Thaler and Sunstein (2008), encourages behaviour without
limiting any options, or providing economic or regulatory incentive.
Recognising that people respond to behaviour change information in
different ways, but also want to be active individuals with an awareness
of their own rights and choices, the principle of nudge is one which has
been increasingly used by policymakers as a 'softer tool' to push people
in a particular direction.

> These [tools] involve working more closely with the citizens, under-
> standing how they are thinking and encouraging them to take – and to
> own – better decisions. It would involve a 'nudge' rather than a push or
> a shout, and would incorporate a 'think', that is government and other

public bodies allowing the citizens to debate and to deliberate so they can decide what is best. (John *et al.*, 2011: 2)

John and colleagues (2011: 2) describe nudges as 'framing choices', providing information and social clues as to the positive choices individuals might make for themselves and society. Rather than work against people's biases, opinions or illogicalities, the idea of nudge seeks to work with them, recognising that people are boundedly rational, that is, they can make rational choices only in the time that they have, with the information available, and within the capacity of their cognitive ability (John *et al.*, 2011). In other words, people are rational to the best of their abilities and context. Working with both psychological principles (for example, that people tend to be creatures of habit, and habits are hard to challenge) and social insights (for instance, the importance of how we are viewed by peers), the idea of nudge seeks to present options rather than one behavioural choice.

To give one example, the Danish Cancer Society has been using nudge to influence the choices we make when eating meals at buffets. It highlights that when faced with an overwhelming number of food choices people have a tendency to sample many things, are influenced by the selections of others and tend to overeat (Laub Hansen, 2012). This is a problem not only for reasons of obesity and weight, but for the longer-term relationship with incidences of cancer. Rather than target this by minimising the options a buffet offers, or reducing the opportunities for eating out, which would be unpopular with the catering industry, the Danish Cancer Society recommend the use of a number of subtle nudges to influence consumer behaviour (Laub Hansen, 2012). These nudges include things like floor arrows encouraging people to visit healthy options as a priority, preparing fruit and vegetables into bite-sized pieces and reducing plate sizes to influence portion control. Whilst subtle, these interventions promoted an increased consumption of healthier foods, as well as offering some benefits for caterers, such as decreased queuing, less waste and increased purchasing of certain products (Laub Hansen, 2012).

The principle of nudge is not without weaknesses. It tends to work best around relatively simple behaviours, rather than those that would be very controversial or challenging. The subtlety of nudge can make such interventions tricky to evaluate and, like most communication efforts, it has a tendency to work most effectively when it comes from a trusted source (John *et al.*, 2011). Like segmentation approaches, nudging people in a particular direction may appear manipulative or deceitful; however, remembering that a nudge will ultimately allow a participant to make their own choice can reduce some of these concerns.

Undertaking a segmentation exercise or using principles around behaviour change more broadly can be both technically complex and expensive and, in addition, segments can quickly, shift, alter or change, particularly around aspects like behaviour and attitude (Eagle *et al.*, 2013; Barnett and Mahony, 2011). Therefore, for many independent research communicators or organisations a detailed segmentation strategy might be beyond the scope of an individual project or activity. Nevertheless, if appropriate, the work carried out by other similar organisations might provide some helpful considerations, tips or clues about those to or with whom you are seeking to communicate.

The 'hard-to-reach'

The desire to create a more complex profile of the relationships between people's lives, behaviours and attitudes may reflect the increasing anxiety that our attention is now demanded by a multitude of communication opportunities. In a media context this is summarised by the term 'cross-media', where the diversity of content, as well as platforms now available to people, leads to 'many different overlapping groups, communities, affiliations, belongings, identities and lifestyles' (Carpentier *et al.*, 2014a: 7). People effectively 'curate' their media use, for instance combining digital and traditional media consumption, thus creating a jigsaw of activities for them around their own preferences, preferred means and interests, leading some researchers to describe individuals as now having a 'media repertoire' or 'media lives' which can be seamless and almost invisible to others (Bjur *et al.*, 2014). The cross-media context also provides new opportunities for involvement in the communication process as previously discussed, including the encouragement of user distribution and sharing, and the creation of audience communities around common interests or fandom (Noguera Vivo *et al.*, 2014). This creates a challenge for the communicator, as already touched upon in the case of journalists, who must think about the best way to capture increasingly individualised and self-motivated users, the 'audience of one' (Lefebvre, 2013); but it can also shroud the ways in which some people, who may lack knowledge, literacy or trust, may not be granted the same access or participation (Carpentier *et al.*, 2014a).

Particular attention has been paid to the concept of 'hard-to-reach' audiences, 'underserved', 'marginalised' or 'disengaged' members of society who may be less visible to research communicators on the basis of a variety of factors. Certain segments of society, such as those that are affluent, vocal or organised, can be more visible and obvious for communication efforts (Eagle *et al.*, 2013), leaving others overlooked. Whilst some elements of this discussion relate to plain old inequality and discrimination, where certain people face prejudice, something which research communicators should clearly seek to avoid, there can also be a moralistic tone to such conversations which potentially mask the assumptions made about particular people, groups or communities. Groups that are characterised as 'hard to reach' may question 'by whom?' (Wilkinson, 2014: 207) as they may not see themselves as being so. Care should be taken that assumptions are not made about particular communities and that their preferences and needs are reflected (Eagle *et al.*, 2013).

In research communication contexts the common assumption might be that people are generally prevented from engaging due to demographic or educational barriers, but there are wider issues to keep in mind. Emily Dawson's (2014a: 212) work on informal, designed environments such as zoos, aquariums, science centres and museums suggests that they can be 'for some' rather than 'all', and that at least in the context of the United Kingdom most visitors tend to be from '[w]hite ethnic backgrounds, middle and upper classes, live in cities and visit with their families or schools'. Across the United States and Europe, although Dawson (2014a) highlights that there is less comparable data available, a similar picture emerges, whereby those in attendance at such sites tend to be younger, with children and from higher social classes. Her work suggests that the needs of those who have been disenfranchised in such settings, including on the bases of ethnicity, gender or low-income, are woefully under-researched. In addition, the needs of people with a disability, who may have issues of physical exclusion, are rarely examined (Dawson, 2014a).

If we spend a few moments to look to the arts setting, similar concerns are frequently raised:

> One of the biggest barriers to audience engagement is the notion held by many that the arts are simply not for them. The 'it's not for me' syndrome is endemic and conspires to exclude people from experiences that could transform their lives. To help overcome this and building on the experience of free admission to museums and galleries, all admission prices should be removed from publicly funded cultural organisations for one week. Once the initial barrier of engagement is overcome, audiences must be given the opportunity to deepen their experience and be introduced to more complex work … A crucial factor in the recommendations I've set out so far is the touring of excellent work. We must provide the opportunity to experience excellence across the whole country. (McMaster, 2008: 7)

Whilst the above quote acknowledges that there are audiences whose needs are not being met around arts engagement it also highlights common assumptions about those who do not engage. Firstly, that lack of participation is a simple question of cost; secondly, that access to a geographical location limits admission; and thirdly, that the problem lies with 'them'; these distort the subtler reasons at play in the view that 'it's not for me'. Such constraints can include things like time, interest or knowledge (Brook, 2011), as well as prior experience (Jensen, 2013). For some, venues for research communication like museums or universities may simply be an enigma; for instance large numbers of people may simply not see a museum as offering any benefits to them as an individual (Falk, 2011).

Where the arts are concerned, settings such as art museums have long been critiqued for their appeal to particular sectors of society and social inclusion is heavily on the agenda (Jensen, 2013; Lewis, 1990; see Chapter 5). However, across both the arts and sciences, while there is a desire for social inclusion in theory, there is also a lack of clear tools to put that into practice, as well as challenges in embedding more participatory practices (Bienkowski, 2014; Lynch, 2009). Hard-to-reach groups are often targeted by 'outreach' activities – further separating the excluded from the core business of such institutions (Jensen, 2013) – or simply provided with a 'new' activity specifically for under-represented groups which might be 'new' to them but has not been tailored in any way to their particular needs or requirements (Dawson, 2014a). This is a particularly important point, as research suggests people can feel even more disenfranchised when they are 'othered', implying to them that they are not the 'ideal' visitor or an experience has not been designed to be relevant to them (Dawson, 2014b). Dawson (2014a) highlights the need for far more complex institutional changes when seeking to create appeal for those that are disenfranchised, including the need for alterations to infrastructure (such as how activities are marketed and ensuring people feel welcome and included within environments), greater community acceptance (awareness amongst the community of such venues that change is needed) and an increased awareness of literacy around such venues; put simply, a need for previously excluded people to be aware of what they can do in such settings and how they can maximise it for their own purposes.

Simply identifying and then meeting a group that may be deemed 'hard-to-reach' is an oversight, which may ignore the more systemic reasons why some people may not identify research communication as being of interest to them. Focusing on the individual, targeting their behaviour – for instance encouraging them to more regularly attend a museum for a perceived social benefit (Brennan *et al.*, 2014) – may distract from the shared and collective nature of inequality; 'the right to change a society is not at the individual's discretion, as this right belongs to the society as a whole' (Brennan *et al.*, 2014: 333). The terminology of being 'hard-to-reach' is therefore quite problematic. Perhaps rather than consider 'hard-to-reach' groups as neglected, invisible or isolated it might be better to remember how we use the term in other ways. 'I've been hard-to-reach' might be something we often say if we have been busy or our attention is elsewhere; thus, remembering people's active choice to engage, or not, in research communication is important.

Summary

In this chapter we have discussed ways in which you might consider working with audiences, participants and publics and the theoretical and practical ramifications these may have in terms of your own research communication activities. What is clear is that the potential reach of research communication is considerable and therefore as a research communicator there are choices to be made around how you consider who can be reached and the people that comprises. In a communication-saturated environment, demands on attention are numerous, and so clear consideration of the right group for your communication effort increases the likelihood of your message having resonance. The relationship between communicator and audience is shifting and changing, and an awareness of this as a research communicator will help you to consider the most suitable engagement for your own particular activity.

Some see the current agenda for inclusion as actually weakening engagement, whereby approaches to increase participation, particularly online, have rendered engagement meaningless: 'connecting or interacting has become a substitute for having something to say' (Furedi, 2004: 89). At first glance it could be assumed that Furedi is criticising people's ability to participate, but in fact he is suggesting that we underestimate people, at times diminishing the quality of what is on offer (for instance in museums or libraries) to the lowest denominator in order to be inclusive. In Furedi's (2004) view this underestimates people's abilities to rise to an experience, as well as the importance of their own aspirations, while also undervaluing the essential essence, quality or intellectual merit of cultural and educational institutions. Ben Goldacre, a well-known voice in science and medical communication, has similarly critiqued the 'indulgent and well-financed' public engagement community as being too 'obsessed with taking the message to everyone, rarely offering stimulating content to the people who are already interested' (Goldacre, 2008: 321).

What does this mean for research communicators? It means care is needed. There is a difference between identifying, understanding and developing activities for a group based on their needs and aspirations, and assuming that they have a particular attitude or requirement for behaviour change. Equally, care should be taken that aspirations for quality in research communication, do not imply that particular groups are of a lesser value or have created their own restrictions to engagement. Work around social inclusion suggests that there are many complex reasons why people may not feel research communication or its venues are for them. Whilst Furedi comments that 'historical experience demonstrates that when the "excluded" want to be "included" they do a very good job of breaking down the barriers to their participation' (Furedi, 2004: 86), the existence of such hurdles in the first place is important to remember.

Further reading

Barnett, C. and Mahony, N., *Segmenting Publics* (Swindon: ESRC/NCCPE, 2011).

John, P., Cotterill, S., Moseley, A., Richardson, L., Smith, G., Stocker, G. and Wales, C., *Nudge. Nudge, Think, Think: Using Experiments to Change Civic Behaviour* (London: Bloomsbury Academic, 2011).

PART II

Approach

4

Face-to-face

In research communication there is a common rallying call encouraging academics to move out of the ivory tower. This concept revolves around the principle that ivory symbolises an impractical and privileged building material, whilst a tower implies a sense of physical, practical and linguistic isolation. The concept was first used in its modern sense to describe the academic community in the nineteenth century, to gently chastise academics on the basis not only of their communication but also of their perceived connectedness with the real world. Thus, whilst there are now multiple opportunities through which researchers are able to communicate – in the media, through popular writing, in online content, and so forth – there remain some particular opportunities to communicate in face-to-face settings, which can be seen to have particular benefits in reaching out from the figurative or otherwise tower.

This chapter will introduce readers to opportunities for face-to-face communication and engagement activities. It will cover key approaches, including participation in the research process, moving through to events and activities you might be involved in, including festivals, cafes, talks, lectures, at generic venues and in museums, science centres and galleries. The chapter will draw on examples from contemporary movements, for instance the use of comedy in communication, the continuing popularity of Café Scientifique and how face-to-face events are being used in research processes.

Why face-to-face?

In today's technological and knowledge-driven society the role of face-to-face communication can appear to be ever diminishing. With a wealth of resources at our finger tips through ever-emerging electronic devices, programmes and apps, we may question why researchers would still consider communicating in face-to-face ways. However, there are important reasons why face-to-face communication has a role in research communication activities.

Firstly, communicating directly with people often allows us to strike up a relationship which it can be difficult to do through other means. It can often be easier to develop a rapport or to empathise with people face-to-face, and to avoid things being misconstrued as can occasionally be the case when communicating electronically. If your research communication is encouraging any form of group or team activity, face-to-face communication can be most straightforward. Even though there are now lots of technologies available to support virtual meeting spaces, having a physical or face-to-face activity is still helpful for complex tasks and information sharing (Stryker and Santoro, 2012).

Secondly, face-to-face communication may, if you want it to, allow people to see you as more than a researcher. Arguably, things like an online profile, or newspaper description of you,[1] can provide a similar essence, and there is growing evidence that computer-mediated communications can simulate the face-to-face experience (Kappas and Krämer, 2011) but such approaches may not allow you the same sense of opportunity to connect with your participants as fellow individuals. In some cases, face-to-face settings can provide more time for informal interaction, be it sharing a coffee during a break in activities or engaging in an informal conversation about the morning's weather, all of which may help a researcher to appear less remote and more grounded in reality. This type of 'modelling' behaviour is often seen to be particularly useful in communication activities which have an educational dimension to them.

Thirdly, face-to-face communication opportunities can provide you with more control over a situation and your message; it allows you control over the anecdotes, insights or experiences you might decide to draw in, to respond flexibly and differently as the situation might require and to think about ways to really engage with your participants. You might communicate through a quote in a newspaper article, but you won't see your readers become excited or glaze over as they read it. In face-to-face communication your participants are highly visible – if a metaphor doesn't work or, conversely, if people are really enthusiastic, you can respond accordingly.

Finally, there are many opportunities for face-to-face communication and, related to that, resources which can be drawn on to support it. If we take museums alone, it is estimated that there are over 55,000 in over 200 countries (ICOM, 2014). If you have a passion for communicating with people directly, then there are highly likely to be opportunities both on the doorstep of your tower and, perhaps more importantly, a few steps away.

Face-to-face opportunities

There is a plethora of face-to-face opportunities for communication available to researchers and participants today. Since the latter decades of the twentieth century there has been a growing trend to map how various countries globally participate in arts and cultural activities (Schuster, 2007; Morrone, 2006) and many of the sites which these surveys ask people about naturally align to locations for the communication of research. Whilst a number of the studies undertaken by individual countries do not allow for direct comparison of rates of participation, primarily due to their methodological variations, there are some general trends which are worthy of note. Schuster (2007) highlights these trends across participation studies from thirty-five different countries including the United States, Australia, New Zealand, Europe, Japan and Brazil. Firstly, whilst activities like going to the cinema, reading and attending sports events have the highest participation rates across countries, this is closely followed by attending museums and historic sites. Next in popularity are attending musical concerts, followed by the theatre, whilst attending the opera or dance tend to have the lowest participation rates. Schuster (2007) notes that these trends, which are similar over a number of countries, seem to be linked to the supply of the activity in an individual country, though he also does not rule out its being associated with demand.

At a European level, data collected via the Eurobarometer shows the highest attendance in cultural events tends to be in Scandinavia and the Netherlands (Brook, 2011), whilst across Europe 37 percent of people say they have visited a museum or gallery at least once in the last 12 months, 31 percent have visited a public library and 28 percent have been to the theatre (TNS Opinion and Social, 2013). When people are asked about reasons for non-participation, lack of time is the most frequently cited barrier, followed by expense and lack of interest, with lack of knowledge/cultural background, perhaps surprisingly, being one of the least-cited reasons (Brook, 2011). Such venues provide a wide variety of opportunities for face-to-face communication. We will now highlight some of the most prominent for research communication specifically.

Lectures, demonstrations and presentations

The opportunity to talk about, demonstrate and present research has not disappeared as communication opportunities have evolved; in fact there are still numerous opportunities that call on researchers to communicate their work in this way. Many universities and research institutions hold regular public talks or lecture series, have visits from commercial operations and, of course, present to their students and other stakeholders through events like seminar series. Universities are also well versed in holding open days, and though these often follow a rather traditional format which is designed to market the institution to potential future students, they are arguably still an opportunity for researchers to refine and develop their communication skills.

Presentations are often critiqued for effectively 'selling' a subject area, which might promote a positive image of research alone and avoid any critical consideration of research (European Commission, 2012). Although by their nature talks and presentations can offer a model for a fairly one-way style of delivery, interaction can be embedded if it is planned for and considered. As a presenter you often have a good degree of control over that which you are presenting and therefore, if appropriate, there is nothing to stop you considering how you might include more questioning, critical or reflexive narratives within such formats.

Although lectures and presentations are certainly one of the more traditional presentation styles, that doesn't mean people aren't interested in making them more novel or creative. For example, you might consider curating a series of presentations which take the format of a Pecha Kucha, a quick-fire presentation style involving twenty slides (often heavily image based) being shown for twenty seconds each. You can see an example of a Pecha Kucha from PechaKucha night, which started in Tokyo and now occurs in over eight hundred cities as a way for designers to showcase their work (www.pechakucha.org/). A presentation slot of under seven minutes really gets researchers to think about their key messages and how to present them. Increasingly popular are models such as 'Unconferences', which use techniques like Open Space Technology to generate on-the-spot agendas and present ideas in far less prepared or formal ways than might have been common in the past. Meanwhile TED Talks have also grown in popularity and, setting aside the fact that they are novel in their open, online dissemination, they also encourage researchers to employ all sorts of narrative, visual and audience engagement-based techniques within a format which would otherwise be relatively traditional. The most popular twenty TED Talks of all time cover a variety of subjects from creativity to statistics, from orgasm to underwater creatures (www.ted.com/playlists/171/the_most_popular_talks_of_all).

Demonstrations were of course first popular amongst scientists showcasing their wares in the eighteenth and nineteenth centuries (Gregory and Miller, 1998) but, to this day, the opportunity to demonstrate elements of one's research also provides opportunities for interaction. It should go without saying that if you are preparing for any live form of experimentation or demonstration within a face-to-face communication activity, you should be exceptionally well practised, have clear explanations and use equipment which is both working and suitable for the environment in which you are presenting (Bultitude, 2010). It's also sensible to have a back-up plan or explanation ready if certain elements of the demonstration simply don't work on the day. Today's researchers will not get away with the graphic dissections, electric shocks and extreme surprises of the past and so it is also vitally important to familiarise yourself with the insurance constraints and health and safety policies of both the venue that is hosting you and your own institution, regardless of your discipline. It is also possible that when demonstrating in this way your 'venue' need not be particularly orientated towards either research or communication. 'Science busking', for example, actively takes research communication to new types of venues and locations. Although presentations and demonstrations often have homes in fairly traditional locations, these are diversifying all the time as John Durant (2013: 2681) sums up: 'Where once you had to know where to look for science outreach, now you're as likely to come across it in a café, a bar, a theatre, or a club as you are in a university or community college extension program.'

One of the major benefits of face-to-face activities, regardless of location, is that you might try out communicating with different groups of people for the first time, often in fairly inexpensive ways which can allow you to be more creative or experimental. Investigate national or local organisations that might be looking for researchers to speak to them; for example, community groups like the University of the Third Age, the Women's Institute or groups aimed at young people, like Guides and Scouts, offer good settings to try out face-to-face communication for the first time.

Schools

Within formal education there are also many opportunities to deliver your research ideas or experiences; presentations, workshops, clubs or school visits can all provide a means to reach the next generation. Schools often appreciate face-to-face activities as these allow students to connect to both research and researchers. This often aligns well with educational agendas encouraging students from different genders or ethnic groups, or from specific aptitudes (those seen as less attracted to subjects or particularly gifted), to consider university or a specific type of career (European Commission, 2012). This can mean that, perhaps unusually for many researchers, the focus of your activity might not be restricted to your research but can also include content about you, what you like doing, what your career involves and how you got there (Bowater and Yeoman, 2013; Mayhew and Hall, 2012).

Of course many formal school activities are also expected to have some kind of connection to the curriculum. It is often fairly straightforward to find out some basic details about what students are expected to cover at different ages through the appropriate government website of the country in which you are communicating, but if you are not sure about how to find that information, ask the organisation, school or teacher with whom you are working. They should be able to provide the basics on what the students are currently covering, which is helpful in orientating any communication plans to the right level. If your own education was some time ago it is important to ask about this. Not only are there likely to have been changes in the curriculum since that time but you may already have been a high achiever in a specific subject area, particularly if you are now working in it professionally, so a broader picture of students' understanding and awareness can be helpful.

In terms of the ways to get involved with schools-based communication there are lots of organisations that can assist; investigate subject ambassador schemes, find out if relevant learned societies have schools-based programmes or investigate if your organisation has an outreach team working with schools with which you could become involved (Bowater and Yeoman, 2013). Schools can be notoriously difficult to 'cold call', finding the appropriate teacher or subject lead through email or telephone is extremely challenging and, unsurprisingly, they are often restrictive to unknown visitors, therefore working with some type of 'mediator' can be helpful.

Like many research communication activities aimed at a broader group of participants, when working with schools it works well to talk about a research area quite broadly, or at least to be prepared that it could provoke some quite general questions. It can be helpful to have a key concept, theme or idea to focus on, particularly one which is likely to be attractive to young people (Mayhew and Hall, 2012), but there is still the likelihood that some questions or ideas that it might provoke will be of a broad nature. Try not to get too tied up in the intricacies of a question not being strictly in your area of expertise, remembering that your audience will see you as an 'ambassador' of your subject. You can be honest if you don't know the response to something, indicating to participants that it's a really interesting question or something to find out more about. Events like competitions and fairs also remain a popular option for schools-based activities, particularly where the sciences are concerned (Bultitude, 2010). They can provide excellent opportunities to work with and support others 'on the ground', as well as in the capacity of a judge or expert who might be consulted. Don't underestimate or talk down to those of a younger age and avoid trying to relate to them too much through jargon or cultural references, unless these are things in which you are naturally interested.

Whilst there are many opportunities to communicate with school- or college-aged young people, this is not the only option. Researchers often look to schools as an obvious focus for communication activities, but these venues have their challenges. There will be young people who are simply not interested, or who don't have the same love of a subject area that you do, whilst others will have a natural interest but may feel reluctant to share this, and so working with such age groups can also be difficult.

Museums, galleries and science centres

Given that there are an estimated 55,000 museums globally, with over 1,000 art galleries in Paris alone, there will be very few researchers who do not have such attractions nearby. Add to this science centres, almost six hundred of which are members of the Association of Science-Technology Centers (ASTC), across forty different countries, and further opportunities for research communication emerge. In addition some university researchers will also have their own institutional collections; for instance, in the United Kingdom it is estimated that there are around four hundred university museums, about a quarter of which are regularly open to the public (Merriman, 2012).

Museums and galleries have become 'hybrid spaces'. Their displays, events and exhibitions, as well as the physical environment of their venue, have diversified, now often comprising shops, information centres and conference venues (Henning, 2006), thus they offer multiple opportunities for engagement amongst researchers. Many modern museums have adopted a 'people-centred' focus, seeking to connect to visitors' own experiences and values, whilst still adhering to certain museum messages which connect visitors to their objects and archives (Hourston Hanks *et al.*, 2012; Henning, 2006: 129). Griffiths (2008) argues that museums have not changed in their thinking as much as we might imagine, as there was always a focus on creating engaging and interactive experiences. Instead she suggests that the term interactivity has changed, with museums now recognising a more dialogic model of visitors centred on their own agency. Museums are, then, more globally conscious, using diversity as a way to attract audiences, and are seeking to be more accessible and democratised in addressing that more diverse audience (Hourston Hanks *et al.*, 2012; Henning, 2006). Thus, assumptions cannot be made that museums offer only one type of experience; instead their programmes can include a variety of activities, from exhibitions and collections to event calendars and adults-only evenings, as well as programmes targeted at young people in both informal and formal education (Merriman, 2012). Science centres are typically characterised by a more interactive flavour and contemporary focus, unrestricted by the tie to a permanent collection. Their focus on revealing the workings of science and encouraging a participant to directly engage with it creates spaces where learning is not entirely predetermined, which is seen to sit in contrast to a traditional, disciplined museum or gallery approach, and to be particularly amenable to contemporary notions of the role of citizens in public engagement (Henning, 2006). Seeking to sit at the heart of some communities as they do, it is also not uncommon to see museums, science centres and galleries playing central roles in local festivals or broader series of events, which also provides opportunities to connect to the wider community through these events.

Exhibitions are a mainstay of these contexts; however, the term exhibition can be used to describe a variety of activities: shows, displays and fairs which can also have multiple purposes (Velarde, 2001). Whilst museums, galleries and science centres will then organise talks, lectures, presentations and exhibitions, interactive activities are also popular within these settings (Bultitude, 2010), sometimes targeted at general visitors but also frequently within formal or informal schools programmes. Workshops, for example, are beneficial because they allow a communicator to provide advice and encouragement, often in a less directive or intimidating way than when presenting formally. Such locations have then been able to mirror, to some degree, the rising popularity of the 'maker' movement and, specifically, 'make and take' activities (Bultitude, 2010) allowing for visitors' participation in new and novel ways in a 'make' which they can then 'take' with them when they go home.

Researchers can foster a personal connection to local venues through a variety of means. For instance, researchers can become involved in refreshing exhibits or designing new interactives and programmes. Although it is common for certain materials and exhibits to 'travel' and be repeated in other locations, many museums, galleries and science centres also have representations of their local areas or are keen to feature locally based research; to have 'roots firmly grounded in the local culture' (Monro, 2009: 196). Investigate if those you enjoy visiting have boards, advisory groups or specific opportunities to volunteer. Volunteering may not be something that you can easily see fitting into your daily life as a researcher, but time commitments are sometimes very moderate or flexible and it can be a good way to make some initial connections. It is also likely that such organisations will contact your organisation if they have a relevant project coming up, so make sure that any online profiles or expert guides show your willingness to engage in these types of activities. Take into account that some small, local institutions in particular have very limited resources or may be operating under charitable status. That could mean offering time or advice free of charge or at a far lower rate than an organisation would typically offer, but there are other rewards from engaging in this way, be they raising a discipline's or an institution's profile or personal benefits to the researcher and any participants.

Festivals and cultural events

Activities in this category can overlap with those that you might consider under talks, demonstrations and presentations, and yet they warrant a separate entry. Why is this the case? There has been a proliferation of these types of cultural events over recent years, which has provided increased opportunities for researchers to communicate and engage with the public. Festivals are proving ever more popular. These are often discipline specific; for instance, there are a wide number of literature, arts and science festivals which, as well as offering other types of activities, offer obvious opportunities for those with relevant interests to attend (Wolinsky, 2010). Additionally, there are festivals which do not have a specific academic focus but which often have zones or spaces that are looking to cater for a variety of interests, allowing those without a specific interest to 'stumble' on research in new and interesting ways (Wolinsky, 2010). Even amongst festivals which are promoting a particular disciplinary identity there is evidence that they can reach people who have a low or limited awareness of a research discipline (Wilkinson, 2012).

Discipline-specific festivals are now common across Europe, as well as other areas of the world, and appear to have a considerable reach. To take one example, the two-week BergamoScienza in Italy attracted 84,000 attendees in 2009 and is a festival where police marshalling has been required, simply due to the scale of the crowds involved and the popularity of the events (Wolinsky, 2010). The Festa Literária Internacional de Paraty or, as it is commonly known, The Flip Festival in Brazil welcomes thousands to its debates with famous authors and literary professors, alongside open-air theatrical and musical events (Festa Literária Internacional de Paraty, 2015). Its success has been so great that it has inspired parallel programmes and activities, including Flupp, a sister festival based in the favelas of Rio de Janeiro, which seeks to broaden literacy and raise awareness of the literature authored by the favelas' residents. Organisations are thinking about novel ways to reach people at such cultural gatherings, for instance the Instituto Gulbenkian de Ciência in Portugal has a long-standing partnership with the Optimus Alive Oeiras music and art festival, permitting its researchers to set up demo activities, art installations and researcher speed-dating activities alongside sold-out music concerts by the likes of international artists such as Coldplay (Leão and Castro, 2012).

Festivals often take place over a few days or a weekend, and 'subject' weeks, days, months or nights are also growing in popularity through-out Europe as well as elsewhere (European Commission, 2012). Unlike a festival, such timed events are not always restricted to specific geographical locations or sites and there are differing views regarding how alike Festivals and 'weeks' are, with festivals typically being seen to offer more high-energy and celebratory activities (Bultitude *et al.*, 2011).To take one example, European Researchers Night, which has been held annually since 2005, includes researchers in over three hundred cities across twenty-four European and neighbouring countries. In 2013 these events, which encourage face-to-face communication and interaction in order to create more personal connections between people and research, were estimated to reach over 1.2 million people, despite being based around smaller, individual events and activities across a number of cities (European Commission, 2014).

What such events, festivals or 'weeks', have in common is a space in time and place which appears to be encouraging increasingly creative opportunities for research communication. With high numbers of visitors attending in friend or family groups, as well as individuals, the activities are often designed to reach diverse interests and age ranges (Jensen and Buckley, 2012). Durant (2013) describes an 'inventiveness' within the festival movement which is seeing activities including story-telling, film, narration and sporting activities create opportunities for research to be better embedded within culture. Perhaps the sheer scope of festival opportunities, or their one-off nature, is leading to what Durant (2013) describes as an increased experimentation around such events. Their temporality can create a sense of occasion and spectacle, or investment either in voluntary terms or for materials, which would be unsustainable over a longer period of time (Jensen and Buckley, 2012). Furthermore, their short-term nature means they are often staffed by researchers and professionals, which is seen to be popular with attendees (Jensen and Buckley, 2012). It is important to remain aware that festivals will not reach everyone; some festivals can be very expensive to attend or are clearly focused on attracting particular social groupings. However, the increased popularity of festivals has meant that some organisations are seeking to more closely coordinate such activities; for example, in the United States there is now a Science Festival Alliance (Durant, 2013; Wolinsky, 2010). Considering events in your local area or looking for any national activities or organising bodies within your home country is one way to find out more about involvement in such activities.

Case study 4.1 Brain Day, Centre for Brain Research, University of Auckland

Brain Awareness Week is an annual international campaign launched by the Dana Foundation of New York. The week aims to raise public awareness of brain research internationally. Since 2004, the Centre for Brain Research at the University of Auckland in New Zealand has used the week to bring to light its activities, composing a series of events during Brain Day to highlight and communicate its work to both public and community partners (www.fmhs.auckland. ac.nz/en/faculty/cbr/brain-day-2015.html). Effectively acting as a health science festival, Brain Day is able to link to many interesting aspects of neuroscience research, including not only the scientific and health-based ramifications of brain research, but also psychological and social dimensions.

Laura Fogg-Rogers organised the festival between 2010 and 2013. As she describes, the festival sought to 'establish engagement and involvement with research, alongside broader aims to raise awareness of brain health and disease … the community focus of the Centre for Brain Research meant that Brain Day was a unique opportunity for scientists to connect and meet with community groups and members of the public'. Held on a Saturday, Brain Day attracts around 3,000 visitors and is free to attend.

Perhaps unusually for a festival of this type, participants are invited to the university itself, rather than to a more public setting. Laura explains the reasons behind this: 'as the festival is organised by the Centre for Brain Research with little sponsorship, we didn't have a huge budget available. However, we wanted the event to be free to encourage as many people as possible to attend. An easy way to do this was to hold the event on university premises, so we sought out the largest conferencing facility in the University of Auckland. While this is still on university territory, its neutrality as a 'business school' meant that we attracted a wider audience, including more families and people without neurological disorders. However, easily accessible underground car parking and mobility friendly rooms meant that we still retained our existing audiences.'

The year 2010 was a 'turning point' for the festival, as Laura describes: 'Moving from the Medical Faculty, which was difficult to reach … enabled easier access for people with mobility issues. Not only that, but the lecture capacity extended from three hundred people per hour to 1,600 per hour – which meant we could run a parallel programme of exciting events … We added in lots more family friendly interactive experiments, social media build-up, arts showcases and musical entertainment, and in 2010, the new festival format was launched.' Over the course of the day the festival now includes a variety of activities, from those designed for young people, including hands-on activities and demonstrations, to talks and lectures from researchers, as well as anatomy displays. Brain Day includes content showcasing music and art links, as well as opportunities to profile relevant community groups and opportunities for participants to sign up for involvement in things like advisory groups and participatory research (Fogg-Rogers et al., 2015). The activities meet the needs both of those who are keen to participate and of those who simply wish to listen and find out more.

We asked Laura whether the link to international Brain Awareness Week was useful to the festival. 'I think it is really important to link festivals into wider social contexts. Feeling that you are part of a wider movement, or can relate your events to other exciting events happening nationally or internationally, means that you can generate a feeling of excitement and anticipation. This is a critical element in a festival, as their nature means that they are time-bound celebrations of research and understanding. Linking to national charities, like the Neurological Foundation of New Zealand, ... helped to generate this buzz. Not only could we build anticipation through social media, newsletters and web emails, but we were also able to generate international publicity after the event.'

Through evaluation of Brain Day over three years, Laura and her colleagues were able to establish that attending lectures was a high priority for many visitors, who often ranked these as 'most useful' and identified them as a good learning opportunity (Fogg-Rogers et al., 2015), despite the wide range of other types of activities on offer. 'We could see the popularity of the lectures just by looking at audience numbers, but this went against all the academic literature stating that transmission communication was out of fashion. We wondered if our audiences really wanted more hands-on science or discussions, and we just weren't giving enough of it to them', says Laura, 'however, the evaluation showed that lectures may be a traditional form of communication, but they are popular for a reason! Our audiences were coming to the event for the joy of learning – either to enhance their own knowledge and interest, or to boost their sense of control in understanding neurological conditions. The lesson for us was don't throw the baby out with the bathwater!'

It's important to bear in mind that even some of the more 'traditional' formats, like a public talk, have been diversified within the Brain Day festival context. To take as an example a live event, 'mind reading' in 2012 saw imaging scientists carry out a live analysis of an MRI scan to ascertain whether someone was being truthful or lying, demonstrating there is still room for creativity in more traditional public talks and presentations. Finally, we asked Laura for her main tips for festival organisers based on this activity: 'Festivals are unique environments, as they generate a buzz around research for a critical period of time. The nature of the festival environment means that you can have lots of different formats all happening simultaneously, and that for me is a key part of the experience.'

Café Scientifique

The Café Scientifique movement, drawing its origins from the French Café Philosophique tradition, is also a growing location for the discussion of academic ideas. With a loose and flexible nature, cafés are held in a variety of locations including coffee shops, bars, pubs, science centres and schools, under a variety of guises and titles, and throughout many countries internationally, including Japan, Kenya, the United States and Brazil (Maile and Griffiths, 2014a; Grand, 2009). Though organisational networks exist, and some cafés are supported by established institutions and groups, they are frequently set up by interested individuals on a voluntary basis, with very little outlay required. Their public nature, away from academic settings, means they are often informal and open to all, the only payment being a potential donation or the purchase of a drink as you participate. Some cafés ask for registration, particularly for popular subjects or speakers, but most operate an open-door policy. Frequently organised on a quieter weeknight, venues provide their establishment on the basis of the bar sales and, whilst many major cities and university localities have them, their informal nature means that cafés also appear in locations which don't have a research 'hub' on the doorstep (Wolinsky, 2010).

Though the Café Scientifique movement was heavily influenced by a focus on science, they have always included consideration of related research themes, drawing on a wider range of speakers, for instance to explore the arts or social and ethical perspectives. Bristol happens to be home to Social Science in the City™, which uses the same model to specifically deliver reflection and discussion on social science topics in cafés, community halls and centres (Maile, 2014). Thus, the reach of cafés can be quite broad, attracting a regular group of people as well as those who might have a specific interest in a subject which happens to be appearing on that occasion. As Maile (2014: 38) describes, 'attendees who come from a range of social and professional backgrounds to listen to research findings and ideas and to think about and discuss them constitutes a form of public engagement that extends beyond any sectional interest'.

Researchers will typically present for only a short time, preferably allowing the opportunity for conversation and discussion to emerge. If you are invited to speak at a café it is likely that you will be asked to leave all typical presentation materials at home. It's not a lecture; instead most cafés will want to see you speaking relatively informally, without the aid of presentational materials or resources, as Grand (2009: 212) sums up: 'changing the venue changes the nature of the debate to make it relevant to those who are participating: in a classroom, you expect to be taught, in a lecture theatre, you expect to get lectured at, but in a cafe, you expect to have a conversation'. Whilst topics are many and varied, a focus on contemporary or 'unfinished research' can provide a good prod for conversation, and though frequently in the United Kingdom there will be one or two speakers, in other countries there might be a panel. Some have facilitators in support, or particular structures to the format for which it is important to prepare (Grand, 2009). In France, for instance, multiple speakers are popular, to avoid giving only one view, whilst in Denmark cafés often involve a scientist and artist for parallel perspectives (Dallas, 2006). Traditionally, Cafés Scientifique were set up with only discussion in mind. At times this may naturally mean discussion will be unsupportive of research and speakers should be open to difficult or challenging questions. If you are considering involvement for the first time, why not attend a few to get a feel for them as a starting point; or, if you are considering setting one up, contact the Café Scientifique network, which has a good deal of useful advice.

Comedy, immersive experiences and generic venues

One step further from discussion events, using comedy to communicate research has started to emerge strongly in the United Kingdom, particularly where science is concerned. Scientists like Brian Cox will often be found talking about science in comedic ways on TV and radio, whilst the likes of Dara O'Briain and Robin Ince are showing that comedy and a science background really can mix (Riesch, 2015; Bowater and Yeoman, 2013). In part, the opportunity for more researchers to become involved in comedy relates to the increasing popularity of the Bright Club movement, which has spread from University College London to over ten different cities around the United Kingdom in a manner not dissimilar to the spread of Café Scientifique (Bright Club, 2014). Of course, aspects of research have long been drawn on for comedic material; 'black' comedy impinges on all sorts of issues that researchers are interested in, from life-and-death medical scenarios to political infighting and domestic life. However, daring to consider such topics in comedic ways can be daunting for researchers, not least because there is the chance to stray into sensitive subject matter and the potential to offend.

If you are considering using humour to communicate your research, carefully consider whether you have a talent for this type of communication. In the Bright Club 'Ten Commandments', the third rule is 'everyone has to be funny', the ninth is 'anyone who won't attend training or put in the time to write a set with jokes in can't perform' (Bright Club, 2014: np). In terms of benefits, humour is often recognised to be a source for engagement and interest, but it can also reduce credibility or trivialise, and relies on a certain level of knowledge in order to recognise the 'joke' (Marsh, 2013; Riesch, 2015). It is also worth remembering that humour is very subjective and, as such, people can interpret the message in very different ways based on their own sense of humour, experiences and views. Your relationship to the target of the humour can also be significant. One interesting example of this is the 'Voice by Choice' sketch (https://vimeo.com/46831064). Written by Lee Ridley, who has cerebral palsy and uses an iPad in his stand-up routines, the short film was created in collaboration with researchers in computing and the arts who are working to improve verbal speech technology based around users' needs. The short film follows three users of voice technology at a speed-dating event, to comedic effect, and has featured at public engagement events and road shows seeking to raise awareness of and engagement with this research (Crest Network, 2015). In the case of this film it has been developed in collaboration with users to very good effect, and whilst often comedy will be used to reclaim authority over stereotypes or language that might, for example, be used against a particular community there can be mixed views on whether this continues to reinforce such depictions (Riesch, 2015).

Where comedy is concerned it is also worth noting that the divisions it can create are leading to some muted questioning of its role within research communication. Use of humour can signify 'insiders' and 'outsiders' who are in on the joke, and typically there is a hierarchical dimension, with all eyes on the comic (Marsh, 2013; Riesch, 2015). One format for science comedy uses the word 'Showoff' in the title (Marsh, 2013; Science Showoff, 2014). Whilst this in itself has an element of 'tongue in cheek', for certain audiences, who already feel marginalised from the research process, comedy may not be the best means of communication. Thus it is important to think about the suitability of a comedic setting, depending on your aims and the nature of the subject matter you are working with, as well as from your audience's perspective.

Comedy, done well, can really engage people in an experience where troubles and concerns are left at the door and there is a shared sense of enjoyment and experience. This reflects a growing trend around 'immersive experiences' which potentially offer interesting avenues for research communication. Immersive settings can include a wide variety of opportunities. For example, in publishing, immersive online sites are allowing teenagers to develop their own fan fiction, including new stories, character relationships and mood boards. One such site, Movellas, which launched in 2012, has 200,000 users per month and an estimated 100,000 stories produced per day (Eyre, 2014). In museums, galleries and science centres we are seeing increasing consideration of how visitors can participate in interconnected activities, for example by using their electronic devices during their visit and then extending this to their home environment. There are also instances of museums using virtual environments to create this sense of a real experience.

> Immersion can be defined as the physical feeling of being in a virtual space. Usually it is achieved by means of sensory interfaces which 'surround' the user. Interaction is related to the user capability of modifying the environment and receiving a feedback to his/her actions. Both immersion and interaction concur to realize what is one of the main goals of a virtual experience: presence, i.e. the belief of actually being in a virtual space. (Carrozzino and Bergamasco, 2010: 453)

Creating virtual interactions in some cases allows for the preservation of certain materials and specimens, as a tool for education and narrative (for example by drawing on other sensory experiences) and to reconstruct events or contexts which would otherwise by inaccessible, or perhaps physically dangerous, to participants (Carrozzino and Bergamasco, 2010). Such experiences would also include the more common use of digital theatres or spaces such as planetariums within such settings (Griffiths, 2008; Sumners *et al.*, 2008). However, used to the extreme, immersion is even allowing for some museums to be partially or entirely internet and virtually based. Box 4.1 provides some examples.

Though such virtual environments are not face-to-face, immersive theatre has also become popular, and though theatre will be considered in more detail in Chapter 5 we will stop to briefly consider immersive theatre here. Whilst it is questioned whether immersive theatre is really 'new' it is seen to be a growing and popular trend within the arts (Alston, 2013; Kidd, 2012; White, 2012). Here the audience is often part of the performance, and though definitions are diverse it can include highly intimate performances in small physical spaces, incorporate the use of technology and different sensory experiences, or occur in everyday locations such as industrial sites, amongst other things (White, 2012). Alston (2013: 128) defines it as 'theatre that surrounds audiences within an aesthetic space in which they are frequently, but not always, free to move and/or participate'. White (2012) highlights that there is an expectation that such experiences will be transformative for participants, with expectations to engage them in active, new and interesting

---

Box 4.1 **Virtual museum and gallery examples**

The Museum of Pure Form www.pureform.org/
Virtual museum of digital art exploring interaction with digitised sculpture, new media, and architectural space.

Smithsonian National Museum of Natural History www.mnh.si.edu/panoramas/#
Although this is a physical museum it also provides a virtual, self-guided, room-by-room walking tour of the whole museum.

Google Cultural Institute www.google.com/culturalinstitute/#!home
The Google Cultural Institute currently comprises exhibits and collections from across the world around three key projects: art, historic moments and world wonders.

United States Holocaust Memorial Museum
www.ushmm.org/information/exhibitions/online-features/online-exhibitions
A series of online exhibitions allowing users to virtually explore a variety of materials by theme.

Inside the Stones www.english-heritage.org.uk/daysout/properties/stonehenge/discover/virtual-tour/
An interactive virtual tour of the Stonehenge monument.

International Museum of Women www.imow.org/home/index
Virtual museum showcasing women's creativity, awareness and action.

Museum with no frontiers www.museumwnf.org/
Presents joint exhibitions and collections across national boundaries and partnerships.

---

ways. This 'stretches' and 'magnifies' the demands on audiences (Alston, 2013: 129), with an expectation that they will contribute verbally or physically, for instance by physically moving with the experience to different spaces, groups or settings. Whilst for novice communicators of research, or those carrying it out as a solo pursuit, it may be difficult to envisage opportunities to communicate in this way there are still aspects which you might consider in relation to your own work. For instance, immersive theatre has been described as being particularly 'premised on the production of experience' (Alston, 2013: 131). Considering how you might build in even a small opportunity for participants to consider their own perspectives, create a sensory connection to your topic or mirror the experience of research, might be subtle tips which you could utilise from such settings. However, as with any activity, you should carefully consider the 'risk' to your participants, taking care to consider any emotional implications, embarrassment or hesitation they might feel in participating, and being particularly mindful of their expectations of an activity, offering them some form of 'guide' through the experience (Alston, 2013).

Immersive experiences remind us that research communication can potentially occur in unexpected locations and many of the face-to-face opportunities mentioned in this chapter can be considered in settings which may not traditionally be associated with research. Sometimes referred to as 'generic venues', such informal locations provide an opportunity to place research in settings that would not typically be expected (Bultitude and Sardo, 2012). Generic venues, environments like parks, shopping centres, transport hubs and social gatherings can be inclusive in different ways, allowing researchers to meet different participants, particularly those who might be intimidated by more traditional research settings like laboratories or universities (Bultitude and Sardo, 2012). Whilst some research communication might specifically set out to make people feel research environments are also open to them, in other cases it might work more effectively to meet on participants' terms. Such generic venues can help participants to feel more relaxed, active in their involvement and positive about being involved, as well as re-engaging or inspiring people who may feel or have thought in the past that they have no interest in a particular area of research (Bultitude and Sardo, 2012).

Research

Finally, in some research settings the boundaries between communication, public engagement and research practices can be far from clear. Approaches such as participatory and action research overlap significantly with public engagement techniques (Maile and Griffiths, 2014a; Kindon *et al.*, 2007). Furthermore, in some definitions, such as Rowe and Frewer's (2005) typology of public engagement, research traditions like surveys and focus groups would fall within the construct of an engagement approach. However, from a research communication perspective, and particularly conversations around 'impact', there can be a tendency to focus on engagement after the fact, rather than before or during research. This neglects that whilst research has an impact on people, people also have an impact on research.

Chapter 8 will consider in more detail public engagement approaches which are participatory, deliberative or designed to engage people with research or policy, many of which are face-to-face. Chapters 6 and Chapter 9 also have information on digital and participatory research engagement. Here it is simply worth noting that engagement in research processes can take multiple forms. In the social sciences particularly, human interactions are complicit in the creation of new knowledge, but equally some artistic works by their nature involve interaction, and some areas of science are reliant on people to garner data, for example in environmental projects. In health-based contexts there is considerable public involvement in research design, partnership and collaborations, through to teaching, advisory and ethical roles (Dickert and Sugarman, 2005).

Participants thus contribute data to the research process, and often this occurs in face-to-face formats. For example, arts-based research, including music, drama, poetry and visual approaches, is being used in settings such as health to elicit representations and generate data, particularly around emotions and experiences that are difficult to articulate through other means, as well as with people who find reading, writing or talking difficult (Lafrenière and Cox, 2012). From the outset, some researchers seek to fully embed people in the design of research, and the involvement of communities, stakeholders or service users may be implicit at all stages of the research process from the design of research questions and the gathering of data to how the results are used (Kindon *et al.*, 2007). Such 'communities of practice' can be used around shared interests or research themes when different stakeholders might have mutual goals (NCCPE, 2014a). In these cases, face-to-face meetings and events might be a commonplace occurrence and communication is not an afterthought in research design but is implicit in the relationships you are building to gather data or answer your research interests.

Case study 4.2 Connected Communities Public Dialogue Day

Since 2011 the Connected Communities programme (http://connected-communities.org/) has supported research on communities, but the programme is not interested in communities simply as a subject of research; rather, it intends to 'connect communities with research, bringing together community-engaged research across a number of core themes' (AHRC, 2015: np). Although it is led by the Arts and Humanities Research Council (AHRC), the idea of connection is central to the programme's ethos, as it involves collaboration between the Research Councils in the United Kingdom. This multi-funder approach ensures that a culture of cross-disciplinary research collaboration is created.

From a research-collaboration perspective, the programme wanted to embed communities within its decision making, as Melanie Knetsch of the Economic and Social Research Council (ESRC) explains in the context of one funding opportunity: 'We felt that as the joint AHRC/ESRC call was focusing on community engagement and mobilisation it was essential for applicants to have a chance to speak with people as part of their proposal development.' One such example of this was a related Public Dialogue Day held in 2012, which formed part of a two-stage research funding application process, as Melanie continues: 'there was an excellent window of opportunity for applicants who were shortlisted, and thus had developed a certain level of a proposal, to speak with the public before submitting a fuller application. We believed this process would ensure that true community and public engagement would be built in from the concept of the research project through to the delivery and beyond.' Four research teams were then invited to participate in the Dialogue Day, prior to their submission to stage two. The intention was that members of the public and community could comment on and constructively engage in a conversation with researchers about their proposals, which might help to further shape their research plans. The dialogue day involved groups of community members moving between each of the four proposals, hearing a brief overview of the plans before an opportunity for in-depth discussion.

One of the major challenges of this, for the researchers, involved its inclusion before funding, with concerns that other research teams might hear ideas or take them up in their own research, as Melanie explains:

> One of the biggest challenges was that each of the shortlisted applicants was in effect in direct competition with each other. We had to set the dialogue up so they all had privacy and couldn't see or hear each other ... All of the public attendees were well briefed before and on the day about not sharing details of one project with another – and it was fantastic to see them take a self-judging stance on this. If one person from the group started to mention another project, other people would remind them not to say anything, which helped establish trust amongst all involved.

The involvement of a facilitating organisation that was experienced in community-based activities meant that researchers were offered support in thinking about the best ways to engage around their ideas, but language was still tricky. As Melanie describes, 'language is always a challenge when you bring different experts and groups together. Having an expert facilitator was key to overcoming this as they created a discussion guide which defined common terms that might be said and outlined the different roles of people on the day, which made it easier for the participants to join the conversation. They also took time out to speak with the grant applicants to ensure that they were very conscious of the words and concepts they might use.'

For the researchers, and the funders that were supporting the activity, it was a somewhat experimental process, and therefore there was uncertainty in advance of the day around what it would involve and what its purpose was. 'We banned the use of PowerPoint presentations', says Melanie 'which meant that the applicants had to think creatively about how to present their ideas and research objectives and methods. I thought this was one of the best parts of the day, as each of the applicants utilised a different approach – some had wall displays and others used objects that could be handed out to represent what they were showing.'

From a participant perspective, being prepared to fully engage was important, so they were provided with suitable information on the research proposals in advance and carefully supported to feel that they could engage in a full conversation. This was evident in findings from the day, which suggested that over 80 percent of participants felt their comments were valuable and that they could express their own views, including those that might be different to the researchers' (Wilkinson, 2013). There were also high levels of agreement that it was helpful to include such activities within research funding processes.

After the activity the researchers involved had a number of weeks to consider the transcripts from their discussions on the day, and how they might incorporate any reflections within their final stage two proposals. One researcher remarked: 'It brought home to us that communities are very diverse ... it was useful to be reminded that communities are made up of people of all different points of view ... we were helped with some of our ideas ... it was interesting hearing people's ideas' (Wilkinson, 2013). Researchers found that comments helped them to sharpen ideas, incorporate feedback and have more confidence in the strengths of their proposals; for some the process also showed the value of community perspectives, and community involvement became a communication activity they planned to embed at regular intervals in their final research plans (Wilkinson, 2013). 'What was noticeable was the significant and positive change in attitudes towards what a public dialogue can offer from both the researchers as well as the attendees', said Melanie after the event. 'When speaking with the research applicants, they were really glad they had come and felt they had come away with valuable insights they could either add to their application or to their ongoing work around communities.'

Melanie suggests that researchers planning similar activities consider the entire process of research: 'I think this was a really innovative way of getting new voices into the design of grant applications ...Our dialogue day showed that people are really interested in what academics do and have some valuable ideas to contribute. With some thinking about the audience and creative planning to stimulate discussions, it is very possible to include new voices at all stages of research. However, an experienced and professional facilitator is definitely worth bringing into any dialogue as they will help ensure all participants have a voice.'

As well as providing data, or influencing research design, it's also possible that your participants may themselves be adopting a role as a 'researcher'. This has become increasingly popular in online contexts, where approaches such as citizen science have really developed a strong influence (see Chapter 9 for further discussion of citizen science), but it is also something which researchers might do in a face-to-face setting, either to develop research capacity amongst participants or because specialist research skills are not essential. Integrating your participants into the research process works well when they will have an incentive for involvement (not necessarily monetary – it can be enjoyment, a game-playing element or altruistic) and activities can be broken down into small tasks, minimising any commitment they have to make (NCCPE, 2014b). It can work less well if very precise data need to be collected or specialist skills or facilities are demanded (NCCPE, 2014b), and it goes without saying that the ethical considerations and appropriateness of involving participants in this way should be carefully considered. Participants should get something out of it; it's not a technique for free labour.

It is likely that the inclusion of a face-to-face approach within your research is something you will already be doing or have considered if it is relevant to your specific discipline. However, what you may not have thought about is how in itself that is a research communication approach; the distinctions between research, learning, action and communication can be subtle (Kindon *et al.*, 2007). Engaging people in your research may in itself influence how you communicate, seeking to construct contributors or subjects as part of the conversation, making their voices the 'centrepiece' rather than about 'them' (Cahill and Torre, 2007). Whilst much research communication may be framed by an output-driven agenda, it is also important to carefully consider and highlight how such communications also influence and are embedded in your research itself, where that is appropriate.

Preparing for face-to-face communication

Audiences and participants, just like students, can easily spot an ill-prepared presenter, so it's crucial to prepare for any face-to-face activity. Karen Bultitude (2010) provides a number of helpful tips on how to prepare, and these are summarised in Box 4.2.

Having a clear set of aims and objectives for an activity from the outset (see Chapter 10) can be extremely helpful in planning content. Contributing to marketing materials or a description of the activity can create 'hooks' for an audience. These could connect to current issues that are popular, whilst still giving an accurate description of your plans so that people know what to expect an activity to involve (Bowater and

---

Box 4.2 Tips for preparing for face-to-face presentation

- Define key messages/aims/learning outcomes.
- Have a plan for timings, resources, responsibilities, and back-up options if the plan changes.
- Stick to your plan and make sure those you are working with also agree to it.
- Play to your strengths, in terms of both your knowledge and communication skills, or collaborating with others if there are aspects you can't offer.
- Be confident but realistic in your aims.
- Do your homework on the participants, timings, purposes, payment and logistics.

Source: Bultitude (2010: 137)

Yeoman, 2013). It's always a good idea to create something bespoke for an audience, so avoid modifying teaching materials or conference presentations. Not only are these likely to be ill-suited to audience needs, but you may be overly familiar with their content, meaning that you do not appear renewed or vibrant when presenting it.

In terms of structuring an activity, expectations and scale are important. Depending on the style of the activity, people may be expecting to engage for a shorter or longer period. Either way, it's a good idea to divide content into manageable chunks. Switching content around every ten minutes or so in a presentation, creating a stopping point after ten to fifteen minutes in a festival activity, or planning in short breaks to allow people time to reflect and to socialise with each other during research engagement activities will help people to stay engaged or move on to something more relevant to them (Wilkinson, 2012). Velarde (2001) provides some useful practical tips for exhibition design that it is also wise to consider when planning a face-to-face activity. He reminds us that people's eyesight and mobility varies, that participants can be engaged through different senses – nose, ears, hands and eyes – and will have certain practical needs (for instance to sit down or to keep an eye on their valuables). Breaks, snacks and meals, as simple as they might be, can make or break a face-to-face activity, and so it is important not to overlook straightforward practicalities.

People are likely to have expectations around participation (Wilkinson *et al.*, 2011a) and, whilst it can be good to challenge these, making an activity appear fresh or interesting, challenging expectations may also mean that participants need more guidance on how to participate. For example, many people are interested to hear a researcher's view, and that can mean they attend such activities with few intentions of making their own contributions (Wilkinson *et al.*, 2011a); this should be respected, but also considered in the design of an activity. There are ways that interaction can be included in a face-to-face activity: setting aside time for questions, creating prompts for discussion, encouraging conversations in small groups or providing materials for people to manipulate and play with – but it is important that participants are prepared to expect this. Again, this comes down to how an activity is promoted, but it might also include how you design the process: people might need time to gather their thoughts, prefer to share their ideas in smaller groupings rather than across a large audience or need some clear prompting that encourages discussion. Interaction can be influenced by participant numbers, and it's very important to consider the impact of large groups. Consider whether facilitation support, audio facilities or a pathway through activities, to interact with people at different times, are needed so as to allow everyone an opportunity to contribute.

Presenting and listening advice

For some face-to-face activities, particularly any that are supported by a particular grant or organisation, it may be that you are given the opportunity to attend specific communication training. Communication training will often incorporate opportunities to practise, as Mayhew and Hall (2012: 551; emphasis in original) describe in their work with teenagers:

> We have found that it is highly valuable – indeed essential – for presenters to do a dry run with a small group of teens before presenting to a full house ... This has proven exceedingly valuable in getting the presentations pitched at the right level and the graphics comprehensible. It also serves to overcome a certain intimidation factor for many presenters concerning the prospect of presenting before an unfamiliar audience. While many of our presenters have initially told us they are experienced at presenting to the public and never do a rehearsal, *every* presenter has told us afterward that the experience was well worth their time.

You may not have the luxury of access to a small group of your participants but there could be family or friends who would be happy to listen to your ideas. Presentation skills are now covered to varying degrees in many undergraduate and postgraduate programmes, yet, faced with the need to give a presentation to a public audience, many people become nervous. Box 4.3 provides some advice for presenters who find this daunting.

There are other important things to remember when presenting face-to-face. These include setting an appropriate pace for a presentation and running to time, considering key messages and reiterating these, speaking clearly and with appropriate language, as well as using effective body language (Dawson *et al.*, 2010). Some researchers feel less confident presenting face-to-face because they are communicating in a second language (Royal Society, 2006), and whilst practice can help with this, at an early point in the presentation a researcher can highlight where they are from as an interesting feature about themselves. Building a connection with an audience helps to create engagement. Whilst you might be very proud and enthusiastic about your research, it is important not to condescend or 'show off' (Velarde, 2001). Instead, Angela Thody (2006) recommends 'flattering' your audience, acknowledging their power and capabilities and instigating a sense of being on a shared journey. A researcher has a difficult job when presenting face-to-face; some people will want to be entertained, others will not, and you need respectability as a researcher, along with a memorable presentation (Thody, 2006).

Whilst you might be considering brushing up on your presentation skills, it is also important to think about how you listen, particularly if you adopt the notion of a shared journey. Listening isn't just about the

---

Box 4.3 Tips for dealing with nerves in face-to-face presentation

- Practise, practise, practise; the more confident you feel in what you are presenting the less nervous you are likely to be.

- Particularly rehearse your opening statements, the point at which you are likely to feel most nervous.

- Notes can be helpful if you are worried about losing your train of thought. Take care that notes are not read verbatim, do not minimise eye contact or create a physical barrier between you and the audience.

- Try to channel nerves into enthusiasm and positivity, using the nervous energy for a practical purpose.

- If you know that you show particular physical signs of nerves, design the activity to detract from these.

- If you do make any minor mistakes, acknowledge them, show you are unruffled and move on.

- Don't be too hard on yourself; remember that many presenters, actors, sports personalities and others channel feelings of nervousness into excellent performance.

words that you hear, it can involve being aware of non-verbal clues, as well as reflecting on what might be unsaid or who is not saying anything. Occasionally people who are very vibrant and enthusiastic communicators can forget the importance of listening, but it is a crucial skill, particularly for those seeking to encourage conversation, as opposed to simply telling people about their research. It is common in many face-to-face formats to have time for people to talk. To do this, researchers often need to remember to keep quiet; don't jump into silences, give people time to think about what they want to say and avoid finishing their sentences. It is important to remember that researchers generally will have more power in the relationship (see Chapter 11). If you are allowing time for participants to converse take care that timings don't slip, reducing the time for any conversation you had planned or, worse, making it difficult for you to listen as people start to shuffle, pack up bags or leave the room. Show full attention to anyone who is speaking and think about using body language that will support and encourage them.

Finally, in face-to-face activities people may say things with which we strongly disagree. Box 4.4 provides suggestions on how to deal with conflict and controversy in face-to-face communication settings. If your subject matter is likely to be controversial or challenging, consider having the support of a facilitator or moderator who will be trained in dealing with such situations and will be able to help alleviate the situation. For the most part, though, people will want to have constructive conversations and it is this element of face-to-face communication that many researchers most enjoy and appreciate (Wilkinson *et al.*, 2011a).

Problematising face-to-face communication

Effective face-to-face communication integrates research communication within the participants' context and is one starting point for building a greater awareness around how people view your research. That is not to say that there aren't pitfalls. Returning to the data on cultural participation across Europe, 37 percent of people say they have visited a museum or gallery at least once in the last twelve months (TNS Opinion and Social, 2013). Contrast this with the 72 percent who have watched or listened to a cultural programme on TV or the radio, or the 66 percent who have read a book, and the figure becomes less impressive (TNS Opinion and Social, 2013).

Face-to-face opportunities can be critiqued for their appeal to typical kinds of audiences – those with existing academic interests or representing particular gender, ethnic and social backgrounds (Maile, 2014) – and, despite the proliferation of events such as festivals, their reach is still relatively small (Jensen and Buckley, 2012). Not all face-to-face

---

Box 4.4 Managing conflict and controversy in face-to-face communication

---

- Anticipate any obviously controversial issues in your research and prepare explanations.
- Don't under- or overplay any controversial angles.
- Be clear about evidence, or where the weight of evidence lies.
- Avoid speculation or comments that could be easily misinterpreted.
- Think about any conflicts of interest (e.g. who funded the research) and be transparent.
- Consider setting ground rules at the beginning of an activity, regarding acceptable behaviour or language. When working with groups allow time to develop these collaboratively.
- Take time before reacting to a comment or statement; think about how to explain responses.
- If someone speaks loudly or argumentatively it might reflect their own anxiety. Avoid raising your voice in response.
- Never get personal about how or why someone might be expressing a particular view.
- If you work in particularly controversial fields (for example animal research) consider additional training and resources that you can access.
- Remember that at times engagement is looking to reveal other perspectives; you may just have to agree to disagree.

Source: Based on Ward (2008)

---

activities are free, so cost can be prohibitive for some. In other cases, familiarity with a venue or confidence to attend may deter people from participating, so it is important to take into account that face-to-face communication does not appeal to everyone (Dawson, 2014b).

When working with other organisations, such as museums or science centres, or even schools, researchers should be aware of the organisation's drivers and idiosyncrasies. Whilst you may have an element of control over the message, its context and the 'noise' surrounding it will be the responsibility of others. For instance, museum narratives can be critiqued for both simplifying and presenting multiple narratives, 'engaging in a "bottom-up" telling of tales, rather than a "top-down" imposition of cultural voice and institutional ethos' (Hourston Hanks *et al.*, 2012: xxii; Kidd, 2012). Both of these framings can be challenging for researchers, who may prefer to see complexity or a certain interpretation as dominant. Other things will also be outside of the researcher's control, participants may ignore instructions, destroy materials and divert from your plans (Velarde, 2001). There can be an element of unpredictability involved in terms of which aspects of your subject may capture interest or direct discussion. If we identify face-to-face spaces as an opportunity for critical discussion and a questioning of interests and exclusion (Maile, 2014), people may express views that you disagree with or be unsupportive of your research. As discussed, your area of research could be particularly controversial or difficult to discuss in such a public context. Thinking about the right face-to-face location for you and the purpose of the activity is, then, even more crucial.

Face-to-face activities can also stir up emotions on the part of your participants. In some settings researchers may be aspiring to have an emotional engagement with participants (see Chapter 5). Lafrenière and Cox (2012: 194) highlight that emotions including 'anger, empathy, empowerment, frustration, guilt, and pride' were recorded as feelings experienced by participants in reaction to a science café focusing on health, whilst emotional reactions to a participatory performance on slavery provoked reactions including 'anger (frequently), fear, shock, sadness and pain' (Kidd, 2012: 77). Inspiring this level of personal involvement may demonstrate the gravitas of an activity, as participants are able to capture the experience and relate it to their own, or recognise their own weaknesses and ignorance, but it is important to consider the risk of provoking memories amongst participants (Kidd, 2012) and any ethical ramifications this could create. For some researchers a sense that discussion of their research could include anything beyond evidence and knowledge, infringing on personal perspectives, feelings or attitudes, may in itself create a negative reaction.

Finally, face-to-face activities can sometimes be a victim of their own success. Many of the examples provided in this chapter have proved popular with participants and therefore are capturing new types of attention. To take as an example Café Scientifique, in some locations, particularly the United States, they have become popular with scientific institutions. Additionally, there has been a growing network of schools using the café principle, where the informal and discussion-based nature is being seen as helpful in increasing teenagers' scientific literacy (Mayhew and Hall, 2012). However, as Grand (2009: 215) cautions, whilst this may 'make it easier to secure speakers for café events, it may also transform the nature and purpose of the original format, potentially giving the perception that cafes are run by and for scientific institutions, rather than by and for the audience'. Many face-to-face activities, that started in 'bottom up' ways, or through small incremental projects and voluntary opportunities, are coming under focus in a policy setting which, as Maile (2014: 29) summarises, 'is now subject to competing discourses and policies focused on evidence-gathering and impact assessment'. Whilst impact will be considered in more detail in later chapters, for many the intentions of face-to-face activities are closely tied to their own personal enjoyment and appreciation of such interactions, and the opportunity to move beyond 'ready-made science' (Jensen and Buckley, 2012). Face-to-face activities often reach out to people in their communities, in spaces of comfort to them, whilst researchers frequently report that they result in thinking about their research in new ways and reigniting their own passion and enthusiasm. Thus, protecting such shared spaces for engagement, sometimes with many, often with few, also appears important.

Summary

Face-to-face communication activities offer a number of benefits to researchers. They can make communication straightforward, lead to empathy and understanding and allow people to more clearly contextualise 'you' amongst the other identities you may have, for instance as a female, young person, hobbyist or member of an ethnic group. As a researcher you may have a very active role in what you decide to communicate, how and when, whilst also being in a position to draw on the infrastructures of others, such as schools, community groups, festival teams, science centres and museums, which can make face-to-face communication a very efficient activity to develop, for those trying out research communication for the first time.

The vast range of face-to-face activities, as evidenced in this chapter, provides a wide range of opportunities for research communication, but also, with some time and thought, lots of opportunities to develop ideas that are novel or creative within a face-to-face arrangement. Communicating face-to-face can be less time demanding than some other communication activities, in that it is often very amenable to other commitments; a school talk here or there, a workshop at a festival or a chat with the local museum may not require the same level of consistent responsiveness as, say, a social media presence. However, they are still demanding in that you need to be well prepared, and some researchers can find the face-to-face nature daunting. Not only are you 'facing' activities when they go well, but also when things do not go quite as planned.

Finally, one of the major assets of face-to-face communication is its context. It offers opportunities to talk to people on their home ground, in spaces where they feel comfortable and relaxed, like bars, shopping centres or at school, as well as to invite them in to venues like universities and science centres or even to be part of the research process itself. Emerging face-to-face settings, like comedy or immersive theatre, or interesting festival formats, extend an invitation to people through their cultural hobbies, musical choices and social interests that are relevant to them. Therefore, while face-to-face activities may never reach such a scale as to impact all or even many, their unique set of benefits makes them an excellent research communication opportunity.

Note

1 It is worth noting that there has been much critical discussion of media depictions of researchers, particularly related to gender and ethnicity (see, for example, Kitzinger *et al.*, 2008).

Further reading

Bowater, L., and Yeoman, K., *Science Communication: A Practical Guide for Scientists* (Oxford: Wiley-Blackwell, 2013).

British Science Association/Science Made Simple, 'Advice for Presenters'. Retrieved 03 December 2014 at: www.britishscienceassociation.org/british-science-festival/advice-presenters.

Maile, S. and Griffiths, D. (eds), *Public Engagement and Social Science*, (Bristol, Policy Press, 2014).

5
Art

Despite C.P. Snow's framing of the arts and science as two cultures with little common ground, art, science and technology have long been bedfellows (Snow, 1993). Advances in science and technology have stimulated developments in the arts as well as acting as inspiration for cultural activities, and visual techniques from the arts have been used to inform and facilitate research across a broad range of disciplines. From Brunelleschi's early work on perspective, through to the modern day, examples of cross 'cultural' impact abound, with artists exploring and exploiting technological developments, as well as drawing inspiration from cutting-edge research, the personalities of researchers or the ethical issues they face. Consider, for example, the development of photography, made possible by advances in chemistry in the nineteenth century and now evolving to incorporate many different physical phenomena, from infra-red through to the artistry involved in hand-colouring electron micrographs. At the same time, photography has become an established art form.

These impacts are not uni-directional from research to art. Artists participated in Captain Cook's voyages as recorders of information, 'to give a more perfect idea thereof than can be formed by written descriptions only' (letter of appointment of John Webber, quoted in Joppien and Smith, 1998). Visualisation, sometimes through crude laboratory drawings, sometimes through more artistic representations, underpins many researchers' work, such as that of Pauling, Watson, Crick and Hoffman. In the context of chemistry, 'the communication of molecules' architectonic essence by little iconic drawings (rather than photographs or etchings), and by ball and stick models, is of proven value ... They didn't synthesize DNA, they reasoned out its structure, almost willing a model into being' (Hoffmann, 2003: np). Furthermore, questions asked by artists can prompt researchers to consider their endeavours in novel ways, leading to new developments. Not to mention that many research-ers apply aesthetic judgements when evaluating their own work. 'When I'm working on a problem, I never think about beauty. I think only how to solve the problem. But when I have finished, if the solution is not beautiful I know it is wrong' (R. Buckminster Fuller).[1]

There has been considerable interest in the past few decades spe-cifically focused on the links between art and natural sciences. To an extent, this reflects the issues raised by C.P. Snow about a cultural sepa-ration between the natural sciences and humanities (perhaps leaving social sciences in some sort of awkward intermediate position), and possibly an assumption that research from the humanities might more naturally find its way into the wider culture through, for example, art and literature. For this reason, at times the discussion in this chapter may appear to focus on exploring the links between natural sciences and the arts. This doesn't mean that the same approaches and issues aren't faced by researchers from the social sciences or humanities but, rather, that these disciplines have not received the same attention from funders (e.g. Wellcome Trust in the United Kingdom; XEROX PARC PAIR in the United States; or Synapse in Australia) or, indeed, the research community.

In this chapter we explore the relationship between research (science, social science and humanities) and the arts. The chapter considers art inspired by research and art that uses research tools and materials within the work itself, as well as research inspired by art. The chapter moves on to explore the relationships between artists and researchers and the potential for the instrumental use of either discipline. It consid-ers audiences for these types of artworks and addresses the potential of what Emma Weitkamp calls 'SciCraft' as a means of engaging audiences with research and technology. From a practical perspective, the chapter explores the processes involved in working collaboratively on creative projects. Furthermore, this chapter focuses on live and visual arts, crafts and DIY culture projects, leaving digital arts to Chapters 6 and 7.

What is art?

The question of what the 'arts' are has been puzzling theorists for generations and the definitions have changed over time. As Belfiore and Bennett (2008) point out, definitions of the arts are both time and place specific, that is, they changed through time and also through location (geographical/cultural), while Shiner argues that modern notions of art are in flux: 'Today you can call virtually anything "art" and get away with it' (Shiner, 2001: 3). Definitions of the arts may, therefore, seem vague and arbitrary in nature. Lewis suggests that 'art could then be defined as a cultural practice that involves the creation of specific and definable object – a play, video or piece of music for example. The function of the object is as a self-conscious, personal, or collective expression of something' (Lewis, 1990: 5). This suggests that, to an extent, art is defined by who makes it and their intentions for the piece.

Belfiore and Bennett (2008) split definitions of art into three areas: essentialist definitions, which seek to capture the qualities and characteristics that constitute art; functional definitions that rely on a notion that art serves a purpose; and institutional definitions, which suggest that the art establishment has the power to determine what is and is not considered art. These difficulties with definitions arise because 'value is not present in the cultural object itself, it is a set of judgements with specific social origins' (Lewis, 1990: 7). As such, art might be judged by aesthetic principles or by the moral or political issues it raises, or any number of other criteria the art critic applies. Furthermore, while certain cultural institutions may be recognised as having the authority to determine what is and is not art, such definitions are not accepted by everyone.

Concepts of art are also being challenged by the inclusion of research tools and technology that gainsay the notion of art as a static enduring object (Miller, 2014; Kac, 2007; Kemp, 2006). Miller reports on early collaborations between artists and engineers, in which the engineering was used to make auto-destructive artworks. Kac notes that artists have become interested in biological techniques (particularly genetics), which are being used to create living artworks which may grow and change. 'Theoretically, many biological artworks may last as long as life exists on the planet, provided that they remain capable of replication and reproduction' (Kac, 2007: 19). Digital artworks are also being created that include built-in change within the programming or allow audience interaction to shape the artistic experience. Artworks such as these may challenge our notions of what art is, as well as questioning the boundaries between art and science.

Arts audiences

A starting point for research communication is often to consider who you want to reach through the project. Different arts approaches are likely to appeal to different groups of people and to provide audiences (or participants) with different experiences and levels of engagement. Equally, we might distinguish between art that is created by an artist (and so might be viewed, read or listened to by an audience) and participatory arts and crafts projects that aim to involve the audience as participants in the project, or approaches that tap into existing forms of

DIY culture. The choice between a traditional, artist-led or a participatory arts approach can have profound implications for project development, not least because they are likely to attract specific audiences or participants (in terms of size and composition), take place in different institutional settings or contexts, require different skills to execute and involve people in different ways. This section initially considers traditional 'audiences' (i.e. those attending exhibitions or performances) and then moves on to explore audiences for participatory arts projects.

One argument often put forward in support of projects designed to bring artists and researchers together is that the resultant 'artwork', whether this be a performance work, an audio or visual artwork, will appeal to different audiences than those traditionally interested in research, whether that research emerges from the realm of science, technology, the social sciences or humanities. Clearly, there are many people who participate in a wide range of cultural opportunities, including both artistic events and more traditional research communication activities, but it has been argued that arts-based approaches can reach beyond the traditional demographic interested in a specific research area (Glinkowski and Bamford, 2009).

Attendance at visual and performing arts events is a minority activity in both Europe and the USA. The 2013 Eurobarometer survey of cultural participation, found that only 35 percent of respondents had attended a concert, 28 percent had been to the theatre and only 18 percent had attended a dance performance or ballet in the past year (TNS Opinion and Social, 2013). A similar percentage (37 percent) of adults in the United States attended live performances (National Endowment for the Arts, 2013). Research over many decades suggests that the strongest predictor of participation in the arts is education, with professionals (e.g. doctors, lawyers) having the highest rates of participation. Borgonovi (2004) identified education in the arts (whether through formal schooling or as part of extracurricular activities, such as dance and music lessons) as the single most important predictor of participation in arts-based cultural events and highlights that price does not appear to be a significant factor in participation, contrary to what many in the policy community have argued. Lewis (1990) argues that since it is the cultural elite that determines what is considered art, this maintains a cultural status quo. Thus, what is determined by the establishment to be 'art' is not necessarily accessible to everyone, for reasons that relate to an individual's cultural capital (which might be accrued through formal education and family-background experiences). Those who do not belong to the cultural elite do not have the cultural capital that enables them to engage with art (and may even lack the cultural capital to enter the building in which art is located). Lewis also argues that the codes used by artists, which signify how the artwork should be interpreted, have developed to be complex and exclusive, which reinforces the need for some level of education in the arts in order to participate fully. Thus, arts practices can reinforce class divisions (as described by Bourdieu). For some non-participants, 'because of the values that dominate subsidised art, the very idea of it is conflated with an alien cultural complexity' (Lewis, 1990: 37). Add to this the complexities of interpreting and engaging with research, and one might wonder, as Reichle (2009) suggests below, whether bringing together artistic, natural or social science ways of knowing might be a step too far for the audience.

> By adapting and adopting scientific methods, processes, and materials, art – whose audience has long since become nebulous and inaccessible – has embarked on a course with an uncertain outcome. On the one side art projects that present living sculptures or transgenic organisms in the context of an exhibition attract a great deal of attention and challenge both institutions and curators, but on the other art out of the laboratory is covered with so many layers of meaning that the reception of newer art trends, like bio art, is fraught with much misunderstanding. Ultimately, it is to be hoped that bridges will not only be built between the Two Cultures and between science and art, but also between science and its technologies and our everyday life so that we are better prepared for the emergence of a biocybernetic humanity. (Reichle, 2009: 216)

Nevertheless, Glinkowski and Bamford's (2009) review of the Wellcome Trust Sci-Art funding scheme suggests that projects which emerge from collaborations between artists and researchers can attract diverse audiences, with some suggestion that the subjects chosen had attracted non-traditional audiences for the arts as well as non-traditional audiences for research. The cross-disciplinary nature of these projects may also mean that they can be shown or performed in a diverse range of venues, from those traditionally associated with the arts (e.g. theatre spaces) to those more traditionally associated with research (such as research laboratories or institutes), with the consequent broadening of likely audience. In exploring performances of *Bloodlines* (http://chime ranetwork.org/bloodlines/), a performance that sought to convey the experience of stem cell transplant, through both drama and music, the venue did seem to influence the background of the audience, with audiences drawn by the science attending performances at science-oriented venues, and those interested in the arts attending arts-oriented venues (Mermikides *et al.*, 2015; Weitkamp and Mermikides, in preparation). Hewer (2003) suggests that the venue also influences audiences' expectations of the exhibition or performance and, as a result, introducing art into a science venue or vice versa can be either a pleasurable surprise or a confusing experience.

David Glowacki is an interesting example of a scientist who in many ways is also an artist. Glowacki is a theoretical chemist at the University of Bristol who explores chemical reactions. However, as you move through his research profile on the Chemistry Department website you come to 'scientific imagination and artistic representation'. In this strand of his research he created *Danceroom Spectroscopy* (http://danceroom-spec.com) as a means of visualising the atomic world he studies. *Danceroom Spectroscopy* has toured internationally, and been performed at venues as diverse as the Z space in San Francisco (an avant-garde arts venue), the World Science Festival in New York, the Bhutan International Festival and the Bristol Proms in the United Kingdom. Although Glowacki collaborated with artists on the project, he is credited with dreaming up the idea.

Participatory projects

An emerging trend in the field of research communication is the idea of engaging participants in craft and performance activities designed to enable dialogue between researchers and the public. Such projects may involve the participants in learning new skills as well as new knowledge; some participants will be drawn to the activity by the research topic, knowing little of the 'craft' that is being performed alongside, while others may be drawn by the craft, knowing little about the research area. Gauntlett (2011) argues that everyday craft and making are important routes to expression and avenues for pleasure and happiness in society. He suggests that the rise of the crafting movement reflects a desire for the personal and authentic in today's consumer world, as well as reflecting a desire to share interests and connect with other like-minded people.

Current participation in artistic activities (such as amateur dramatic productions) is similar to attendance at artist exhibitions and performances. Around 38 percent of the population of the European Union reports actively engaging in an artistic activity in 2013, the most popular of which was dancing (35 percent) (TNS Opinion and Social, 2013). Participation is not uniform across Europe, with the highest participation rates in northern European countries and the lowest in southern and eastern Europe. Age and education also influence participation, with younger people and those with more years of formal education taking part in larger numbers. A recent survey in the United States using a slightly broader definition of the arts to include craft activities, such as weaving, suggests that around half the population engages in at least one arts or craft activity (National Endowment for the Arts, 2013); while around a quarter of Australians participate in arts and crafts activities, such as jewellery making and photography (Australia Council for the Arts, 2010). These numbers suggest that there is a potential audience for projects that seek to combine research communication with arts and craft activities, and there is a history of using these approaches in health education, to give one example, which could usefully inform the design and development of such activities.

In the context of research communication, then, craft offers an opportunity to engage people with science which can align well with discussions around public engagement with science and technology (Chapter 8), and projects are emerging, such as MS: The Big Knit, that involve participants in a crafting activity (in this case knitting a neuron) and discussion about related scientific issues (e.g. neurology related to multiple sclerosis; http://knitaneuron.blogspot.co.uk/). While little research has yet explored emerging SciCraft practice, there are suggestions that this type of project might attract different audiences than traditional research communication activities, and may also provide a platform for discussion that is viewed as 'safe' by participants (Featherstone and Pope, 2011). Participating in creative projects may not only provide an opportunity to learn about research, but may also help participants to acquire skills and competence more broadly. Research in the field of community arts–health projects, for example, suggests that these types of project can have a range of benefits for participants that go beyond any learning gained about the health topic. For example, Brodzinski (2010: 17) argues that '[t]he collaborative and improvisatory process of making a piece of work and the journey of discovery it entails may be more significant in terms of impact on self-esteem, community building and so forth, than what is produced at the end of the project'.

MS: The Big Knit (Featherstone and Pope, 2011) linked the public and neuroscientists together through the creation of knitted neurons, and in the process facilitated discussions. Participants with prior interests in both MS and knitting were attracted to the project. The finished artworks, which were constructed from the participants' knitted neurons, necessarily looked handmade, but this project was not primarily about the product. Instead it aimed to create a space in which discussion could happen. However, it raised the issue of quality and the position of the finished 'artwork' in the project. Lewis (1990) notes that quality is potentially a problem for community art projects, with the products often looking amateurish. This suggests the importance of devising evaluation criteria linked to individual project objectives – quality can then be judged against these outcomes specifically (e.g. quality of discussion, professional delivery of the project rather than a high-quality finished artwork).

Participatory arts events can also be appropriate for engaging children. Atopic Arts, a project run by Ascus together with Eczema Outreach

Scotland, brought families and artists together to explore the emotional impacts of eczema. The workshops involved clay modelling and pillow painting and encouraged children to reflect on their experience of eczema while creating a space for them to present their dreams, fears and fantasies. The artists worked with a designer to use their experiences from the workshop to create a portable exhibition pack to promote eczema awareness in Scotland. This is a similar approach to that taken by Dr Lorna Warren, who works with older women (see Case study 5.1).

Case study 5.1 Look At Me! Engaging older women with research

Dr Lorna Warren, Senior Lecturer in Social Policy at the University of Sheffield, is committed to doing research with, rather than on, people. Through years of working with diverse groups of women, Lorna has tended to use participatory research practice, and this led naturally to thinking about how she communicates her research. 'As academics we privilege talk and text. But when you go into people's homes, they show you around the house, they get out the family album or they show you objects. So I'm *seeing* their lives and I realised I wasn't really putting this back into my research,' says Lorna. So when she was contacted by Clare McManus, Director of arts organisation Eventus, it seemed natural to put together a funding application to the New Dynamics of Aging programme, a multidisciplinary research programme funded by several United Kingdom research councils that seeks to improve the quality of life of older people, for a project that would combine both visual research and public engagement.

Look At Me! involved older women (aged from forty-three to ninety-six) in workshops where they discussed aging and cultural and media representations of aging. The project used three approaches: art therapy techniques, photo therapy and community arts practice. Participants were encouraged to produce images that were honest, challenging and humorous, using whatever medium they felt comfortable with. This led to artworks including sculpture, painting and collage as well as photographs designed to trouble widely held stereotypes. Artworks created by the women individually, and jointly with the photographers, were exhibited to the public in three venues in Sheffield, England. Lorna, whose research has focused on the social care of older people, says 'the visual is part of people's narratives. Communities where there are language problems, where people aren't as comfortable with the conceptual, can engage with the visual. Everybody can engage with images. And everybody can take what they want from them, which of course makes your research trickier.'

Using arts-based approaches might limit involvement to those people who are already interested in the arts and it was clear that some participants were drawn to the project because it involved artistic activities, but others just wanted to try something new. 'If you are trying something out for the first time, there is a degree of "Oh will I be able to do this".' In order to encourage input from a wide range of women, including those who would not, as individuals, have responded to a university research request, Eventus used its knowledge of Sheffield's regeneration areas to recruit women through community groups. The women and their organisations were then involved in the recruitment of the photographers they would work with to produce images. The women didn't have to create the artworks themselves, but they did decide together with the photographers how to approach the project. 'In this group, there wasn't that anxiety about being able to make the works of art, but it was still an artistic process,' explains Lorna. She believes that this approach enabled women to participate (the oldest of whom was ninety-six) who might not have been able to participate in traditional research methodologies, such as in-depth interviewing, which can be very tiring for participants.

Working with arts-based organisations presented some challenges, notably around working practices. As an example, Lorna cites differences in their approach to gaining participants' consent. 'When you work with arts-based organisations, they work in a very different way. Our expectation in the university is that we get consent before we do anything. Most of the organisations we worked with work on trust. Eventus was used to reaching out to members of the community, doing some work with them, building trust and then getting them to sign the consent form and I think that is just as valid.' Other tensions arise when there are different motivations for becoming involved in the project, such as freelance artists who may prioritise their own career over wider project goals. 'You kind of hope when you run a research project that everyone is singing from the same hymn sheet, but you can never quite be sure. It's always worth trying to have those conversations.'

About the project, Lorna says 'I've never laughed as much. It was joyous and a real sense of connections. Having fun and making a political point.' She felt that the project had allowed her to capture stages of life that we often don't capture in research, though she acknowledges that it can be a challenge to balance the need to maintain your criticality as a researcher and yet provide and participate in an experience which is enjoyable for the participants. Although the project has now finished, Lorna is still working with many of the participants and continues to work on disseminating the findings of the project. Very often these activities end up being undertaken in her own time; raising questions about how such activities could be funded in the increasingly rigid and constrained environment of UK universities. For Lorna, public engagement and research are integrally intermingled and dissemination is all part of the process. 'All the UK funding bodies are now talking impact. And for years I've been doing this participatory research and haven't got that far. But now people are realising that if you are going to achieve public engagement and impact, this is exactly the way that you do it.'

Collaborative practice

In considering SciArt or even encouraging collaborations between researchers and artists we should be mindful that research, particularly the natural and social sciences, uses different knowledge practices than artists do. For example, what constitutes research in these different fields can be quite different and have very different intended outcomes. As Zwijnenberg (2009) points out, arts and sciences are separate knowledge domains with their own institutional products and expectations. These can be very different and it can be difficult for someone not trained in the discipline to understand the complexity of these distinct research processes. Furthermore, the way that the product of the research is expressed might also be quite different: how do those whose research domain values academic journal publications value an artist's body of work? Zwijnenberg (2009) reminds us that the product of one knowledge domain should not be judged by the standards of the other. These different practices and expectations can create conflicts, particularly in the areas of project design, expectations and working methodologies. Notwithstanding these differences, examples of coalescence, where artistic and scientific processes merge, are beginning to emerge.

Both artistic and research organisations are showing an interest in building collaborative projects between artists and scientists, though their motives are not always clear. Zwijnenberg (2009) suggests that scientific research challenges our views of the world and that artists seek to explore these challenges in their work; in essence suggesting that for artists, science is a stimulus for creating works that interrogate the human condition. While this is undoubtedly true and a key stimulus for some, Dowell and Weitkamp (2010) point out a rather more prosaic driver: the emergence in the UK, at least, of specific funding streams, such as the Wellcome Trust's Arts Awards, a scheme that is designed to enable 'the creation of a new artistic work' that has biomedical content. Dowell and Weitkamp (2010) also point out that the theatre practitioners interviewed were also interested in exploring the new ideas that science presented; so, while funding may be a stimulus for this type of project, it is not the only factor that influences an artist's decision to explore emerging research. Similarly, in their evaluation of the Wellcome Trust's SciArt funding scheme that ran from 1996–2006, Glinkowski and Bamford (2009: 64) observed that 'the attraction of entering into art–science collaborations was a sense of the beguiling mystique attached to the other discipline'. Notwithstanding the suggestions in both Glinkowski and Bamford's (2009) work and Dowell and Weitkamp's (2010) that researchers are open to collaborating with artists, Zwijnenberg (2009) argues that scientists rarely see art as contributing to their work. Instead, as Dowell and Weitkamp (2010) found, scientists see these forms of collaboration primarily as a means of public engagement, rather than as a process of developing their own thinking or practice, raising questions about the extent to which collaborations of this nature really move beyond what Hilton (2014: 112) calls 'a contrived exercise in cultural relations' to produce 'genuinely valuable scientific and artistic output'. Box 5.1 provides examples of initiatives designed to bring artists and scientists together. Because these are schemes that match artists with scientists, they each cover a range of arts practice and all provide sufficient materials to give a flavour for what is possible.

Box 5.1 Example projects bringing artists and researchers together

---

– The University of Chicago's Arts/Science initiative encourages collaborations between artists and researchers in the social and natural sciences, with the specific intention to stimulate transdisciplinary work that will break new ground in both the arts and sciences. Interactive videos explore a number of projects created through this scheme. http://artsscience-media.uchicago.edu/#Homepage

– The European Digital Art and Science Network is a European-funded project that aims to bring digital artists together with researchers. The network aims to foster intercultural collaborations and interdisciplinary exchange between researchers and digital artists. http://www.aec.at/artandscience/

– The Synergy Project, funded by the National Science Foundation in the USA, brings together artists together with researchers. Artworks produced during the collaboration are exhibited to the public. Videos on the website illustrate the range of approaches taken. http://science360.gov/series/synergy-project-experiment-art-science-collaboration/13c20997-be8f-48a8-8d18-5bbfe37378ef

---

Although few and far between, there are examples of scientists who acknowledge the value to their research of working with artists (Arends and Slater, 2004). Pearce, Diamond and Bream (2003) suggest that it is the different ways of thinking that make art/science collaborations effective: artists can provide lateral thinking, facilitate the socialisation and humanisation of technology, challenge dominant structures and contribute to invention. Frankel and Whitesides (2007: 7) highlight the power of images to communicate science, both to those outside the field and also, importantly, to those within a given field, as 'a single image organises a deluge of information in a form that is easy to understand. An image that is rich in composition and colour always catches the eye. And what catches the eye, catches the mind.' Nadrian Seeman, a structural scientist, also highlights the potential of visual representation for scientists, arguing that non-photographic visual representations can lead to new ways of looking:

> If we look at non-photographic art, it is often a little different from the mental image we may have had of the subject before we looked at the artwork. Sometimes these differences lead to ideas, because they force us to think of the images differently. As a structural scientist, I have found that these differences can lead to notions and experiments. (Seeman, 2014: 144)

Ox and Lowenberg (2012) suggest a rather different view of SciArt, one focused on collaboration. They argue that we may have moved

> beyond an initial phase – that of artists having relationships with engineers who help them create new instruments to use for making their art, and artists serving scientists by helping to represent scientific concepts for the public. Today *art and technology* seems to have lost its reason for being and relinquished its place to something quite different: *art/science*, which refers to worldviews, conceptual systems and research based on equal contributions from differently trained minds. (Ox and Lowenberg, 2012: 2; emphasis in original)

Ox and Lowenberg advocate collaborations on a deeper level than those which see 'scientists as filling a knowledge gap, providing them with information and understanding that they [the artists] lacked' (Dowell and Weitkamp, 2010: 896). Likewise, Ede (2008) identifies the potential for artists to engage on equal terms with scientists who themselves have ethical concerns about aspects of science. As she writes,

> Such collaborations may present a particular challenge to artists who don't want to make work that is simply 'issue-based' and to scientists who may be afraid that important arguments might be devalued by lightweight irony. But in the best works, such doubts can be resolved, and particularly with a view to our deep concerns about our imperilled environment and with questions of ownership [e.g. patenting of life forms] and the global economy, they must increasingly be. (Ede, 2008: 6)

Those working across disciplines can expect to be changed by the experience, as Edwards (2008: 54) argues; 'art enters the science cultural institution for the same ostensible reason that science enters the art institution, to serve the institutional mission, not to question it, not to change it from what it is. But once the art arrives, it inevitably goes further and begins engaging minds and provoking them.' Under the direction of Peter Fehlhammer, the Deutsches Museum proactively engaged with artists, bringing 'art into the science museum to challenge and to disturb, to show the complexity of art and science and the dialog that must take place between the two' (Edwards, 2008: 62), and not primarily to communicate science – a purpose similar to that of Ariane Koek in setting up the Arts@CERN programme.

Case study 5.2 Arts@CERN

Arts@CERN (http://arts.web.cern.ch/) seeks to stimulate creative collisions between artists and researchers. They're called creative collisions because they are designed to create a space where the unexpected can happen. 'So it's an experiment, just like the experiments here at CERN,' says Ariane Koek, International Arts at CERN and curator of Collide@CERN. The programme has three strands: 1) an artists in residence strand, Collide@CERN, 2) a visiting artists programme and 3) an arts-research strand, called Accelerate@CERN. All three strands are designed to facilitate idea generation for the artists involved. But it is not only the artists who are changed by the residency; scientists also report that the residencies change them, changing their way of thinking about their own research as well as providing more general benefits in terms of communication skills or general well-being.

Starting from the premise that the ideas of science are a springboard for the imagination, Ariane Koek has developed a programme with a difference. 'It's a curated experience,' explains Ariane. This means that artists aren't just given an office and told to get on with it; instead Ariane creates an experience specifically for the artist, which at a minimum will comprise physics lectures and opportunities to meet physicists. For both the Collide@CERN and Accelerate@CERN programmes the artist is also paired with an inspiration partner (a scientist) for the duration of the visit, and contact often doesn't stop there. As Ariane explained, 'Wonderful collisions happen between the artist and the scientist. Julius von Bismark and James Wells, his inspiration partner in 2012, have been creating a piece of work which just spontaneously happened [after the residency]. It will be a big public art piece. That's a lovely unexpected outcome.'

This vision for an arts programme that links particle physics and the arts has its origin in Ariane's own desire to step out of her comfort zone when she won a Clore fellowship for leadership in the arts. Rather than attach herself to a traditional arts venue, Ariane chose to come to CERN. At the end of her three-month stay she produced a proposal for CERN to develop an artists-in-residence programme. 'I argued that to be a cultural force in the twenty-first century it's not enough to be at the forefront of science and technology, you need to be science plus technology plus art,' says Ariane. The programme she developed in many ways mirrors the experiences of scientists themselves.

Artists' applications are reviewed by a panel comprising experts in the arts and scientists, a process not unlike the peer review process used in research-funding applications and while all the artists participating in residencies have produced artworks, this is not an outcome on which they are judged. As Ariane explains, 'I believe we've become too product focused. We've lost trust in the creative process. We've lost trust in artists. But a piece of artwork takes as long as it takes. You can't constrain it. If you say the piece must be finished in three months, then yes you will have a piece which might describe the science or illustrate the science. But it won't have that something extra, that art has.'

Communication is not the main purpose of the Arts@CERN programme, but it is an important aspect. Ariane believes that artistic works that explore scientific ideas attract new audiences to science. 'The arts reach the hearts and parts which science communication alone can't reach.' And it seems to work. Ariane explains that the world première of Gilles Jobin's work, *Quantum*, which was held at the CMS (Compact Muon Solenoid) detector in CERN, drew in an audience interested primarily in dance, many of whom, despite living near CERN, had never visited. 'They were gobsmacked, by the dance but also by this mysterious, underground machine,' recalls Ariane. Performances also occurred during CERN open days and it was apparent that people had come specifically for the dance performance, and then participated in the open day activities. In a review of the work that has emerged from the first three years of the Arts@ CERN programme, Ariane estimates that the artworks have reached around 7 million-arts oriented people around the world.

Benefits and challenges

For truly collaborative projects, the potential for creativity in arts/science project groups may be greater than in more homogeneous groups because the group diversity encourages individuals to build ideas using a wider range of knowledge domains. Such projects are not without their challenges. They stretch and challenge creators by exposing participants to new types of practice and thinking and require compromise on both sides. Hara *et al.* (2003) points out that collaborative practice involves taking risks and trusting others in the process of negotiating project boundaries, agreed meaning and shared responsibility, while Pearce, Diamond and Bream (2003) note that collaborative working exposes you to contrasting communication styles, working practices and temperaments. Miller (2014) highlights problems of language and communication as well as the need to acknowledge the contributions of all parties (examples abound of artworks attributed only to the artist, with no acknowledgement of the involvement and input of scientist or engineer). Some of these differences are differences between individuals and so might be encountered in any type of collaboration or team working, but some differences, for example in expectations of the 'product' of the collaboration, expectations of the roles and contributions of the different disciplines or working practices (akin to what Wenger (1998) terms community of practice) of the different disciplines may exacerbate these tensions. Box 5.2 provides some suggested tips for collaborative working.

Box 5.2 Practical tips on collaborative working

Language: Disciplines use language in different ways, and attempts to communicate across disciplines can lead to unavoidable reduction in the nuances of understanding. Patience and time are needed to explore understandings. Brokers (people able to speak both languages) can be helpful facilitators of this process.

Relationships: In some collaborations there can be a tendency for one group to see themselves as advisors or 'teachers'. This position must be interrogated rather than accepted without question if collaborations are to move to more equal footings.

Purpose: The purpose (both artistic and research) of the project should be clarified early on so as to avoid a mismatch in expectations.

Compromise: Collaborations involve shared ownership and this inevitably involves compromises. A common problem is the balance to be struck between accurately representing the research and artistic merit, though other compromises are also inevitable.

Valuing and acknowledging contributions: Early on establish ways to value the contributions of both parties, both through the working practices established as the project develops and also when exhibiting or performing the final artwork.

Time and resources: Recognise that this type of project takes time and that collaborations may also develop over time. Equally, different partners may have different expectations of what is a reasonable or necessary time or resource commitment and different ideas about what contributions require payment.

Researchers engaging with arts, then, need to consider their role in relation to the artists and institutions with whom they work. Are they providing inspiration? Are they co-creating a work of art and, if so, what is their role in this process? Who might the audience be, what are their expectations and how are they to be involved? How might the 'success' of such collaborations be judged? These are just a few of the questions that arise when considering research communication with the arts, but they are important questions to address at the start of any collaboration.

Impacts and expectations

A strong current running through debates about the impact of the arts is a concern on the part of many artists about the instrumental use of the arts. Calls for 'art for art's sake' may be seen in some senses as a response to calls for art to justify its worth (or public funding) by demonstrating social impacts. These debates extend back into the nineteenth century, and so have a rather longer history than the current drive amongst the wider research community to demonstrate the 'impact' of research, but the debate has many parallels; so-called 'blue sky research' tends to use the 'unexpected benefits' argument in this context, which is hardly different to saying 'research for research's sake'. Nevertheless, in the context of research communication, it is worth exploring the types of impacts that artistic approaches might have on audiences as a means of placing this approach to communication in the wider context of research communication strategies. Whilst we will explore impact and evaluation in more detail in Chapter 10, it is worth pausing for a moment here to consider in more detail the specific considerations the arts bring to these discussions.

Holden (2006) identified three types of cultural value that may arise from the arts: intrinsic, instrumental and institutional. Intrinsic value relates to subjective experiences, and so is difficult to measure and value. It includes aspects of the arts, such as aesthetic, historical and symbolic value, but can include factors such as authenticity which address concepts of price and worth and how these might be judged. Public and professional audiences may focus on this type of impact when discussing the effects of artistic experiences. Instrumental impacts are those which have social or economic benefits, such as improved educational attainment or health and well-being. These tend to be of most interest to funders and policymakers, and so are often the focus of attempts to measure value, though Holden believes this is an insufficient measure of the cultural value of the arts. Finally, institutional value consists of the ways that an arts institution relates to the public and how it influences wider public values. As such, it is of relevance to the public, but may be of less interest to professionals, policymakers or funders.

Beliefs about the impact of the arts have changed throughout history and both positive and negative effects are claimed for artistic experiences. Plato, for example, believed that the arts had a corrupting influence, a belief that has persisted to some extent throughout history. Exploring the history of views of the arts, Belfiore and Bennett (2008) identify six ways in which the arts have historically been viewed as having an impact on society which span the three categories identified by Holden: catharsis, personal well-being, education and self-development, moral improvement, political power, and social stratification and identity creation. A seventh theme, that of autonomy and rejection of instrumentality, focuses on the independent value of the arts, regardless of the effect they may have on the audience. Among the seven themes, some are more easily measured than others.

Experience of the arts may have specific educational or self-development impacts through, for example, artistic experiences that widen intellectual horizons, helping us to make sense of the world as well as promoting creativity and skill development; such aims are often seen in community arts programmes and may link to research communication objectives. Applied theatre, for example, may be designed to integrate into the curriculum or to work toward a specific health or social benefit, and community arts projects often seek to influence the community in which they are conducted. Brodzinski (2010) summarises the likely impacts of applied arts and health projects in four areas:

- Educational – projects may be designed to deliver a specific message in an engaging way.
- Community development – projects may seek to encourage a sense of community through collective creativity and at the same time identify community needs (e.g. health or social needs).
- Skills development – projects may offer an opportunity for participants to gain creative skills and enhance personal well-being.
- 'Pure' art – artworks may be presented in new settings (such as hospitals, family doctors' surgeries) without an overt health-related aim other than that which might be expected from improving the visual landscape of the setting.

Notice that most of the areas above do not include specific clinical benefits (with the exception of community development, which may have the goal of identifying health needs that could then be addressed through clinical provision). This has been an ongoing issue for applied arts and health projects, which typically involve interdisciplinary teams of clinicians and artists. Clinicians (and sometimes funders) may expect to see evidence of clinical benefit from such projects, which may not be realistic or easily measurable. As Brodzinski (2010: 11) notes, 'there is, then, a recognition of the efficacy of arts in health, but the field is struggling to develop a framework within which to reflect on the impact of such work'.

While we do not wish to in any way suggest that the arts do not have intrinsic worth, from a practical point of view, it may be desirable or necessary to evaluate the impact of projects developed through collaboration between researchers and artists. As Brodzinski suggests, identifying the intended impact of a project enables you to articulate a framework around which the project may be evaluated (see Chapter 10), whether through formal or informal means. Nevertheless, there is considerable debate about how such evaluation might be undertaken and framed. For example, Galloway suggests that '[a]rguably, the main issue for advancing our understanding of the effects of arts interventions is ontological; it is not research methods but the most effective "orientation" or "logic of enquiry"'; consequently, the crucial question that still needs answering is 'what types of research *approach* are best suited to investigating the social effects of the arts?' (Galloway 2009: 126; original emphasis). Similarly, Belfiore and Bennett (2010) argue that there is a need to move beyond the 'toolkit' approach to arts evaluation and to question long-held assumptions about what the impacts of the arts might be, whether positive or negative. As such, 'before "impact" and its measurement can be discussed in any meaningful way, we need a better understanding of the interaction between people and the arts' (Belfiore and Bennett, 2010: 125). Thus, they suggest a research agenda that 'aims at an open enquiry of the problems, both theoretical and methodological, which are inherent in the project of understanding the response of individuals to the arts and trying to investigate empirically the extent and nature of the effects of the aesthetic experience' (Belfiore and Bennett, 2010: 139).

As these authors suggest, there is a need for a greater understanding of the effects of arts experiences on participants, and research is exploring what these might be – a gap which evaluation can begin to address. We therefore suggest that at the early stages of an arts-research project some time is set aside to explore and consider what impacts might be appropriate or desirable from the project; these might be effects relevant to participants, but equally it might be appropriate to consider the impacts of the project on the project creators. This will allow you to articulate a theory of change around which to build your evaluation (Galloway, 2009). Appropriate evaluation tools can then be identified which might consider both process and product. Evaluation allows participants to reflect on the extent to which a project has met their expectations and enables those elements that work well or fail to meet expectations, whether they are related to process or product, to be interrogated and adjusted for future projects.

Summary

What can we expect from collaborations between researchers and artists? Certainly we can expect creativity and novelty. We might also anticipate that such approaches will reach new or under-served audiences. Examples such as MS: The Big Knit suggest that craft-based approaches may facilitate dialogue and discussion, although it can be challenging to recruit researchers to contribute to such projects, as they can require substantial time commitments and place researchers in contexts which are unfamiliar and uncomfortable (Featherstone, personal communication). Such approaches, however, are not without issues: arts-based approaches might go some way to reaching new audiences, but these are still likely to be audiences that are already socially engaged, with what Bourdieu would call significant cultural capital. Reaching out to under-served audiences requires a careful and thoughtful choice of partner organisations and cultural venues. You need to go to where the audience or participants are and beware of the invisible barriers that prevent some groups from engaging at all. This isn't to say that projects combining research and the arts can't reach new audiences, but just to highlight that it is not a given that such projects will reach beyond the 'usual suspects'. As Anker and Nelkin (2004: 194) eloquently point out in relation to art exploring the field of genetics:

> Visual art can help to explicate and popularise an often obscure science, translating difficult information and illustrating complex social issues in persuasive and culturally meaningful ways, but artists cannot really communicate concepts in science that are beyond – and even defy – common understanding. Rather, their work reflects their individual responses and social concerns. Moreover, art has its own deliberate obscurities and complexities that follow from its unique historical and symbolic associations. There may be better ways to communicate and popularise science.

Reward structures for researchers do not necessarily prioritise or explicitly value public engagement, and this applies equally to all forms of public engagement. While there is a growing pressure on researchers around the world to demonstrate the 'impact' of their work, there are no clear metrics for doing so. Furthermore, this pressure to demonstrate impact may encourage researchers to consider the arts as a 'handmaiden' able to facilitate this aspect of their work. As a result, there can be a tendency within the science and health communities to view the arts as a vehicle or tool through which to communicate. This instrumental use of the arts in the service of other disciplines leads to projects better described as ones that 'happen' to use arts. Of course, the opposite is also possible: artists may engage with scientific concepts in ways that might best be described as instrumental (the science is merely the vehicle through which ideas are explored). The issue, then, is to discover ways that allow both the art and the science to maintain their integrity.

The pressure to undertake public engagement is not unique to research-ers. While art may be everywhere, the process which separated 'fine art' from craft also in many ways separated art from society and Ede argues that the public is in many ways better informed about contemporary science than it is about contemporary art (Ede, 2008). Shiner (2001: 269) contends that a 'major trend of the past thirty years has tried to reinte-grate art with life, from the intimately personal to the broadly political'. This trend seeks to bring art to wider audiences, or to place art outside of traditional art venues, including public spaces. Major art museums and galleries around the world now have public outreach or engage-ment strategies, including galleries such as the Fundació Joan Miró in Barcelona, which has a programme designed to facilitate understanding of the museum's content, aimed at children and adults; Denver Museum of Arts, which hosts artists in workshop spaces where visitors can inter-act with artists at work; and the National Museums of Liverpool, which has proactively sought through Positive Images, a programme designed to explore local heritage, to engage those groups who would not nor-mally consider taking part in a museum experience. When it comes to developing new works of art to be sited in public spaces, artists may now meet with members of the local community as well as the art establish-ment with a view to creating artworks that both are inviting spaces for the local community and also provide aesthetic interest. Such approaches might also serve to widen access and increase audiences to more traditional art venues, and examples of artworks are springing up that move 'away from the modern ideals of the autonomous artist and the self-referential work to embrace a democratic vision of collaboration, service, and social function' (Shiner, 2001: 301). These issues about public engagement with the arts and the approaches used to tackle them look remarkably similar to approaches used for public engagement with research. Perhaps these two communities, artists and researchers, and their respective institu-tions could learn much from working together more frequently.

Notes

1 Source: http://wikiquote.org/wiki/Buckminster_Fuller.

Further reading

Miller, A.I., *Colliding Worlds: How Cutting-Edge Science Is Redefining Contemporary Art* (New York: W.W. Norton and Company, 2014).

Pauwels, L. (ed.), *Visual Cultures of Science: Rethinking Representational Practices in Knowledge Building and Science Communication* (Hannover, NH: Dartmouth College Press, 2006).

Reichle, I., *Art in the Age of Technoscience. Genetic Engineering, Robotics, and Artificial Life in Contemporary Art* (New York: Springer–Wein, 2009).

Wilson, S., *Art + Science Now: How Scientific Research and Technological Innovation Are Becoming Key to 21st-Century Aesthetics* (London: Thames and Hudson, 2010).

6

Digital

Web 2.0 technologies open up many new opportunities to engage publics at all stages of the research process, from design, through data collection and processing, to dissemination, and in a variety of different ways. These can range from fairly passive approaches that provide content for those seeking information (e.g. via project web pages) to highly interactive approaches, such as games and apps. These projects are enabled by a growth in technology, both hardware and software, that enables interaction and engagement and makes it easier for individuals to create their own digital projects. It is now relatively easy to create a website or other presence for your research on the internet, allowing researchers to become publishers of their own content, though other approaches, such as app development, may require specialist skills and interdisciplinary collaboration.

Much of the growth in digital public engagement projects comes about because it is now so much easier to create and share content on the web, using what are now commonly referred to as Web 2.0 technologies. Web 2.0, a term first coined by DiNucci in 1990, refers to the underlying architecture which allows information to be shared and repurposed across a range of digital devices, including computers, gaming platforms and mobile phones. Pew Research Centre's Internet and American Life Project suggests that the term gained popularity because Web 2.0 'provided a useful, if imperfect, conceptual umbrella under which analysts, marketers and other stakeholders in the tech field could huddle the new generation of internet applications and businesses that were emerging to form the "participatory Web" as we know it today: Think blogs, wikis, social networking, etc.' (Pew Internet Research Centre 2010; Fox and Madden, 2006: np). Web 2.0 is applied to a wide range of technologies, some of which will be discussed in greater detail in Chapter 7, from mechanisms that allow information to be collated and represented (e.g. news aggregators), through to tools that make it easy to create your own digital places and spaces. As with all such tools, they can be used both actively and passively by users, who may choose to read what others have produced or indeed create their own mashups and repurposed materials.

Web 2.0 technologies have made it possible for anyone to become a content producer, or what Bruns (2006) calls a 'produser', eliminating the need for a middleman or gatekeeper who traditionally mediates access to older, more expensive media and technologies (e.g. journalists or web designers). This has the advantage that researchers can now reach many potential publics directly by engaging in digital communication opportunities. It has the disadvantage that the digital space is becoming very crowded, and being heard amid the cacophony of digital noise is no simple matter. Whereas previously working with a press office, for example, may have been your only option to attract attention to your research in a media context, today you can write your own website content, getting the message out in your terms and words, with as much or as little detail as you choose. This demands new skills of researchers, in terms of both technical and communication skills. It is now up to you to make sure your writing is appropriate for the audience you hope to reach. Furthermore, that journalist or other mediator (in the traditional media system) had an existing readership or audience, and your website may well have limited reach unless you are either very lucky and are quoted by someone with a big following or are very persistent in marketing it.

So, how is the busy researcher to capitalise on these opportunities? This chapter considers the growing ecology of digital tools and opportunities for research communication and engagement. The primary focus in this chapter is on communication about research and the plethora of ways that publics encounter research online. It is designed to help you think about the tools you might use to engage audiences with your research (and the tools you might personally prefer to avoid). It is primarily about communication and engagement rather than participation, which is covered in Chapters 8 and 9. The decision on what to include in this chapter, and what to leave to the social media chapter, is, to an extent, arbitrary and there is inevitably some overlap between the chapters. There are also many digital projects and approaches which we simply did not have the space to cover; in the world of Web 2.0 your communication efforts are limited only by your imagination (and technical skill).

Who's online, doing what?

We are now in an era of widespread, though unequal, internet use. In the United States, for example, 87 percent of adults use the internet, with 97 percent of eighteen to twenty-nine-year-olds accessing this technology (Fox and Rainie, 2014). Seventy-one percent of these users access the internet every day. Contrast this with 6 percent of the population in Afghanistan accessing the internet and 29 percent of people living in Thailand in 2013 (World Bank, 2015), and a more mixed picture emerges. Internet use in Europe is also patchy, though still much higher than in many countries of Africa or Asia, with several countries having over 40 percent of the population never having used the internet (Portugal, Greece, Bulgaria and Romania), while countries such as Finland, the Netherlands and Norway all have fewer than 10 percent of the population who claim not to use the internet (Anon, 2012). In Europe, as in the United States, age is the largest predictor of non-use, with those over fifty-five accounting for the majority of non-users. These figures illustrate that internet access is not universally used or available, something which must be considered if you are trying to engage certain groups with your research.

Users also access the internet in a variety of ways. In the United States, 68 percent of adults access the internet using mobile devices, such as phones, and 58 percent of adults in the United States now own smartphones (Pew Research Centre, 2012). Use of mobile phones to access the internet also varies by age; in Europe, for example, around 40 percent of sixteen to thirty-four-year-olds access the internet through these devices, with lower rates in older groups (Anon, 2012). Arora (2012) argues that digital spaces are not without constraints and that 'digital ghettos' are emerging, comprising people who are unable or unwilling to engage in this sphere. Thus, 'contrary to democratic and utopian notions of Web 2.0, is a reality where there are deep segmentations, segregations and social struggles in accessing these privileged digital domains' (Arora, 2012: 605).

Information and communication dominate activities online: amongst American adults, 94 percent use the internet for email, 87 percent use search engines, 83 percent search for health information and 74 percent read news online (Pew Research Centre, 2010). Fifty-three percent of European internet users were using social networks in 2012, and 19 percent used file-sharing sites. However, only 20 percent indicate that they have read and posted opinions on civic or political issues via blogs or social networks, though this ranges from just under 50 percent in Finland to around 5 percent in Belgium (Anon, 2012).

Despite the large number of people online, the potential hegemony of mainstream media remains a contentious issue. At the heart of the debate is the difference between push and pull media. As Malin (2011) argues, mainstream media may have advantages over digital media because they are streamed into our homes, enabling routine and ritualised use of content. Through ritual use of particular programmes, we give these media the opportunity to promote the salience of certain topics. In contrast, the internet is inherently a pull medium; that is to say, we have to actively seek content rather than waiting for it to appear through our routine viewing and listening experiences. This can present a challenge to the research communicator using digital tools, particularly if they are trying to reach groups who are not already interested in their subject area. Search algorithms, which determine what material is presented to the user and in what order, accentuate the problem of the long tail (large number of sites with relatively few visitors) for those seeking to communicate their research via the internet, as they tend to prioritise popular pages over those with less traffic. 'This means that unlike the more traditional medium of broadcast television, which focusses user attention on a common program or advertisement, these top sites offer users an experience unique to their search terms and browsing patterns. Not every Facebook user will, or even can, see the same things when they visit the site' (Malin, 2011: 192). Although the challenge of being 'found' cannot be understated, reaching the already-interested is becoming easier; as the internet has become more sophisticated, users are more regularly provided with sites and suggestions of interest to them based on their current usage or through recommendations via their social networks.

Access on the move

Mobile devices are also changing the way that we access information. Phones, for example, are personal, portable and available when we are on the move. Worldwide, mobile phone subscriptions have reached 96 percent on a population basis, with many countries showing greater than 100 percent penetration (ITU, 2014a). These figures may include 'dead' subscriptions, as well as people with more than one mobile phone subscription. While there are still differences between developed and developing countries, mobile phones have been widely adopted throughout the world and 78 percent of mobile subscriptions are now in developing countries. Mobile phone penetration can be high even amongst the least-developed countries; Cambodia, for example, has mobile penetration rates of 132 percent, thanks to a very competitive telecoms market (ITU, 2014b).

Mobile phones are used in ways we might expect: that is, for keeping in contact with friends and family through voice calls, text messaging and email access. But with smartphone ownership increasing, new uses for phones are emerging. InsightsNow (2012) suggests seven emerging ways that people use mobile phones: for 'me time' (e.g. access to entertainment), 'socialising', 'shopping', 'accomplishing' (e.g. managing finances, health), 'preparation' (e.g. planning activities), 'discovery' (seeking information) and 'self-expression' (participating in hobbies). Of these, 'me time' is by far the largest use identified by InsightsNow, but many of the categories identified might also be considered leisure activities, suggesting that public engagement approaches that tap into leisure interests might be fruitful. Looked at another way, we could consider how smartphones are used to access data and information (which would also cross many of the categories above). Smartphones are predicted to account for 67 percent of data downloaded via mobile devices (compared with laptops at 14 percent and tablets at 11 percent) (ITU, 2014b). According to the Pew Research Centre (2012), 56 percent of Americans use their mobile phone to browse the internet. There clearly is scope for public engagement using mobile technology; but interestingly, according to the InsightsNow report, around 68 percent of these leisure activities occur in the home, so we should be careful about making assumptions regarding the location of mobile users.

Digital spaces and places

In the context of 'visitors' (to websites), it is useful to consider why those visitors might arrive at a given site and what they might be looking for in terms of interaction. Arora (2012) suggests that Web 2.0 spaces fall into five groups: utilitarian-driven; aesthetic-driven; context-driven; play-driven; and value-driven. These spaces are performed and maintained by individuals and offer a useful way to think about the ways that people engage in the digital sphere. They also suggest issues that you might consider in designing a digital engagement. Of course, any given individual is likely to use a variety of different Web 2.0 spaces for different purposes.

- *Utilitarian-driven spaces* tend to be functional, with a focus on utility. This view of the internet emerged from the idea of the internet as providing an 'information superhighway', that is, access to an enormous volume of information that might be valued or put to use by individual users.
- *Aesthetic-driven spaces* acknowledge the needs of people for personalisation and creativity. Users can manipulate the spaces they occupy, though often within only a limited range of choices. This allows users to manifest their voice in the production, for example, of content. The ability to personalise a space into one in which you are comfortable may determine whether or not you engage with a particular internet space (e.g. Twitter, blogging software). Aesthetic aspects may influence which spaces you feel comfortable

engaging in, and also allow you to present your identity more clearly online.

- *Context-driven spaces* reflect the fact that we bring with us to the online world expectations and prejudices about certain types of public and private spaces. For example, museums have certain cultural connotations and these connotations may well transfer into an online presence. Likewise, we can identify differences between social networks such as LinkedIn (predominantly seen as work or professionally related) and Facebook (which might be seen as a more public, leisure-oriented pursuit). While different users may have slightly different expectations of spaces, it is useful to consider the likely context of the space when considering a communications activity. Ask yourself who usually engages in this space and why, and design your activity to address these users and their needs.

- *Play-driven spaces* use the term 'play' broadly. While such spaces include games and gaming websites, play can also be used in work spaces or to enhance customer loyalty. Increasingly, sites are emerging that seek to combine serious aims (such as education) with game elements, in a trend referred to as gamification. Fun spaces can be associated with attempts at behaviour change. An example from the 'real world' is the Stockholm underground stairs that were retrofitted to look and behave like piano keys, in an attempt to encourage commuters to climb the stairs rather than stand on the escalator.[1]

- *Value-driven spaces* seek to connect to our sentiments and, by pulling on our values, to retain our attention. These spaces may connect to people's needs to explore new worlds or ideas, or they may connect to specific cultural interests as a means of creating a 'visiting public'.

As Baym (2009) notes, there is a tendency online to think of everything as 'new', yet from both a research and a practice perspective it can be useful to think about how a project or communication strategy might translate from the 'real' to the 'virtual' world. This doesn't mean that adaptation to a new context isn't needed, but it does mean that we shouldn't always seek to create something completely different online. Since people take concepts and expectations from one realm to the other, communicators need to think about what impact these concepts will have on project design. For example, what expectations do your audience bring with them that might affect their interaction with your research? Equally, you need to consider what concepts or expectations you may take with you into the online world. If you've worked successfully with traditional media, you may have unrealistic expectations of website traffic, for example. The different types of spaces identified above both can shed light on the types of places and spaces in which you would feel comfortable interacting (not everyone finds SecondLife a comfortable place, for example) and also suggest some elements you might need to consider if you are trying to reach a particular group with your communications activity.

There are other ways that we can conceptualise online spaces and places beyond their purposes. Baym (2009) suggests we should consider seven features of digital places (temporal structure, social cues, storage, replicability, reach, mobility and, perhaps the most important, interactivity), which might feature in different ways on websites. The temporal structure of a medium determines whether communication is synchronous or asynchronous. Birch and Weitkamp (2010), for example, found a temporal disconnect when it comes to listeners interacting with the online fora associated with podcasts. These users typically listen to podcasts offline and so must make a special effort to reconnect to the internet if they are to contribute to online discussions; this presents a barrier to online interactivity for all but the most committed listeners. Considering the temporal structure of the medium is, therefore, an important factor if your primary interest is to generate synchronous interaction with users, for instance through discussion.

Social cues, those factors that provide context and meanings to messages, can be problematic online. With face-to-face (or body-to-body) communication, we have access to the full range of social cues, from body language through to tone of voice, and these help us interpret whether a person is being, for example, ironic. In the digital sphere, some of these cues may be missing, making it harder to interpret a message in the way it was intended. Communicators need to consider the context of the digital space, what users expect and the richness of the medium (in terms of what social cues it provides; see Chapter 7 for further discussion on media richness) when developing communication to ensure message suitability and integrity. Likewise it can be important to consider how long the message will be available online and how this might affect framing. Storage presents a problem both in terms of maintaining access to digital work (which may become incompatible with updated software, causing material to have to be removed or expensively updated) and in terms of removing outdated or inappropriate content. Recent changes in legislation mean that you have a right to be forgotten online, but removing content may not be easy if the content has been quoted by others. The issue of content being used by others (replicated) may also cause concerns about copyright and ownership, as well as issues of misquotation or simply the research being superseded by new thinking.

Digital media has the potential to reach large and diverse audiences, but in practice getting noticed is not so easy. Few of us will be as lucky as @LegoAcademics to attract 14,000 Twitter followers in less than a week (Cramb, 2014); despite the marketing hype, going viral is not easy to achieve, and most researchers will have to work hard to secure an online audience. However, if you have a clearly defined group you wish to reach (such as a local community or specific interest group), then the narrowcasting that is possible online can help you reach those people most likely to be interested in or affected by your work.

As we have seen above, there is a growing use of portable digital devices (such as smartphones and tablets) which can connect to the internet in a variety of geographical locations. Particularly for those who want to engage audiences in specific geographical areas, this mobility opens up new possibilities for engagement with research. QR code trails, for example, can provide users with additional information about historical sites or natural features, though uptake can be problematic. Rio de Janeiro, for example, embedded QR codes in pavements at various points in the city in 2013. The black-and-white cobbled QR codes mimic the black-and-white mosaic pavements that are a symbol of the city and also provide tourists with useful additional information (in a variety of languages), including historic details related to specific tourist landmarks like the Arpoador boulder at Ipanema Beach. Developments in technology are also enabling digital overlays onto existing landscapes that show, for instance, archaeological research (for example the Virtual Romans mobile app, developed by De Montfort University (http://digi talbuildingheritage.our.dmu.ac.uk/2014/02/0/virtual-romans-mobile-device-app-launch/), see Case study 6.2).

Current trends in public engagement focus on interaction and dialogue, both of which require interactivity. But interactivity in the digital sphere occurs at many different levels, from the ability to change the aesthetic aspects of your Twitter home page, to social interaction, whether in real time via a chat function or simply the ability to post your views about a YouTube video. Thus we might see interactivity as lying on a continuum (Figure 6.1) from fairly passive engagement (watching a video) to projects which require the audience to engage actively, such as games that require the user to make choices or perform actions.

A related (but distinct) issue is that of interaction: the extent to which the project allows or encourages interaction (synchronous or asynchronous) between researchers and the public. Here we might consider websites or projects with no easy way for readers or users to contact the researcher as offering no interaction, while a project which facilitates live chat with a researcher enables interaction. Of course there are many levels in between, from the simple 'like' buttons on YouTube that offer a

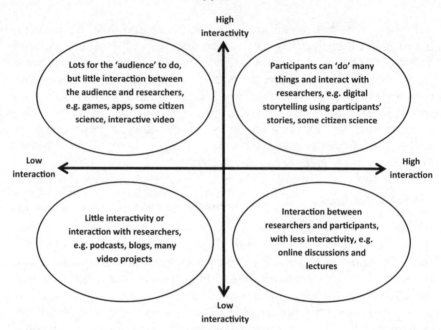

Figure 6.1 Interactivity and interaction seen as dimensions of public engagement projects

public 'rating' system, to projects which collate and curate oral histories or other public contributions. As a creator, you need to consider what level of interactivity and interaction you wish to enable; the visitors will then choose an appropriate level of interactivity and interaction for their purposes. So, in designing any digital engagement project, there are a number of questions you need to address. For example, what level of interaction do you want to have with your audience? What level of interaction do they want to have with you? Do you want to build in interactivity (but not necessarily interaction), perhaps drawing on principles of gamification in the design of your digital project? These are questions that need to be considered at the planning (and funding) stage of the project and will have implications for your ongoing commitment and involvement in the project, as well as for the skills needed to create the project in the first place.

Interaction and interactivity are not the only facets of digital communication you might consider, but they are the aspects focused on in this chapter. Below we will consider digital engagement tools that illustrate different facets of interaction and interactivity as examples of how these two elements might be employed in digital research communication: video projects; digital storytelling; gamification, games and apps.

Video projects

Video may be seen as a fairly passive engagement tool for the audience, allowing them to sit back and watch and thereby requiring neither inter-activity nor interaction. However, these projects can capitalise on the potential for interaction. Consider the science video project The Periodic Table of Videos (PTOV), a collaboration between chemist Martyn Poliakoff and journalist and filmmaker Brady Haran. The project seeks to interest the public in chemistry through the use of short videos about the elements. The website associated with the project organises the videos using the periodic table, a visual representation of the elements originally conceived by Dimitri Mendeleev. The videos range from explanatory videos that explore the history of a particular element (e.g. niobium) to those discussing the properties of specific elements, including showing the explosive properties of some elements (e.g. potassium).

Although professionally produced, the videos have a homemade, unscripted quality that may contribute to their appeal. Exploring news videos online, Peer and Ksiazek (2011) argue that popular (as judged by number of views) videos broadly adhere to professional media-production standards (e.g. steady shots, good-quality audio and visual imagery), and Haran brings these qualities to the PTOV project. However, when it comes to content, there is considerable flexibility and potential for innovation in the way you tell a story in a video intended for online consumption. Kim (2012) suggests that YouTube video content, while influenced by the mainstream media genre, tends to be short, humorous and accessible – characteristics not always associated with mainstream broadcast programming. This suggests that people may be looking for something slightly different when accessing online videos than what they expect of TV broadcasts.

Judging from viewer figures, PTOV has managed to grab the interest of a large segment of the public, through its combination of filming techniques (which are clearly professional but retain a homemade edge), conversational narrative, personalities (Poliakoff appears as the stereo-typical mad scientist), impressive bangs and demonstrations. By May 2013, there were 478 videos on the site (far more than there are ele-ments) and overall the project had received over 41 million views. Even with such large viewing figures, Haran and Poliakoff (2011) point out that it is not easy to measure the 'impact' of the project (see Chapter 10). As they point out, 'one "view" cannot distinguish between a high-school teacher showing the video to an entire class or one individual watching the same video numerous times' (Haran and Poliakoff, 2011: 181). Viewing figures give a sense of the reach of the project, but PTOV has additionally engaged with the comments facilities offered by YouTube as a way to increase interaction, both with themselves and between viewers. Haran and Poliakoff have explored the comments received (either posted on YouTube or received via email) as another way to assess the impact of the project and the extent to which it has created conversations online. They give the examples of viewers asking questions that are then answered by other viewers (many-to-many interaction), as well as questions they receive and answer (many-to-one interaction), highlighting some of the ways that the impact of a project like this could be conceptualised and measured and highlighting that the question of impact requires some thought in the digital sphere.

Practically, video projects require a collaborative effort, such as that between Poliakoff and Haran or between Jilli Rose and Nicholas Carlile, who created the award-winning short animation *Sticky* (see Case study 6.1). For both Poliakoff and Carlile, collaboration came about through the interests of the filmmaker, who sought the involvement of the researchers. While you may be approached by a filmmaker (or other professional such as an artist) to collaborate on a project, researchers interested in working in these areas might also take more proactive approaches. In the case of film, it might be worth attending specific film festivals and networking with filmmakers to generate interest (for example South by Southwest in the USA, or the Sheffield doc fest in the UK). Closer to home, if your research institution includes academics interested in film, you might consider approaching them with a view to creating a joint project that meets both of your research interests and might potentially be funded through either a research proposal or specific public engagement funding scheme. Other models of production are also possible, from projects organised at the university level (e.g. https://vine.co/universityofkansas), to those that seek to inspire others to create their content, such as Dance your PhD (http://gonzolabs.org/dance/), a contest for PhD students to present their research in dance form. In the case of Dance your PhD, the project probably does not involve professional filmmakers at all, as the entrants presumably rely on their friends and family to film the dances they create. These projects all aim to reach broad audiences, but there are also examples of video projects designed to reach specific audiences, such as the Science for Environment Policy video packages produced on behalf of the European Commission and designed to reach environmental policymakers.

Video projects don't necessarily require substantial funding, though long-lived projects such as the Periodic Table of Videos will require ongoing support. Researchers wanting to initiate their own video project might seek funding as part of their dissemination plans, and thereby cover the costs of filming and editing. Jilli Rose used a crowd-funding approach for *Sticky*, while Dance your PhD is sponsored by the American Association for the Advancement of Science. PTOV has funding from a wide range of sources, including both Nottingham University (where Poliakoff works), research funders and charitable trusts, highlighting the wide range of funders who might contribute to such a project.

As with all digital projects, getting noticed is often the problem. This may not solely be down to the effort you put into marketing your project, but also to the practices and processes embedded within the distribution platforms that privilege the content of already popular users. Van Dijck (2013a) calculates that around 4 percent of YouTube users upload 75 percent of the videos, basing his calculations on a study by Ding *et al.* (2011). As van Dijck argues, this suggests that YouTube's 'algorithms thus explicitly undercut the impression that most YouTubers are active "produsers" and that all uploaders are treated equally' (van Dijck, 2013a: 116). Getting noticed as a researcher in the long tail of narrowcast activities is not easy. Careful consideration needs to be given regarding the audience you hope to reach and why they might be interested in what you have to say. Perhaps PTOV was lucky, or perhaps its approach struck a particular cord, but achieving such a high viewership is likely to be challenging and it is important to set realistic expectations on both the number of viewers you are likely to reach and the types of interactions you might generate through the videos.

Case study 6.1 Sticky, animation and science communication

Serendipity seems to coalesce around Nicholas Carlile, an Island Ecologist based in Australia and rediscoverer of living specimens of the Lord Howe Island phasmid (*Dryococelus australis*), a giant stick insect around fifteen centimetres long. Rats arriving on the damaged and beached supply ship SS *Makambo* in 1918 were thought to have wiped out the Lord Howe stick insect in the 1920s, though climbing expeditions to a nearby rock, Ball's Pyramid, since the 1960s found a few dead specimens. 'We regularly received requests to climb Ball's Pyramid to look for the insect, but the climbing teams rarely if ever included entomologists', Nicholas, who works for the Office of Environment and Heritage in New South Wales, explains. 'So we decided to mount our own expedition.'

It took four years to get approval, but finally the team were on their way. After a week of waiting for weather to allow them access to the Pyramid they eventually had a 'window' of twenty-four hours for searching. They found evidence of phasmids on the afternoon of the first day, but as the creatures are nocturnal the team had to mount a night-time climb before sighting two live insects. The insects appeared to live during daylight hours in hollows beneath just one bush on this, the world's tallest sea stack.

This lucky encounter with this incredibly rare phasmid was mirrored a few years later when filmmaker and animator Jilli Rose got in touch with Nicholas about a film she had in mind. The result of their collaboration is the award-winning film *Sticky* (http://vimeo.com/76647062).

Jilli's initial idea was to produce an animation with only a musical sound track, but on hearing Nicholas speak she realised he could narrate the story giving a personal insight into the rediscovery. 'She gave me ten questions and wanted off-the-cuff answers,' Nicholas recalls. It took two and a half hours across two sessions for Nicholas to record his responses to the questions. He sent the recordings to Jilli and then didn't hear anything more until she had produced the final edit.

'I wouldn't have ended the film the way she did, but she had her reasons,' he says, highlighting the need for researchers to be flexible when working with artists or the media. 'Artists have different perspectives and ways of presenting information which connect with our emotions and feelings.'

Jilli had picked up on Nicholas's passion to prevent extinctions and his excitement in the discovery of a species thought to be extinct. Having Nicholas narrate the film allows him to convey these feelings directly to the viewer. Jilli also wove his ideas into the animations, for example, using the imagery of the extinct Tasmanian tiger as a guide and metaphor for the problems of extinction within the film. The Tasmanian tiger happens to be a particular interest of Nicholas's and he was delighted to see the way she had incorporated its image as a subtle reminder of what we have lost.

Finding ways to express your passion is one of Nicholas's key tips for anyone seeking to communicate their research, whether they are giving a media interview or working with arts practitioners. 'Passion makes you interesting to listen to,' he advises. 'It gives you a positive delivery and energy.' If you can use this excitement to intrigue an interviewer or potential collaborator, then you may win a little extra time to explain your research.

Nicholas's passion comes across clearly in the narration of *Sticky* and you can hear why Jilli was keen to incorporate his voice directly. 'There is a real synergy between science and the arts,' says Nicholas. 'Both are trying to reach the unobtainable. It's a beautiful marriage because you are both trying to achieve something special.' If you have the chance to work with artists or filmmakers, take the risk – you never know quite where it will take you.

Digital storytelling

Digital stories are short, multimedia videos told by ordinary people and usually 'distributed' using web-based platforms. At first glance, digital storytelling may seem quite similar to other video projects. What makes it different is a focus on the individual. Digital stories are told by individuals, expressing their personal narrative. Stories may be told using still or moving images, though purists may argue against the use of moving images, which are combined with audio (spoken or music) and textual elements. Emphasis is usually placed on the personal and emotional quality of the film, rather than on the production qualities. 'The personal narrative, told in the storyteller's unique voice, is central to the process of creating a story and is given priority in the arrangement of symbolic elements. Narrative accessibility, warmth, and presence are prioritized over formal experimentation or innovative "new" uses for technologies' (Burgess, 2006: 207). Burgess argues that digital stories are 'based in everyday communicative practices – telling personal stories, collecting, and sharing personal images – but remixed with the textual idioms of television and film; and transformed into publicly accessible culture through the use of digital tools for production and distribution' (Burgess, 2006: 210).

From a research communication perspective, digital storytelling can allow you to tell your own story or to curate the stories of your research participants. In a two-minute story, 'Carmen', a community-based HIV researcher, explores why she became an HIV researcher (http://www.youtube.com/watch?v=m7pIPR-jC64). The story explores the origins of Carmen's interest in HIV, reflecting on when she first heard the term, through to her first experiences of people dying alone in an HIV ward. The story reflects the core elements of digital stories: it offers a personal perspective, telling the author's story in her own voice. The story is simple and the narrative easy to follow, though both are brought to life through the inclusion of examples that illustrate points she makes quite subtly. This is a story about one person and what motivates her, but research can generate many stories which, when collected together, offer a powerful insight into a community or issue. Consider the Nagasaki Archive (http://n.mapping.jp/index_en.html). This archive has collected together photographs, maps and historical information and is working with high school students to collect the memories of survivors of the atomic bomb (in Japanese). This project combines these individual voices with historical research to create an archive that provides both a single, overarching digital story as well as poignant individual stories. Carmen's story and the Nagasaki archive are both similar and different. Both offer personal insights and both tell a story. The linear story that Carmen presents allows limited interactivity (you can post a comment or like the video), while the Nagasaki Archive allows visitors to plot their own story narrative, depending on the stories they choose to read or watch and the order in which they are accessed. While not strictly research communication, the film *Highrise* offers another approach to digital storytelling that could be adopted by research communicators working in collaboration with others. *Highrise*, an award-winning interactive

film from Canada, takes a similar approach to the Nagasaki Archive
in that it tells the stories of individuals but presents them in a way that

---

Box 6.1 **Digital story examples**

The Centre for Digital Storytelling provides a number of examples of
digital stories produced through its workshops. http://storycenter.org/

Capturing Wales: BBC Wales has produced a number of digital stories
with people from Wales. The archived website also includes resources
for producing digital stories. www.bbc.co.uk/wales/audiovideo/sites/
galleries/pages/digitalstorytelling.shtml

The Are You Happy Project combines elements of digital storytelling and
professional filmmaking. This project asks people around the world 'Are
you happy?', following the approach of Marceline Loridan and Nadine
Baillot fifty years ago in Paris. www.theareyouhappyproject.org/about

Untold Stories encourages migrants to tell the story of their lives. http://
blog.libver.gr/en/?page_id=28

---

allows the viewer to choose where to go and to whom to listen. *Highrise*
presents the stories of people living in high-rise buildings around the
world. This project combines professional filmmaking by Katerina Cizek
with individuals' digital stories. *Highrise* provides a curated window on
individual lives and gives an indication of what is possible with sufficient
funding. Digital stories come in all shapes and sizes; the examples in Box
6.1 will give you some sense of the possibilities of this medium.

Anyone with access to a computer can make a digital story.[2] The
focus on authenticity over production values means that there are excellent examples of 'home-made' films. The starting point when creating a
digital story is to define a simple core message: something that can be
said in two to three minutes. Once you have identified your message,
you can start to draft a script and gather together the visual material
(still photographs and video) that will form the basis for the story.
Review your script critically, asking yourself whether it can be simpli-
fied further, and also whether you have included specifics rather than
generalities. Remember that less is often more in the context of a two-
minute story. It's also important to think about the language you use.
For researchers used to communicating about their research in an objective way, the personal approach of digital storytelling may be uncomfortable. Clarity is important, since the spoken word is ephemeral, in
contrast to written words, which can be mulled over until the meaning

is clear. Read your script out loud and rework any text that you stumble over. You need to find your own voice and style using language that rolls easily off your tongue.

Once you have a script you are happy with and a selection of images and/or video, it's time to produce a storyboard. The storyboard is the guide you will use when you are ready to put your visual images and audio into the programme with which you've chosen to make your final film, such as Adobe Producer, iMovie or Windows Movie Maker. It's worth spending time to get the storyboard right so that you are clear how the text and visuals will work together. Even so, your storyboard does not need to be a work of art, but rather a functional piece that links images to specific parts to the script. Once you have your story-board ready you can record your audio file and import pictures into your chosen filmmaking software to make your rough cut. This you can polish using the tools within the programme (e.g. fading pictures, adding text).

Making a digital story is a creative process and 'where Web 1.0 was all about downloads, Web 2.0 is about uploads too' (Wheeler, 2012: 23). The availability of Web 2.0 tools is one of the reasons why 'people everywhere are using the web to broadcast, publish and share their ideas, opinions and creative works to the rest of the world.' (Wheeler, 2012: 23). Making your own digital story or enabling your research participants to share theirs taps into this facet of popular culture. As Wheeler (2012: 23) suggests, there has been a 'massive, unprecedented surge in self-publication and personal broadcasting', made possible by the digital tools. The process of creating a digital story is fairly simple, but as with all digital projects, being 'found' amongst this morass of popular content is not so easy. Chapter 7 explores how to raise your digital profile (and draw viewers to films or other resources you produce).

Gamification, games and apps

Games offer a route to interactive engagement with research, though often this interactivity comes without direct interaction with research-ers. Designing engaging games is no simple matter and this is one area where researchers are likely to need to work collaboratively with games designers who have the technical (e.g. programming and marketing) skills needed to produce successful games. There are examples of hubs, such as the Pervasive Media Studio in Bristol and Utrecht University's Centre for the Study of Digital Games and Play, which bring compa-nies or individuals working in the creative industries together with academics. Exploring these types of academic–industry meeting places may suggest opportunities for researchers interested in using digital tools. Associations such as the DiGRA (Digital Games Research Association) may also help to broker contact between academics and games designers.

It might seem obvious, but a key aspect of any game is that it is played, which leads us to consider a key concept from digital cultures research: playfulness. Playfulness is usually considered as either a state within a person or a state of a person that involves a sense of humour and spontaneity. According to Arrasvuori *et al.* (2011), playfulness can motivate engagement in a number of ways: pleasure can motivate and enhance learning; challenge, fantasy and curiosity may make routine tasks more enjoyable; and pleasant experiences can increase users' focus. It is these motivational factors that make this approach appealing for research communication, particularly if you are seeking to reach an audience that is otherwise unlikely to engage with your research.

Since the seminal work of Huizinga in 1955 'Homo Ludens: a study of the play elements of culture' (Huizinga, 2014), much has been written about playfulness and its importance in culture. Dovey and Kennedy (2006: 20) argue that 'the emergence of the computer game as a form of mass entertainment has prompted a return to theories of play which, we argue, have significant utility in understanding our relationships with mediated culture as a whole, as well as contemporary technoculture more specifically'. They suggest that the computer game allows us to 'act out all kinds of mediated fantasies; we can run championship winning sports teams, indulge in militarized gore fests, become a kick-ass riot girl or spell-casting witch' (Dovey and Kennedy, 2006: 41).

Games are being used to engage the public in the research process, for example, Fraxinus; a Facebook game designed to support research on ash dieback disease, and Fold.it, a game to support research on protein folding. These are examples of citizen science projects (see Chapter 9) that have turned routine elements of research into games as a means of using the public's interest in playing games to further research ends. Sometimes called 'serious games', games may be designed for specific educational purposes, for example in major-incident medical management (Knight *et al.*, 2010), or have social agendas, such as the game Darfur is Dying, which seeks to raise awareness of genocide, and Ayiti (https://ayiti.globalkids.org/game/), which encourages players to consider poverty and the trade offs that ensue.

There are also examples where research underpins the storyline of a more traditional game. Cascade, which is in development by the games developers Fayju, draws on Dr Jody Mason's research. Mason, an Alzheimer's researcher at the University of Bath, has advised the game's designers on the scientific content of the project; but for Fayju one of the key aims is 'to raise awareness of Alzheimer's disease and the desperate need for further research'. The project has received funding from the Wellcome Trust through the co-production awards (broadcast, games and film). According to Fayju, 'In this "simulation" you interact by piloting a space craft around the cell and blasting the enzymes whose unchecked actions are leading the onslaught of Alzheimer's Disease' (Bushell, 2015). Jack the Ripper 125 (http://jtr. aurochdigital.com/), also in early development, is using game elements to create a 'playable' documentary about Jack the Ripper. This project draws on the media and digital cultures research of Patrick Crogan from the University of the West of England, Bristol and Janet Jones of Middlesex University, as well as the games design expertise of Tomas Rawlings of Auroch Digital. Players explore the 'notions of crime, news reporting and ethics' in a virtual environment where they can 'interact with characters, discover clues and piece together the story, drawing parallels between contemporary society and this infamous crime'.

The observation that video games 'can demonstrably motivate users to engage with them with unparalleled intensity and duration, game elements should be able to make other, non-game products and services more enjoyable and engaging' (Deterding *et al.*, 2011: 10), has led researchers and games designers to explore whether game elements can be used in other contexts, including both education and business. Deterding *et al.* (2011) refer to this use of game elements in non-game contexts as 'gamification', and most authors now make a distinction between 'gamification' and designing games. Gamification can also be used in public engagement projects, for example the Virtual Romans app (see Case study 6.2).

Case study 6.2 Virtual Romans – merging technology and archaeology

Drawing on the skills of an interdisciplinary research team enabled researchers at De Montfort University to create an app that allows users to explore Leicester as it was in AD 210. The original research explored how creative technologies, and in particular artificial life, could help us understand life in the Roman era. Nick Higgett, Principal Lecturer at De Montfort University, wanted to make the research on Roman Leicester and 3D technologies accessible to the public.

'The 3D technology could show people what Roman Leicester was like, and it was really pushing the technology boundaries at the time. So we wanted to make some public-facing outcomes from the research and experimentation,' Nick said.

The app[3] is not the only public-engagement element of the project, which also includes a website where you can view 3D objects and buildings and a kiosk at the Jewry Wall Museum in Leicester. The app uses GPS technology to determine where you are in the city and then shows you what Leicester would have looked like in AD 210. 'The app shows you what the buildings were like and you can walk inside and explore them virtually,' Nick explained.

This type of approach could be used for other historical sites, to show what they looked like or to allow users to explore a site in more detail. Nick is already working on another app to show how Glossop, in Derbyshire, looked during the Industrial Revolution and as the town changed during post-industrialisation in the 1980s.

Creating this type of app means bringing together people with different skills – either technological or, in Nick's case, experts in a particular location or historical era. 'In creating Virtual Romans, we were guided all the way by Dr Richard Buckley at Leicester University who excavated a lot of the sites that we reconstructed,' Nick said.

There were multiple motivations for the activity: 'I didn't want this to just sit in some lab somewhere. It was important that people could see what we'd done, in terms of the reconstruction,' Nick explained. 'Also, part of our funding was from Leicester City Council, through the museums service, and so public outcomes were an expected part of the grant.'

In terms of the public audiences, to an extent the app will appeal most to people living in Leicester and the East Midlands of the UK who are able to experience it within the city itself, and in creating the app Nick had in mind primarily visitors to the Jewry Wall Museum.

As with many types of public engagement, making people aware of the project is a key factor in its success. Nick believes that you need to allow time for publicity activities or your research will be lost amongst the large number of apps clamouring for people's attention.

Those interested in creating interactive digital projects might consider the growing opportunities for gaming, gamification and playful experiences available through both computer-based and mobile platforms, a number of which have been discussed above. The growth of the tablet market, along with the variety of mobile platforms, means that you are likely to have to make some early decisions about the operating system you will use for your projects (Teacher *et al.*, 2013). This may depend on which platforms are most popular in your geographical region, if you are interested in local or national reach. While there are tools available that allow you to create your own app, for most researchers constructing an app or game related to their research is likely to involve third parties with technical expertise in order to produce high-quality user experiences. The large number of games and apps now available means that the public can have quite high expectations in terms of both visual design and game mechanics.

Users' needs

Whatever type of digital project you are considering, whether a simple video or a complex citizen science project, early on you need to consider the needs of your audience or participants. In assessing information, most people are looking for accessibility, relevance and credibility. All three need to be carefully considered in digital communication. Accessibility is not just about availability, but is comprised of discoverability (how easily it can be found) and comprehensibility (Metzger and Flanagin, 2011: 48): 'Consequently, information producers must consider carefully ways in which they craft, position, and disseminate their information to maximize its accessibility to target audiences.' Effective use of Web 2.0 technologies requires going where the audience is, rather than creating entirely new communication platforms. So, in developing digital communication projects it might be worth thinking about how you can work with existing platforms, rather than, say, creating your own website to host materials. 'The most effective communication channels are not necessarily novel – rather, they are those that take advantage of where people already habitually and routinely gather, share, and communicate with one another' (Metzger and Flanagin, 2011: 55).

Relevance is of course a subjective term that reflects the extent to which the information or dissemination activity meets the subjective perceived needs of the individuals at the receiving end. However, as a communicator, you can think about how you frame your project to highlight its relevance to potential participants or audiences. Consider why they might be interested in what you have to say and ask yourself the 'so what' questions – so what is important about this research? So what should the audience do with this information?

Credibility is linked to relevance; information that is judged as not credible is also rejected as not relevant. Credibility may relate to judgements about the source of the information and may include evaluation of endorsements by known and trusted 'others' in their social networks. 'Thus, evidence-based health and medical information accessed via Web 2.0 technologies can gain credibility by offering (a) authoritative researcher- or government-produced information and (b) information from people who are fellow sufferers and thus possess experiential credibility' (Metzger and Flanagin, 2011: 53). Making clear the research that underpins your digital engagement project can go some way to addressing this first aspect of credibility, as will highlighting the expertise of the project participants. Other aspects of credibility may be less in your control, once your project is public, as you may be relying on trusted members of social networks to promote the project and raise awareness of it.

Digital communication strategies also make demands of the audience. While many projects may simply require you to 'sit and watch' a video, participating in others may demand some level of information technology literacy or ownership of certain types of technology. Increasingly, popular culture demands transliteracy skills from its audience. The audience may no longer be seen as passive, but instead an active participant in the creation and dissemination of information. Now the audience must 'be able to create, organise and share content, and communicate across, and through, a variety of social media, discussion groups, mobile devices and other services that are commonly available' (Wheeler, 2012: 17). In choosing certain types of communication routes over others, we are inevitably selecting a subset of the potential audience; engaging with those that have the skills to use particular technologies, the time to participate and an interest in that particular medium of communication. It is, therefore, important to recognise that digital communication does not replace other types of communication. Instead, we need to 'recognise the significance of each tool, and how each can be used effectively in all its variations, and also in combination with other tools' (Wheeler, 2012: 18).

Summary

One of the reasons for exploring digital research communication is the growth in the amount of time we spend online. After all, one of the key principles of research communication is to go where the audience is. In this chapter we've explored several possibilities for digital research communication. But are these really what the 'audience' wants? In relation to medical evidence, Bernhardt *et al.* (2011) argue that current practice in research dissemination does not match the information needs or preferences of users and that researchers should consider ways of embedding Web 2.0 technologies in their dissemination practice. What they term dissemination 2.0 'takes advantage of the core foundations of Web 2.0 applications – collaboration, participation, multi-directional information exchange – to improve current dissemination activities and advance the translation of research to practice' (Bernhardt *et al.*, 2011: 36). Although Bernhardt *et al.* are largely thinking about translating research into clinical practice, there are parallels for the communication of research to public groups most likely to benefit from the research. Moving forward, when designing digital communication projects, consideration should be given to the 'interaction' domain. Some of the projects identified here, even when they use relatively one-way media, such as the Periodic Table of Videos, do allow for interaction, albeit often asynchronous interaction. Others, notably games, afford significant interactivity with much less potential for interaction. As Web 2.0 tools mature and researchers become familiar with their potential, new approaches that afford greater opportunities for interaction are bound to emerge.

In this chapter we have explored only a small subset of the potential digital approaches to research communication today. New tools yet to be created will no doubt open further opportunities for digital engagement and for a researcher it can seem daunting to engage in this sphere. Start with tools with which you are familiar, so as to reduce your technological learning curve, and think about how these could be combined in creative ways to share your research with those who might benefit or be interested. Consider how much interaction you would like to have with these publics and how much time you have available for such interactions. It's all well and good to encourage interaction and comment, but do you actually have the time to respond, should you generate demand? Set realistic expectations of yourself, as well as of your audience. Also consider whether there are others, with specific skill sets, such as filmmakers or games designers, who might provide skills you do not have. Bringing in such expertise can greatly enhance the quality of the finished project. They may involve costs that can be built into research-funding proposals. Equally, there may be funding schemes to which you can apply that specifically fund public-engagement projects of this type.

Notes

1 This is an attempt to tackle the obesity epidemic by encouraging activity. You can see the experiment at: www.youtube.com/watch?v=2lXh2noaPyw.
2 The Digital Empowerment project, funded by the European Commission, has produced a useful guide to digital storytelling. www.digem.eu/.
3 Additional information on the Virtual Romans project can be found at: www.romanleicester.dmu.ac.uk/. The Virtual Romans app is available from: https://itunes.apple.com/us/app/virtual-romans/id704260926?ls=1&mt=8.

Further reading

Arora, P., 'Typology of Web 2.0 spheres: understanding the cultural dimensions of social media spaces', *Current Sociology*, 60:5 (2012) 599–618.

Bruns, A., *Blogs, Wikipedia, Second Life and Beyond, From Production to Produsage* (Oxford: Peter Lang, 2006).

Dovey, J. and Kennedy, H.W., *Game Cultures* (Buckingham, UK: Open University Press, 2006).

7

Social media

In this chapter we will consider how you might use a variety of media to communicate your research to both the public and your peers. The chapter is intended for those new to using media (traditional or social) for research communication and does not seek to provide a comprehensive overview of the potential ways media might be used, but rather offers examples as a jumping-off point for your own endeavours.

The chapter briefly covers writing for traditional media, before moving on to consider your digital profile and the practicalities of using social media for research communication. We define social media as those internet-based tools and platforms that allow individuals to create content, some of which also facilitate conversations and networking between individuals. Social media offer the potential of many-to-many communication, though in practice we also see both few-to-many (for example high-profile Twitter or YouTube accounts that have many followers) and few-to-few (for example, some LinkedIn Groups have only a few hundred members, but many of these members post regularly and comment on each other's posts) communication through these channels. The chapter considers how you can use social media to reach your peers, potentially increasing the academic impact of your work, as well as approaches to reaching stakeholders and interested publics with your findings. These tools and approaches can also be used earlier in the research process to seek input and feedback on developing ideas, helping to shape applied research so that it meets citizen or stakeholder needs, though this is not a primary focus for this chapter.

Traditional media

Many researchers interested in disseminating their findings to a wider audience turn initially to the mainstream (or traditional) media – both print and broadcast – usually focusing on opportunities to feature in the 'news'. And it is certainly true that traditional media offer potentially large audiences for your research findings, though securing journalists' interest in your work may not be so simple. Nonetheless, these mainstream media are often seen as the bread and butter of research communication efforts and researchers are usually supported by a (often extremely busy) press office provided by their employing institutions. Approaching your institution's press office may result in the construction and issuing of a media release, a short, one- to two-page 'story' that highlights the key findings of your research. Such releases are usually pegged to an 'event', the publication of a journal paper, awarding of new research funding, presentations at conferences and such like. For 'stories' deemed to be of wider interest or with particular visual appeal, the press office may also create video footage or a VNR (video news release) to encourage and support uptake amongst broadcast journalists. Media releases are designed to stimulate journalists' interest in the subject, and while some journalists may simply summarise this release, most are likely to want to talk to you before publication. Thus, the press office also plays a vital role in fielding calls from journalists, letting you know who would like an interview and for which media (publication, programme) they are producing a story. If you are helpful and are able to discuss your research in clear language suitable for their readers, listeners or viewers, leaving out jargon and explaining concepts, then they are likely to keep your details, calling you in future when they need expert comment about other related research or news events.

As many guides and books have already been written about getting your research into the media and working with journalists (see Table 7.1 for a few examples of online, freely accessible guides), this chapter largely focuses on opportunities for you to write stories for public consumption (e.g. magazine articles and how to approach editors), and opportunities for communication using social media such as Twitter and Pinterest. While we urge you to make use of traditional media opportunities for dissemination, this chapter explores how researchers can make best use of digital tools to create a strong digital profile and, as such, it has some crossover with Chapter 6. Given the high use of digital media and search engines by those seeking information on particular topics (including journalists researching stories), your digital media communications can play an important part in your wider public profile.

Table 7.1 Guides to working with the media

Organisation	Guide
Arts and Humanities Research Council (AHRC): Researcher Toolkit: Working with the Media for Arts and Humanities Researchers. Available from: www.ahrc.ac.uk/News-and-Events/Media-Centre/Documents/Toolkit%20-%20Working%20 with%20the%20Media%20 for%20Arts%20 and%20Humanities%20 Researchers.pdf	The guide explores what makes a good story, focusing specifically on finding human angles for arts and humanities research. It uses the TRUTH (Timely, Relevant, Unique, Topical, Human) text for judging the media-worthiness of research.
Centres for Disease Control: Media Outreach Guide Available from: www.cdc.gov/SafeChild/ images/SafeChild_MEDIA%20 GUIDE-a.pdf	Aimed at health professionals, but much more broadly relevant, this guide outlines the steps needed to proactively seek media coverage, including identifying spokespeople and also monitoring the coverage you receive.
European Commission: Guide to Successful Communications. Available from: https://ec. europa.eu/research/science-society/science-communication/ index_en.htm	This interactive guide outlines the process of developing a communications strategy, covering media relations, websites and other types of publications as well as providing case studies from European Commission-funded projects.
Panos: Working with the Media: A Guide for Researchers. Available from: http://r4d.dfid. gov.uk/PDF/Outputs/Panos/relay_ researchers_guide.pdf	Produced by Panos, the Chronic Poverty Research Centre (CPRC) and the Overseas Development Institute (ODI), this guide highlights the importance of thinking about media communication from the outset. It provides tips on creating messages, identifying and working with journalists who might be interested in your research.
Science Media Centre (New Zealand): Desk Guide for Scientists: Working with the Media. Available from: www. sciencemediacentre.co.nz/wp-	Highlighting the importance of working with the media, the guide moves on to explore what journalists are looking for and provides insights into the

Table 7.1 (cont.)

Organisation	Guide
content/upload/2014/04/SMC-Desk-Guide-for-Scientists.pdf	working lives of journalists to help researchers understand their constraints.
Science Media Centre (UK) has produced a number of publications aimed at scientists working with the media. Available from: www.sciencemediacentre. org/publications/ publications-for-scientists/	Guides cover different aspects of media work, including: why engage with news media, top tips for media work and communicating uncertainty in a soundbite.

Writing for popular publications

Writing is part of any researcher's daily grind, whether it is funding applications or research papers for publication, but few researchers proactively seek opportunities to write for more popular or general audiences. That's not to say that we won't, if asked, write pieces for professional magazines, and many researchers do take advantage of these opportunities. But how does one go about proactively seeking opportunities to write about one's research for a wider audience, and anyway, why spend the time to do so?

To answer the second question first, popular and professional magazines can introduce a much wider audience to your research than can be reached through academic publications. By carefully choosing publications for which to write, you can make your research accessible to those most likely to be influenced by the findings, whether that is through changes to policy, practice, lifestyle or attitudes (see also Chapter 10). If you, rather than a journalist, are writing the story, then you are in control of how that story is told, allowing you to highlight aspects of your research most relevant to readers. This can be particularly appealing to those working in sensitive areas where there may be concerns about how research will be presented by mainstream media. When writing, bear in mind the readership and what they do (or do not) already know about the subject area and their likely interests; writing the article yourself is not a licence to insert caveats or qualifications into your findings. You are acting in a role similar to that of a journalist and need to ensure that the level of explanation is appropriate to the readers (see Box 7.1 for tips on writing for popular publications).

Now to the trickier question of how to proactively seek opportunities

---

Box 7.1 **Ten tips on writing for popular publications**

---

1 *Seduce your reader*: the opening paragraph is the most important and should be designed to drawn in the reader.
2 *Plan your story*: before you begin writing, outline the story arc so you know where you are beginning and ending.
3 *Transition from topic to topic*: stories need to flow, so think about how you link paragraphs.
4 *Analogies, but not clichés*: find ways to explain your research, using either analogies or metaphors. This helps make the prose vivid for the reader as well as providing helpful tools for explanations. Avoid clichés, though – these lead to bland stories.
5 *Avoid jargon*: all research disciplines have their own languages; it's vitally important to explain any jargon that's necessary, or you will lose readers.
6 *Think about the reader*: most writers have a mental picture of the person for whom they are writing. These pictures help you write in language appropriate for that person (how would you explain your research to your aunt or non-academic friends?).
7 *Be active, not passive*: writing is much more interesting when written using the active voice.
8 *Concrete examples (and non-examples)*: give concrete explanations. Sometimes it is just as useful to give counter examples, or examples of what does not follow from findings.
9 *Consider what readers already know or believe*: it can be very hard to argue against established beliefs. If you are arguing against a strongly held belief or stereotype you may need to think carefully about how you approach this so as not to have your argument rejected out of hand.
10 *Read your work aloud*: it helps you to hear the rhythm of the language.

For more examples and tips, see Blum *et al.* (2006).

---

to write about your research. The first decision is one of time. How much time are you prepared to devote to writing for non-academic audiences? If you are prepared to spend the time to write regularly, consider setting up a blog (see below). But if, as is likely to be the case for most researchers just embarking on public writing, you are not ready to make this commitment, or if you want to reach a specific group of professionals, then it's time to explore professional and popular publications. For specific groups, like conservation charities or health professionals, there are likely to be a few specialist magazines (online and in print) that cater for them specifically. There is a vast array of publications for which you could write, and a key consideration will be identifying the right publication for your research and the audience(s) that you would like to reach. Draw up a shortlist of publications, then read them thoroughly to understand the style and type of articles that they publish. Most publications, whether print or online, have their own specific style, and you will need to fit into this. If the articles are normally 2,000 words, it's no good writing 5,000. Neither the editors nor the readers will have patience for this out-of-character piece. So before putting pen to paper, whether for a full manuscript or a pitch, thoroughly investigate the publication.

Once you've settled on a publication for which you'd like to write, explore the submission process and identify key editorial staff. Professional and business-to-business magazines often have quite small editorial teams, so look for a contact that handles submissions. More popular publications, such as *New Scientist* or *Newsweek*, will have a number of editorial staff and you will need to find the one who seems most appropriate (sometimes this is simply the 'features' editor, but some magazines have editors for different subjects or sections). At this stage, have a look to see if the publication offers any guidance on submitting manuscripts or ideas for stories; some magazines provide specific details on what they are looking for from authors, such as *American Scientist* (www.americanscientist.org/about/page/submission-guidelines) or *Pacific Standard Magazine* (www.psmag.com/page/write-us). In some cases the publication will ask for ideas to be submitted, essentially a pitch (see Box 7.2) which outlines the planned story; in other cases they may ask for complete manuscripts to be submitted, so it's important to check early on what is required. There are also an increasing number of online magazines that offer academics the opportunity to write articles for public consumption, such as *The Conversation* (https://theconversation.com/become-an-author) and *Aeon* (http://aeon.co/magazine/about/). Again, these are likely to request submission of ideas which are then considered by the editorial office and commissioned.

Print magazines work many months in advance, so, for work that has seasonal relevance, get in touch with the magazine at least six months before the relevant 'season' or event (e.g. such as elections or seasonal illnesses). Digital publications tend to have shorter turn-around times, although it can still take them several weeks to respond to a pitch. Once you've hooked the editor, work scrupulously to the agreed deadlines. While some editors may be willing to wait for a late piece, many won't, and a missed deadline may mean that the piece you've worked hard to produce is rejected. It may also damage

---

Box 7.2 Pitching to editors

A pitch is the way you sell your idea to an editor. Pitches are short (often only a few paragraphs) and designed to tempt the editor, making them want to know more. Typically, the pitch outlines the problem you plan to address, often giving some facts and figures that put it into perspective. Then you tantalise the editor with the issues to be discussed in the article. Indicate how long the article will be (this needs to take account of the constraints within the magazine itself as well as your own assessment of the topic) and whether you can provide any images (if this is appropriate for both the subject and publication). If you've had any other popular articles published, then you can include these as examples that demonstrate your ability to write (for a non-academic audience). Finally, make sure that it is clear how the editor can contact you (preferably by phone and email). For further guidance on pitching stories to editors, see Sumner and Miller (2013).

In preparing a pitch, it's very important to take into account any instructions the magazine provides. This is your ONLY opportunity to convince them that you can do the job; so, is it vitally important not only that you show an appreciation of their magazine, but also that you demonstrate your flare for writing!

---

your longer-term relationship with that editor, who may consider you unreliable.

Developing a digital profile

Writing for traditional media outlets has the advantage that it taps directly into an audience already established by the newspaper, magazine or journal. Many of these publications are also now available online, so interviews and writing intended for traditional media may also now form part of your digital profile. But you can do much more to consolidate and shape your digital profile by carefully choosing to engage with other online tools, whether they be classic websites (such as institutional websites), social media, such as Facebook and Pinterest, or the array of 'in between' media, such as blogs and Twitter, which are being used both in ways that are like social media and as traditional broadcast media (see, for example, Bruner, 2013 on Twitter use). You may be surprised to find that you have an existing digital profile drawn from the online media that you (or colleagues) use, and it can be insightful to explore this (see Box 7.3 for suggestions on how to explore your existing digital profile).

Researchers and academics are engaging with the plethora of online

---

Box 7.3 Explore your digital profile

Investigate your existing digital profile by putting your name and a few appropriate keywords into various search engines (it is important to use more than one search engine, as results can vary). Try a few different search terms if you have a common name or are very active online in both your personal and professional life. In the digital realm, personal and professional lives can collide, so be aware that your online hobbies may be just as likely to appear in a search list about you as your professional activities, and consider how these different realms might affect both personal and professional relationships.

Explore the results to see where you can be 'found' online and what this says about you as a scholar. This is your existing digital profile and the basis from which you might develop your profile further. It is important to consider what this profile says about you and whether this is the message you wish to portray. If not, then you might need to reconsider some of the ways that you engage with online media. The good news is that in most cases people explore only the first page of links returned by a search engine and it is possible to change the order in which links appear by taking an active role in your online life.

It can also be worth exploring the digital profile of someone in your field whom you judge to have a strong digital profile. What are they doing that you could also do?

---

tools available to them, and for a variety of reasons from professional networking and self-promotion to goals linked to increasing the impact of their research amongst stakeholders or the public. Academics also engage with a wide range of digital tools, from institutional websites and professional networks, like ResearchGate, LinkedIn and Academia. edu, through to more popular media, such as Twitter and Facebook (van Noorden, 2014). Some of these may be used primarily for professional purposes, others primarily for social purposes, but both will form part of your overall digital profile.

The value of academic social networking remains in question. In a survey by *Nature* (van Noorden, 2014: 127), amongst the researchers most active on academic social networks '[t]he most-selected activity on both ResearchGate and Academia.edu was simply maintaining a profile in case someone wanted to get in touch – suggesting that many researchers regard their profiles as a way to boost their professional presence online'. This contrasts with the more public social media, such as Twitter. In the survey by *Nature*, while only 13 percent of respondents used Twitter regularly, half of those that did used it to follow conversations about their research field and 40 percent claimed to comment on research issues raised through the medium. For most users, though, social media are mainly tools for monitoring: keeping up to date (e.g. finding out about new papers) and listening (e.g. finding out about current debates) (see, for example, McCormick, 2014 and Bruner, 2013).

For those who decide to move beyond monitoring (or lurking, as it's called in social media), you need to consider how you will present yourself online, including the relationship between your professional and private online activities. Barbour and Marshall (2012) identified five personas that academics typically use when presenting themselves online:

- Formal Self – this persona uses digital media to present their key achievements, using these tools to demonstrate their knowledge and expertise. This type of online presentation may avoid interaction in favour of a broadcast-style approach to communication.
- Public Self – still focusing on the traditional academic structures, this public persona interacts with others, seeking to network and sharing ideas. This networking allows researchers to locate their thinking in wider academic debates.
- Comprehensive Self – similar to the way that many people use social networks, it blurs the lines between one's career and outside interests. In this persona, academics will combine discussion of their professional activities with organising their social lives and communicating with friends and family. This approach allows greater public access to personal lives.
- Teaching Self – unlike the other constructed online selves, this persona focuses on using digital tools to connect with students, particularly the so-called Generation Y and Digital Natives. In this context, an academic's persona becomes an extension of the institution's intranet or other online teaching spaces.
- Uncontainable Self – covers those academics who do not seek purposefully to manage their online presence. The uncontained self is created by others and may be positive or negative, depending on who is creating the content.

The uncontainable self may highlight the risks of not creating your own digital profile. Bik and Goldstein (2013: np) admonish researchers to engage in the digital sphere to further their careers and increase their profile, suggesting that a lack of online presence may be damaging; 'in today's technology-driven world, lack of an online presence can severely limit a researcher's visibility, and runs the risk that undesirable search results appear before desirable ones.' They provide practical advice, such as:

- Establish a professional website – to avoid undesirable search results.
- Locate pertinent conversations – identify people with common interests, using social media such as Twitter.
- Interact with a diverse range of people online – they argue that the digital sphere is all about conversations.

However, they also note that, online, you will primarily reach people who are already interested in your subject area, and also that it can be challenging to navigate the deluge of information available through social media. Reaching an already interested audience is not necessarily problematic. Professor Melissa Terras, of University College London, argues that social media activity can have a positive impact on traditional metrics used by academics to judge the 'worth' of research. She provides evidence, on her blog, of the impact of her own blogging and Tweeting activities on the number of downloads of her research papers (Terras, 2012). Bik and Goldstein (2013) suggest that an effective online digital profile can provide a useful opportunity to network with other researchers, leading to new research collaborations or ways of thinking about your own research. They also suggest that these public digital engagements have real-world impacts, for example by bringing your research to the attention of potential research users and the broader public (see Chapter 10).

Which leads to the question, who reads my social media posts? In most contexts, we tailor our communication to the audience that we think is listening. For example, we decide what terminology to use and what level of explanation is needed. Knowing who the audience or readers are, therefore, helps to design appropriate research communication. However, 'as in much computer-mediated communication, a tweet's actual readers differ from its producer's imagined audience' (Marwick and boyd, 2011: 117). Furthermore, there are several issues with identifying social media readerships; for example, on Twitter the number of followers can be counted and it is even possible to explore followers' biographies. However, just because someone follows you does not mean they read your tweets. And if your profile is public or you make use of hashtags, then you may have readers who are not followers. Furthermore, tweets may be retweeted, altered with or without attribution, and there are a number of tools which 'allow users to repost tweets to Facebook, MySpace, and blogs' (Marwick and boyd, 2011: 117). This presents a challenge for users of social media in general: how to strike a balance between the social norms of presenting information and phatic communication, which add authenticity, and a desire for privacy. According to Marwick and boyd (2011: 124), '[t]he tension

between revealing and concealing usually errs on the side of concealing on Twitter, but even users who do not post anything scandalous
must formulate tweets and choose discussion topics based on imagined
audience judgment'. This can be particularly problematic if you are
using social media both for professional communication and to maintain personal friendships and family relationships. 'For most [social
media] users, there is a distinct difference between one's professional
persona, addressed mainly to co-workers and employers, and one's self-
communication towards "friends"' (van Dijck, 2013b: 199). How do
you negotiate your imaginings of the interests of these two groups, what
they might consider appropriate communications or, indeed, what you
wish these different groups to know about you? Many people negotiate
this problem by maintaining separate accounts for work and friends, or
use different social media to connect with different groups. But however
you decide to work with social media, imagining your audience is a key
starting point.

Social media have come under scrutiny and criticism from scholars,
particularly in relation to their economic models. While Fuchs (2014)
would agree that social media are technologies that facilitate engagement and interaction, he raises concerns that the creativity and knowledge generation made possible through these technologies will also lead
to exploitation. Fuchs (2014: 60) argues that 'visibility is a central
resource in contemporary culture that powerful actors, such as media
corporations, can buy'. This may be overt, in the form of adverts, for
example the promoted tweets on Twitter, or it may be covert, in the
form of advertisers paying popular YouTube video makers to create and
post promotional videos. While many vloggers (video bloggers) may
indicate that they were paid to produce a particular video, this has not
always been the case. As of November 2014, in the United Kingdom the
Advertising Standards Authority (2014) has specified that such videos
must now be clearly labelled as advertising. It is likely that other regula-
tors may follow suit, but, as YouTube crosses borders, it may be some
time before all such content is reliably labelled.

Some of the respondents to the survey by *Nature* also raised concerns
about the economic motives or business plans of the platforms researchers used for communication (van Noorden, 2014). As researchers, we
may sign up to a social media platform whose professed ideals are consistent with our own (e.g. making our publications more widely accessible), but what happens when that platform is bought by a commercial
company with a view to making money out of our individual activities?
The same, of course, can be said of the large public social networks
and the ways that they seek to monetise the collective and individual
creativity of their users; there has been much discussion of the way that

companies such as Google and Facebook use the information we wittingly and unwittingly provide (see, for example, Fuchs, 2014).

Practical engagement

Kaplan and Haenlein (2010) present a typology of social media that is useful in orienting the way we think about practical engagements (Figure 7.1). The typology relates different types of social media to two media theories – media richness theory and social presence theory – and considers two aspects of social interaction: self-presentation (the way present ourselves) and self-disclosure (the amount we divulge about ourselves). Media richness (Daft and Lengel, 1986) considers how the amount of information contained in media helps to resolve ambiguity

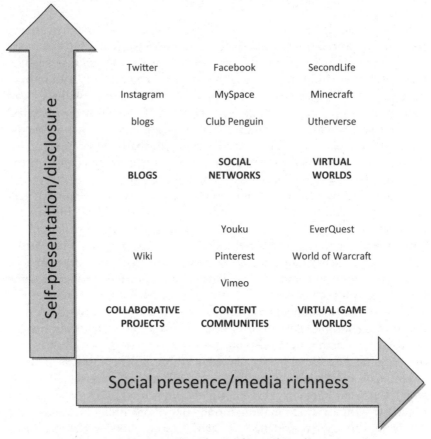

Figure 7.1 Typology of social media
Source: Adapted from Kaplan and Haenlein (2010)

and uncertainty in communication. Social presence (Short *et al.*, 1976) considers the amount and nature of the contact possible between individuals (e.g. in a social media context the ways that social cues are present through written, visual or auditory material) and comprises elements of intimacy and immediacy. Kaplan and Haenlein (2010) argue that blogs are high on self-presentation/disclosure but low on social presence/ media richness, because the author has control over the medium and there is relatively little opportunity for interaction or intimacy. In this sense, blogs might be considered as offering little opportunity (beyond asynchronous comments functions) for interaction. Thus they might be seen as primarily a tool to disseminate research findings or enhance a researcher's career through providing a platform for their views. In contrast, virtual worlds, such as Second Life, are high on both self-presentation/self-disclosure and social presence/media richness because they allow both synchronous communication (that is, avatars can talk or communicate in writing in real time) and the opportunity for text, visual and auditory communication (through labelling, graphics and inclusion of audio or video recordings which can be played either synchronously or asynchronously). The discussion below considers different approaches to social media communication within this framework of self-presentation/self-disclosure and media richness as this highlights the expectations of the audience and also the factors a researcher might consider before embarking on a particular approach.

Entering the blogosphere: written, audio and video blogging

Blogs come in all shapes and sizes, from microblogging via Twitter, to blogs hosted on institutional websites, and increasingly blogs are combining media formats. The blogosphere has grown rapidly and a number of researchers are now active in this arena using platforms such as Technorati, WordPress and Nature Blogs to manage individual blogs, as well as contributing invited posts to blogs such as the *Guardian* newspaper blogs. Depending on the software used, you can embed audio and video, which can also be shared on other channels such as YouTube. Including these tools increases media richness and potentially broadens the appeal of a blog to those less likely to engage with the written word. Regardless of the media you embed, a blog can be distinguished from other types of multimedia projects because it uses a diary entry format, where posts appear typically in reverse chronological order. Blogs also typically use a more personal writing style than traditional media, allowing the author's presence to be felt in the writing.

Hitchcock (2014) argues that blogging is an integral part of academic life; it is a way that researchers can enter the public sphere and contribute to their public roles, not unlike contributions to letters pages and public lectures. Similarly, Ewins (2005) argues that blogs can be used to consolidate and build a public narrative around your research and to build academic networks. Mewburn and Thomson (2013) suggest that for many academics the purpose of blogging is to communicate with other academics and to 'talk back' to an increasingly managerial academic administration. As Hitchcock (2014: np) says, 'Twitter and blogs, and embarrassingly enthusiastic drunken conversations at parties, are not add-ons to academic research, but a simple reflection of the passion that underpins it.' The personal writing style of most blogs means that the author's presence can often be easily seen (making them high on social presence) and this in turn can make research seem more human and less abstract, although authors may wish to consider how much of their personality they disclose.

Blogs may be seen as a route to communicate with a broad, public audience, and even as opportunities to enter into debates about emerging scientific and social issues (see Case study 7.1 and Box 7.4). They can also be used as a means to test ideas that are not quite ready for publication. As Gregory (2009:14) notes, 'blogs are valued for their hybrid quality: poised somewhere between the formal and informal, they can be a useful space for research that doesn't fit into traditional categories, such as research outputs that are not big enough (or quite ready) for a whole formal paper but are worth sharing or which take more risks with data than would survive peer review'. The relationship between blogging and research publication is a complex one, as blogs do constitute publication. However, most blog posts are relatively short (at least, compared with research papers) and unlikely to present data in sufficient detail to jeopardise future publication. And they can provide a useful way to elicit feedback on ideas, though they offer only limited interactivity (people read content and listen to audio or watch video, but only a very few post comments) and this is typically asynchronous, requiring the reader to return for any updates or further comments from the author.

Blogs have developed out of a counter-culture movement that seeks to enable participation in public discourses, and for many this means that readers should also be allowed to join the discussion, voicing their opinions. Reader comments can be thoughtful and contribute insights that ultimately improve research. On the other hand, trolls abound and bloggers can expect irrelevant and even hateful comments to be posted, making it important to have a thick skin, particularly for female bloggers who choose not to hide their gender (Thorpe and Rogers, 2011). For this reason, some bloggers prefer not to allow readers to post comments and use their blogs more as a means of presenting their ideas on a topic. Either way, blogging can help to raise your profile and may lead

---

Box 7.4 **Top tips for academic bloggers**

Popular academic bloggers Dr Tom Crick and Professor Alan Winfield have come up with ten top tips for academic bloggers (adapted below from Crick and Winfield, 2013), which should help you develop a successful blog.

1   *Write about yourself*: people are as interested in who you are and what you do as they are in your research.

2   *Find your voice*: academic blogs come in all shapes and sizes. Find a voice and style that suits you. This may take some time, so expect your blog to evolve.

3   *What is the purpose of your blog*: be clear about what and why you are blogging so that the content is coherent. It's also worth thinking about what you want to achieve with your blog, as this will help keep you on track.

4   *Be clearly identifiable*: don't use a moniker or hide behind anonymity. For your blog to add to your academic role, you, and your academic role, need to be clearly identifiable. It's also worth being clear whether you are blogging on behalf of your university or independently.

5   *Think about how controversial you want to be*: as a rule, don't say anything on a blog that you wouldn't be prepared to say in any other public forum. Controversy can seem like a great way to get noticed, but consider whether it might affect your future career prospects, particularly if you are a younger academic.

6   *Blog posts are publications*: do consider what information you release and whether it might jeopardise future publications or patents.

7   *Let your university know you are blogging*: some universities positively encourage blogging, others may be more reticent. While you may not need permission to set up your own independent blog it is probably best if your manager knows about it.

8   *Set a realistic goal in terms of blogging frequency*: blogging takes time, and that is time away from other activities. Equally, readers come to expect posts, so you need to set realistic expectations.

9   *Market your blog*: if you don't tell people about your blog, you are unlikely to have any readers. Social media activities can help draw readers to your blog.

10 *Only blog because you want to*: blogging can be fun and something you look forward to, it should not be one more job to be ticked off on the list of academic chores.

to other media opportunities. The trick is to write interesting content that gets quoted on other blogs or in mainstream media.

From a producer's perspective, blogs take many forms, though in general they are more informal than traditional academic writing. In their study of one hundred academic blogs, Mewburn and Thomson (2013) identified various writing genres, including: reportage (reporting new information from conferences), journalistic (synthesising multiple sources), essays (informal and formal), pedagogic, confidential (using a personal tone) and satirical. Although journalistic blogs appear in the list, it is worth remembering that bloggers are not journalists (although many journalists also blog). This means that bloggers, while they may subscribe to many journalistic principles and seek to write sparkling and engaging posts, do not have to follow established journalistic routines and practices. As Chalmers (2009: 76) notes, 'there is no onus on bloggers to be balanced in what they say or to seek opinion from both sides of an argument'. This presents a particular challenge for the reader, who may not easily be able to tell whether a particular blogger has an axe to grind.

Case study 7.1 Garnering blog readership

Although he had been a blogger since 2006, it was only after he joined Twitter that Professor Alan Winfield, of the University of the West of England, Bristol, started to notice an increase in his readership figures. 'I started to notice my readership increased when I started tweeting about new blog posts,' Alan says. 'My followers would "favourite" the tweet, retweet it or even recommend the blog post in their own words, and then very quickly I was reaching thousands of potential readers for each post.'

Not surprisingly, then, marketing is essential if you want more than a handful of readers. Twitter is not the only social network that can be used to promote a blog; LinkedIn and Facebook, amongst others, also offer opportunities. The trick is to use media with which you are familiar and comfortable and that ideally you are already using, because it is not just about sending promotional tweets about new posts, you also need to engage with your community. In relation to Twitter, Alan says, 'You need to tweet about other things and engage in conversations, at least two to three times per week. From time to time this gives you a chance to mention that you've blogged about an issue before, drawing new readers to older posts. It's not overt marketing, more a case of contributing information and opinion.'

Good content and regular blogging are essential, as are finding your own voice and style. Some bloggers like to post frequent but short posts, while others prefer to produce longer essays on a less frequent basis. The key is consistency, so that readers know how often to expect posts. It is far better to blog once or twice a month than to set off blogging every week and then to disappear for a month or two. As Alan says, 'Don't set yourself unrealistic expectations on how often you will blog. This will only make you feel under pressure and disappoint readers.' And don't forget to reply to comments that people post on your blog. 'This can be time consuming, but it is an important part of blogging as it adds an element of interaction,' Alan believes.

Alan thinks that blogging can fill a range of public engagement roles. Some of his posts focus specifically on his research, new papers or talks he is giving, but he also blogs about topical issues in robotics, such as philosophical issues, ethics and science fiction. 'These posts are not directly linked to my research, but are triggered by wider social issues,' he says. This places his research within a broader social discourse on robotics and allows him to engage actively in this discourse.

Blogs also lead to other media opportunities. This is at least partly because many journalists engage with social media and use it as a source of story ideas. 'It's not hard to identify science journalists in your country as they often include their Twitter handles on news articles and other media profiles. That means that when you've blogged about a forthcoming paper or conference presentation, you can be proactive and message individual journalists directly on Twitter.' Timing is critical, as Alan explains: 'The blog post needs to be published before the conference to give journalists a reason to publish or broadcast the story.' News is just that, something that has either just happened or is about to happen. Journalists aren't going to be so interested in your blog post about a paper that came out several months ago.

Individual blog posts can vary tremendously in length, both between blogs and within an individual blog, microblogs, such as Twitter, being an obvious exception. The very short nature of Twitter posts makes this platform more suited to news and promotion. Exploring how people use Twitter suggests that it is primarily used as a broadcast platform, marketing tool, diary or social platform (Marwick and boyd, 2011). Marwick and boyd (2011) found that people used Twitter to strengthen and maintain digital intimacy amongst friends, some of whom might be friends also in the real world. Many others though, saw Twitter as a strategic tool, used to develop and maintain a 'personal brand' or digital profile. Hearn (2008: 198), for example, argues that '[t]he function of the branded self is purely rhetorical; its goal is to produce cultural value and, potentially, material profit', and raises concerns that the commodification of our lives has led to 'flexible' personalities that change affiliations when the wind blows differently. In this context, the creation and maintenance of our digital profiles as researchers encourages us think about how we might 'exploit every opportunity', but through this process we may 'grow increasingly cynical as we recognize that work is a game and that its rules do not require respect, but only adaptation' (Hearn, 2008: 213). So, while we encourage you to think about your digital profile, it is also important that your communication is authentic. Consider why you are engaging with these media and how these engagements meet both your needs as a researcher and the needs of those with whom you are in contact, and design your approach to using them accordingly.

Whole projects can be created around video as we have seen in Chapter 6, but video can also be used to enhance a written blog, or even take the form of a videoblog, or vlog as they are known, hosted on sites such as YouTube. Audio or video formats offer a potentially richer media experience than text-only formats, and may be particularly appropriate for some types of research (e.g. fieldwork may naturally suggest the collection of sound or image files which might enhance a blog). Twenty-seven percent of adults in the United States who use the internet have posted a video online and 72 percent of them watch online videos on sites such as YouTube and Vimeo (Pew Research Centre, 2013). Audio formats are equally appealing, allowing users to listen to audio programmes while going about their daily lives (Birch and Weitkamp, 2010), although these mobile environments may prove distracting. Gay *et al.* (2006) suggest that in the case of astronomy podcasts there is a bias toward listeners in the twenty-five to forty-four age range and that, while listeners had a variety of educational backgrounds, most had a university-level education. As with written blogs, podcasting and vodcasting allow researchers to reach their publics directly, without the need for a middleman (e.g. a broadcaster).

When it comes to podcasts, there are many opportunities for researchers. Some of these arrive through processes not unlike those associated with mainstream media: that is, the podcast producer invites the researcher as a guest on their show. However, the relatively low cost of high-quality digital recording equipment and the free availability of editing software (such as Audacity) gives researchers the opportunity to create their own high-quality audio outputs and there are a number of interesting examples of audio-based research communication projects, some of which also engage with the mainstream media, such as The Naked Scientists, Astronomy Cast and Footnoting History.

Producing high-quality video, particularly on your own, is more challenging. Given the large amounts of high-quality video online, it is worth considering whether you can produce material of sufficient quality before embarking on video blogs. By and large, we are not talking about putting your recorded lectures online, although there are many fine examples of public lectures that have been recorded (usually professionally) and made available online, for example the TED Talks and TedX channels and the Royal Institution's Christmas Lectures. As with any communication, in creating a podcast or vodcast you need to first think about the listener. Redfern (2009: 180) notes that 'the intimacy of the medium can bring a greater level of attention and make it quite possible to explain complex ideas. But it has to be clear and free of jargon.' While Redfern recommends underestimating the knowledge of your listeners, you should never underestimate their intelligence.

Quality, not just of audio or video, but of content, is also a consideration. There are plenty of poor-quality podcasts, but there are also an increasing number of high-quality shows. 'Suddenly, professional radio producers have competition not only from established rival broadcasters but also from the publishers of newspapers and magazines, science organisations and the aforementioned pro-ams' (Redfern, 2009: 190). Markman (2012) identified the opportunity to produce radio on their own terms as a key motivating factor for podcast producers and that securing and interacting with their audience helped to maintain momentum and interest in the genre. Nevertheless, blogging, whether written, audio or video, should not be undertaken lightly and concerns have been raised, in academic and other spheres, about the impact of unwise online profiles on future career prospects. Hitchcock and others warn the academic blogger to take care about this public profile: 'remember that everything from Academia.edu, to Twitter, to Facebook and Flickr, is a form of publication, and should be taken seriously as such. If you would not say it in an academic review, or in the questions following a public lecture, don't say it on Twitter' (Hitchcock, 2014: np). Time is also a factor in considering whether or not to blog or vlog. While there is perhaps less reputational danger in intermittent blogging, such practices rarely win you readers. Chalmers (2009: 76) cautions that 'maintaining a high quality blog can take up a serious fraction of a researcher's day job'.

Pinterest, Flickr and visual communication

A number of social platforms focus specifically on the visual rather than written or spoken words. Depending on the nature of the images included, these sites can offer greater media richness than more text-based approaches, particularly if you make use of the caption options to provide context for the images. You will need to consider what balance to strike between self-presentation and self-disclosure, particularly if you use the same account for personal and professional images. Platforms such as Pinterest, where curators collect and present tagged visual images, and Flickr and Instagram, photo-sharing sites, also offer opportunities to communicate your research. Most research is about people, ideas or events; images can make your ideas and achievements more tangible. Like many blogs and YouTube feeds, Pinterest, Flickr and Instagram are platforms designed for sharing and offer users the opportunity to comment on posts (images). Pinterest, for example, allows 'curators' to create virtual scrapbooks of images, which may be drawn from their own photos and graphics, or from other websites. For example, FEM Inc provides a curated collection of powerful female characters in entertainment (www.pinterest.com/feminc/boards/). Curators can provide a relatively long commentary providing information and context about the image, and others can post additional comments, in the style of many blogs. Instagram uses a similar format, although the images are normally your own.

Jessica Leveto, of Kent State University, USA (www.pinterest.com/profjess/) has identified a number of ways that Pinterest can be used by academics and has presented these in an infographic.[1] In the infographic, Leveto suggests ways that Pinterest can be used for research, teaching and public engagement:

- Archival functions
  - identify and save relevant visual resources
  - locate images to visualise topics
  - collaborate with colleagues for research and teaching
  - create a photo journal of your research
- Teaching functions
  - curate resources for 'virtual' field trips
  - demonstrate the applied nature of abstract concepts
  - collaborate with students
- Public engagement/dissemination
  - public engagement
  - bring research to life with a visual biography.

Flickr has developed a reputation as a place to source images through Creative Commons licensing, but it also has potential for public engagement if your topic is amenable to photography. For example, the National Oceanic and Atmospheric Administration in the United States posts photos with explanatory captions (www.flickr.com/photos/noaaimages/with/14018146303/), while the US Natural History Museum has a Flickr gallery devoted to its bug collections (www.flickr.com/photos/nhm_beetle_id/). Flickr users have a number of licensing options to choose from which they can apply to the images they upload. These range from free use with attribution through to more restricted uses, such as a restriction for non-commercial use or a no-derivatives license that prevents others making works derived from your images. If you decide to post your own photos on Flickr or similar sites you need to consider any restrictions you might place on their use.

Instagram has grown tremendously in popularity, thanks to the easy-to-use mobile app that allows you to instantly upload photos from your smartphone to your Instagram page. Unless you actively make your account private, anyone can see the photos you upload, leading to some concerns about the images uploaded by some more vulnerable groups, such as teenagers. You can caption uploaded images to provide some context and explanation for the images presented. A number of research organisations are now using Instagram for research communication, including NASA's Marscuriosity site (https://instagram.com/marscuriosity/), which has unretouched images from the mission, and the archaeology photos from the Institute of Field Research (https://instagram.com/ifr_global/). The University of Bergen (https://instagram.com/unibergen) uses Instagram to present a wide range of research and to offer a snapshot look at the day-to-day lives of researchers at the university.

If your research is visual in nature it is worth considering these and other similar platforms as sites for research communication either on their own or combined with other approaches. The key is to have visual material. That could be in the form of infographics explaining your research, or photos or images created during the research process. Equally, photos or images created as part of outreach or public engagement work could be included (see, for example, the Glasgow School of Art Flickr stream www.flickr.com/photos/glasgowschoolart), although you need permission from participants if your photos include recognisable images of other people (see Chapter 11).

Facebook, Myspace and social networking

Few studies have explored the potential of social networks for research communication, though there is much research exploring the socio-cultural impact of Facebook. Despite the lack of research on the potential of using Facebook to communicate research, many research organisations are setting up Facebook pages, such as the European Space Agency, and there are a growing number of social network pages devoted to research projects, such as the EU-funded Perseus project. These sites may be used to provide updates on research activities or project results, or as a more general tool to stimulate interest in the subject area, for example by providing a stream of interesting images. Furthermore, many universities see Facebook as a marketing tool, setting up pages with a view to attracting new students. As an individual researcher, you can either create a regular Facebook page (as physicist and BBC presenter Jim Al-Khalili has done) where you have friends with whom you interact or create an organisation page that allows you to have followers or fans, such as the page created by physicist and BBC presenter Professor Brian Cox.

Social networks tend to be high on both self-presentation/disclosure and media richness. As many of these sites are used primarily for social (non-work) interaction, there is an expectation that individuals will engage in a relatively high degree of self-presentation. In fact, there is concern that individuals may disclose too much of their activities, and for researchers there is a need to consider carefully how you use these spaces: is this a leisure or professional activity, or do you combine the two?

A study of the Monterey Bay Aquarium Research Institute's (MBARI) Facebook page, explored the MBARI's approach to public engagement via Facebook, with a view to understanding whether its Facebook activity could have an impact on ocean literacy (Fauville *et al.*, 2015). The study sought to understand how posting strategy and content influenced the reach of a story, as well as how fans interacted with the site. As an institution, the MBARI does not have 'friends' on its Facebook page (friends are people who share information on Facebook) but only 'fans' (a user who likes a particular Facebook page). The study explored the factors that affected organic reach (the number of 'fans' seeing a post) and viral reach (the extent to which 'fans' shared MBARI stories with their friends). It found that visual material is more likely than textual material to engage Facebook users: posts that included images and video reached more 'fans' and their friends than did text only or text with a link posts, highlighting the need to consider media richness in planning any communication activities using these media. It is important to note that this study was specifically of Facebook, and so the findings may not be relevant to other, more professional social networks such as LinkedIn. The study also highlighted the importance of regular posting; optimum reach was achieved when five stories were posted each week.

Facebook also proved to be a good platform to enable citizens to ask questions about marine science and receive expert responses, thereby enabling a degree of interaction between researchers and the public. However, it did not promote discussion between 'fans'; fans reported not engaging in discussion or comment themselves, for fear of being wrong. Furthermore, there was a sense that fans were not interested in the opinions of other fans. However, there was some evidence that fans did enter into discussion about MBARI Facebook posts amongst their own friends. Fauville *et al.* (2015) conclude that Facebook provides an opportunity to engage those who already have an interest in the oceans, and that through the sharing of stories by fans, this type of platform may widen reach to those who would not otherwise encounter ocean research.

Social network sites have the potential to provide rich media environments, combining text, visual and audio content. They also offer the opportunity, and perhaps in some cases the expectation, of greater dialogic interaction than platforms such as blogs and Flickr. In the case of institutions, we might expect fairly high levels of self-presentation and low levels of self-disclosure. However, in the case of individuals, there is likely to be a tension between self-presentation and self-disclosure, particularly if you intend to use the site for both professional contacts and friends.

Second Life and virtual worlds

Potentially the most media-rich environments, virtual worlds, combine images, text and synchronous audio communication. Self-presentation, through design of your avatar, also tends to be high and the opportunity to speak to people means there is inevitably a degree of self-disclosure. Virtual worlds are online communities where users interact via an avatar, a two- or three-dimensional computer graphic. Virtual worlds fall into two classes, those focused on entertainment, typically games such as World of Warcraft, and those focused on social interaction, such as Second Life. While there are opportunities for research communication in gaming environments, these are constrained by the game rules. This section will focus on the more open-ended experiences of social virtual worlds (SVWs), exploring the opportunities afforded by Second Life, one of the largest such communities.

SVWs like Second Life enable a wide range of virtual interactions, from attending concerts or public lectures, through to e-commerce and e-education. It is, therefore, possible to undertake most types of public engagement activities you might conduct in the real world in these virtual worlds. Furthermore, you are not geographically bound, enabling you to interact (potentially) with people who live anywhere in the real world, including those who may have difficulty with real-world access due to either mobility or psychological issues – such as agoraphobia. However, you do interact in real time, so the practicalities of running an event for people on the other side of the world mean that either you, or they, are keeping unsocial hours.

Research is beginning to understand why people use SVWs. Zhou *et al.* (2011) categorise uses of SVWs as functional, experiential and social; in their study, the primary functional uses of Second Life are learning and shopping, while exploring the environment itself was the primary experiential motivation for using Second Life. Social goals include meeting and interacting with people with similar values and interests. Although these broad motivations hold for most users, Zhou *et al.* (2011) found variations in specific motivations, depending on individuals' psychological needs. Hassouneh and Brengman (2014) identified seven types of SVW users: role players, relationship seekers, manipulators, achievement seekers, friendship seekers, uninvolved and escapists. This study found friendship to be the main reason people used Second Life, though around 25 percent of respondents appeared to have a 'job' in Second Life (such as designing clothing for avatars, being a DJ at a club or even as a photographer, as well as world builders and designers). As in Zhou *et al.*'s study, the opportunity to make money, through playing games, making and selling items or having another type of job, is one reason people participate in these environments; Second Life has its own currency (Linden dollars), but this can be converted to real-world currencies (e.g. American dollars). The opportunity to experiment and try out different roles is also important to Second Life users: 'In free-form SVWs, users can easily own several avatars, have a job in-world, and create different characters and virtual lives. Trying an avatar of the opposite gender seems to interest users too, with ten percent of male respondents and around four percent of the females using an avatar of the opposite gender as their main one' (Hassouneh and Brengman, 2014: 337).

The social aspect of SVWs comes through in most studies of user motivations. Eisenbeiss *et al.* (2012) categorised Second Life users into three groups: 'Socialisers', 'Creativity seekers' and 'Refugees'. These groupings suggest some strategies for moving real-world research engagement into this virtual environment:

- Socialisers are looking for social interaction. This suggests that public engagement activities that draw on opportunities for interaction and socialising, for example Science Cafés, may work well for these users. Eisenbeiss *et al.* (2012) also suggest that socialisers, because they are communicating with each other, may provide word-of-mouth publicity for regular events.
- Creativity seekers are looking for opportunities for creative expression, and so communication opportunities that allow them to explore their own creativity might work well. This could include online 'making' or 'hackathon' events (hackathon describes playful, intensive activities that draw designers, computer programmers and others together to co-create software and objects, using for example Arduino).
- Refugees seek opportunities to escape from their daily lives. This segment of users might engage with research communication approaches that involve role play, for example, becoming a virtual anthropologist.

Second Life has been adopted as a learning tool in higher education, with a number of universities having a presence (e.g. University of the West of England, Bristol; Arkansas State University). Learning environments are being created, such as Leicester University's Saami Tent (which provides a 3D immersive experience for students studying archaeology and ancient history, allowing them to explore Saami objects and experience gender roles within the Saami community). These environments allow students to practise skills relevant to their area of study which it would be hard to provide in the real world, such as access to rare objects, or to practise laboratory skills in a virtual world before undertaking real-world practicals. Second Life is also being tested as a platform for distance learning (for example, the University of the West of England's MA in Education in Virtual Worlds), enabling students from around the world to participate in the same course (although this may mean they are attending classes in the middle of the night).

Museums and art galleries have also created virtual presences (see Chapter 4), such as the Exploratorium Science Center in the USA (www.exploratorium.edu/worlds/secondlife/). Some of these venues offer potential collaboration partners for public engagement activities, which may be useful for those interested in exploring the opportunities of the medium. Cafés, such as the Kira Café (www.kira.org), may offer opportunities for public lectures and discussions about your work. Djorgovski *et al.* (2012) report that popular science lectures were one of the most successful aspects of the MICA (Meta-Institute for Computational Astrophysics) project, which included activities ranging from scientific collaboration meetings and informal gatherings, through to public lectures. MICA public lectures were typically attended by fifty to seventy avatars and the outreach programme included 'Ask an Astronomer' sessions, which were popular with science enthusiasts (Djorgovski *et al.*, 2012). Djorgovski *et al.* (2012: 55) argue that SVWs break some of the traditional barriers faced by people in attending public lectures, which include geographical limitations, and also social barriers:

> One important feature of VWs is that they lower the social barriers in most human interactions, and education is no exception. People who attended our popular lectures and informal discussions would generally not attempt (or not even have an opportunity) to make comparable contacts in real life. This levelling of an educational playing field may have a huge, beneficial social impact.

Case study 7.2 **Second Life: Science Circle**

Science Circle provides a space to talk about research and education in the virtual social world Second Life. Founded by Chantal Snoek and Jes Stannard, Science Circle brings together twelve universities from across four continents, two marine research laboratories, The Exploratorium (a science centre in the United States) and NASA Education. Diversity is key in this group, as the circle aims to connect people from different disciplines and inspire creativity and inventiveness, globally.

'For me, the Science Circle's biggest success is the reliable activity it has maintained in its years of operation. No other educational group I have come cross in Second Life has lasted or kept an active group as long as the Science Circle,' explains Jes Stannard. But keeping the Circle going has its challenges too, as Jes explains: 'Keeping members active over the internet is a huge challenge. Making a virtual world appealing to those in real life is a challenge too; new technology is also hard to get across to some educators.'

The Circle operates like an informal seminar series, but one aimed at a much wider audience than the departmental seminars we might encounter in universities today. Not only do attendees come from a range of disciplinary backgrounds, but they represent a diverse range of countries and include members working in industry as well as educational settings. Jes highlights that '[a]ll ages are welcome at our presentations; we have had members and attendants of seventy-plus years old. And I was nineteen when I joined Science Circle, we have had a few younger ones too.'

Circle members give presentations and offer field trips on a variety of topics, ranging from history and palaeontology to computer science and quantum physics. Past presentations include:

- Transmathematica – a survey of recent results on division by zero
- Augmented Mind
- Transcending Culture in International Settings.

Videos of most presentations are available on the Science Circle YouTube channel and notes or slides are available on the Science Circle website, so those unable to attend in person can also access the resources.

Second Life allows presenters to both show slides and use audio functions. This means that you can interact with your audience. Presentations might take a traditional public lecture format with questions asked at the end, or more informal discussion. Field trips or visits to other sites are typically more of a guided tour of the site, allowing participants to ask questions and interact with objects along the way.

Second Life affords many opportunities for public engagement and research communication, but it does take time to learn how to navigate it effectively. Jes warns that new users should 'prepare for a steep learning curve; Second Life can be quite overwhelming when you first log in-world'. She advises new users to explore the world and find out what others are doing before embarking on their own research communication activities. 'Educators already share their work in Second Life and they are worth looking at,' she adds.

Strategy and social media

With such a plethora of social media opportunities, where should you begin? Unlike traditional media, where you might be offered the opportunity to write a one-off article about your research or a recent project, social media requires ongoing commitment. As Fauville *et al.*'s (2014) research and Winfield's recommendations for bloggers suggest, social media requires regular activity. It's no good setting up a blog and posting only once, nor will you gain many followers to a Twitter account which you visit and post on monthly. So the first issue to address is to consider how much time you can devote to your social media activities. Deciding how much time you are willing and able to spend on these activities will shape your decisions regarding which platforms and how many platforms you might realistically use. There are tools which can streamline your activities across platforms (such as Hootsuite and Tweetdeck), ensuring that you automatically tweet about new blog posts, for example, or linking Twitter and Facebook accounts, but while these tools can improve efficiency, they will not do all the work for you.

Next you should identify your social media objectives. These might relate to the impact of your research, such as increasing downloads of academic papers, or it might be that you are interested in reaching a particular stakeholder group that might use your research. Equally, your objectives might relate to public engagement or even to increasing enrolment on a degree or postgraduate degree programme. The important thing is to think carefully about what you would like to achieve through social media and what is realistic. It's fine to have some aspirational objectives, but it is useful to have some fairly achievable objectives too. Spend a little time at the planning stage thinking about what success might look like in relation to social media activities, as this will help you to measure the impact of your media activities (see Chapter 10). Tools are available that will help you measure the impact of social media activity, and increasingly there is interest in the academic community to harness these to assess the wider impact of research (see Box 7.5).

Having identified your social media objectives, it's time to think about what platform(s) are most appropriate and likely to lead to success. If you are mainly interested in reaching other academics, then choose one of the academic social networks, such as ResearchGate or Mendeley. If

---

Box 7.5 Altmetrics

Social media tools are available to help assess the impact of your social media activities. There is some discussion in academic circles about how these measures, collectively known as altmetrics, might be incorporated, alongside traditional citations, in measures of academic esteem and impact. The website altmetrics.org, provides a summary of how altmetrics are being used and a guide to some of the tools available. These focus mainly on tools to collect altmetrics for research papers. There are also tools designed specifically to measure the impact of your social media activities, such as Klout and Topsy. New tools appear regularly, so it is best to explore what is available once you embark on social media activities.

---

you are seeking to reach a stakeholder group, research what platforms they typically use. Or perhaps there is a particular style of communication that appeals to you or that fits with the nature of the data you collect, such as image-based approaches.

Whatever platforms and objectives you set, we recommend being realistic and starting small. It is easier to find the time to manage one or two social media accounts effectively than it is to jump in all guns blazing and scattering a limited amount of interaction across a number of platforms. Also, remember to review and evaluate your activities on a regular basis. Are the platforms achieving what you set out to accomplish? If not, consider how you might change your interaction with the platform or whether there are other strategies you can use to increase your success. If it really isn't working, then let it go and try another. Social media tools are largely free to use, at least at a basic level, allowing you to give them a try and to see what works best for you and your research.

Summary

Opportunities to reach stakeholders and the public have changed rapidly over the past few decades, and while traditional media continue to provide a route to increasing awareness of new research, new tools are facilitating a range of novel ways to engage the public and stakeholders with research. Whereas academics might typically have approached traditional media at the end stages of the research process, as a further dissemination tool, these new tools have a role to play throughout the research process, from the generation of ideas and the honing of research questions, though to dissemination of findings. This not only could offer the public greater input into the design of research projects, but also gives researchers the opportunity to share and communicate about the process of research, allowing the public glimpses into the ivory tower.

This chapter has looked briefly at proactive ways to engage with traditional media, as well as exploring creative approaches to communicate your research via networks such as Twitter, Flickr and Second Life. These new platforms have challenges: in terms of how best to manage the time you dedicate to communication and engagement; choice of platform that meets both your needs and the needs of the publics you are trying to reach; and in terms of measuring the impact of your communications through these channels. It also brings about the need to consider your overall digital profile and the relationship between your professional and private lives: in what ways are you happy for these to merge, and what strategies might you employ to keep them separate?

Note

1 Jessica Leveto's academic uses of Pinterest graphic can be found at: www.pinterest.com/pin/72268768995272025/.

Further reading

Blum, D., Knudson, M. and Henig, R.M., *A Field Guide for Science Writers*, 2nd edition (Oxford: Oxford University Press, 2006).
Van Noorden, R., 'Scientists and the social network', *Nature*, 512 (2014) 126–9.

8

Political

As we have discussed in previous chapters, there are a wide variety of opportunities to communicate with publics, but beyond these exist other scenarios for engagement, including engagement with policy frameworks, which can also have their challenges. As with communication with a public audience, doubts can arise as to how to access, convey and work with stakeholders who are focused on political issues of governance; but just as in work with publics, increasing awareness of policymakers' needs, operational practices and access routes can assist researchers in communicating with such stakeholders. In addition, the policymaking sphere exists not only as a possible communication channel but also as a framework in which a great deal of engagement activity is occurring. Many of the approaches to engagement through which researchers seek to consider their work have emerged from democratic framings of participation and such settings are also explored within this chapter, as context for researchers keen to use such approaches, along with the citizens' role in such negotiations.

Deliberation

When we think about democracy it is almost impossible to ignore the role of *demos* or *people* within it; 'democracy means a form of government in which, in contradistinction to monarchies and aristocracies, the people rule. Democracy entails a political community in which there is some form of *political equality* among the people' (Held, 2006, emphasis in original). However, from the outset of democratic structures in ancient Greece to the modern day, democratic regimes represent tremendous variety in their definition, in particular with regard to the participation of their citizens. Such democracies have been plagued throughout history with questions surrounding who can participate (with regard to wealth, property, title, occupation, literacy, gender and race) and how active that participation should be. Historically, these approaches have been associated to two main models of democracy: direct or participatory democracy, where citizens are directly involved in decision making, and liberal or representative democracy, in which elected officials represent the interests and views of citizens (Held, 2006). Whilst democracies now largely represent the pluralist notion of one person, one vote, politics in both the public and private spheres remains focused on questions around how, who and why people can participate and engage in political decision making, and relatively recently these issues have generated even greater interest with the recognition of a third approach to democracy (Held, 2006), that of deliberative democracy, which is perhaps most relevant to researchers seeking to communicate their work.

Participatory approaches within the political framework lie at the heart of deliberative democracy, and thus align considerably with calls to engage within research processes. Deliberation, which involves careful discussion and debate of a subject in order that decisions can be publicly defended, was most notably visible with the establishment of civil and criminal juries in the seventeenth century. Although the jury model – the gathering of a group of citizens to provide an impartial verdict – is occasionally problematic, the use of juries in legal settings is well respected and it is a responsibility which is, in the main, taken seriously by lay participants who recognise and appreciate the considerable power that such roles hold. The social importance of the jury model in law has, then, significantly influenced the public's view of deliberative processes more widely, bringing a social significance and authority to their influence (Gastil and Richards, 2013; O'Mahony, 2013).

Beyond this legal setting, a more widespread uptake of deliberative theory emerged in the 1970s and 1980s and subsequently various versions of deliberative democracy have developed. Like many concepts in the field of communication, definitions of 'deliberation' are open to differing framings and have raised both conceptual and practical questions (Korthals, 2013), and it is certainly not the case that deliberation includes only the jury model. However, broadly, it might be argued that approaches incorporating deliberation sought to compensate for some of the faults found within historical democratic models. For instance, informed deliberation amongst citizens reduces the long-held concern that democratic decision making can be swayed by the short-sighted concerns of the masses rather than the minority views held by those with greater levels of expertise, particularly in political eras of sound bite and celebrity (Held, 2006). In other words, providing people with information, and the time to consider it, seeks to allow more considered decision making, which can include decision making on scientific, social and research-based issues. Deliberation also provides opportunities to explore issues that are more personalised and local in nature, contributing to political decision making that can be defended on its basis within the contexts to which it is relevant and recognising individual citizens as agents rather than as observers in political settings (O'Mahony, 2013).

> Deliberative democrats make a very distinctive case; that is, they contend that no set of values or particular perspectives can lay claim to being correct and valid by themselves, but they are valid only in so far as they are justified. Moreover individual points of view need to be tested in and through social encounters which take account of the point of view of others – the moral point of view. (Held, 2006: 233)

This style of deliberation centrally privileges the concept of 'reason', but avoids a reductionist definition. Reason is not restricted 'to established "reasoners"', the role of experts (and perhaps we might consider here researchers) alone and forms of reasoning including only reified knowledge (O'Mahony, 2013: 130). Instead, reason can be taken to mean that 'all are open to be persuaded by the arguments of others' (O'Mahony, 2013: 130). The rise in new media technologies, new social movements and changes to communicative paradigms have allowed for more deliberative opportunities to arise (O'Mahony, 2013). Furthermore, providing opportunities for citizens to deliberate, question and probe important social issues became obviously prominent with regard to many aspects of science and technological research at the turn of the new millennium. At this time society had become more technologically dependent and driven, with more governance decisions taken over broader constituencies (for example, international regulatory frameworks), decision-making power moved to technocratic elites which often neglected the wider social issues presented by research (Heinelt, 2010; Held, 2006). Technological issues became pervasive in their potential to have an impact on all members of society (Heinelt, 2010), while a gulf developed in public trust regarding how governments dealt with emerging issues of innovation. This led to the proposition that improved deliberation, dialogue and engagement in political decision making could restore public trust (see Chapter 1) in both research and governance. Deliberative approaches have emerged at a time, then, when public satisfaction with traditional political decision making appeared to have been eroded.

Case study 8.1 The People's Campaign for Decentralised Planning

Kerala, an Indian state comprising approximately thirty million people, could be an unexpected place to have a strong deliberative history. As a state, it is responsive to national polices, and yet it has managed to cultivate circumstances for deliberative democracy amongst its population to which many countries have only aspired. Its citizens had not previously been given many opportunities to participate, nor had local governments been able to exercise a great deal of local control (Heller et al., 2007). The state's population size is also the equivalent to that of some nations – another reason why it is perhaps an unusual location for civic participation at a local level.

Yet deliberative democracy has been used in a number of contexts within Kerala, including, but not restricted to, local government, sustainable development, working conditions and health reforms. The most significant driver for this was the People's Campaign for Decentralised Planning. Originating from a left-wing government in the mid-1990s, the People's Campaign allocated over a third of the state's budget to local constituencies (which constituted over 1,000 localities) to manage. At a practical level this meant that local people would be first engaged on their priorities, followed by involvement in the delivery of resulting projects, and were given new control over how budgets were used. Importantly, this meant that people could 'shape' rather than just 'choose' local policies (Heller et al., 2007: 629). The People's Campaign was not only a local investment in decision making; it was also about mobilising citizens to be active. Over 100,000 citizens received training as part of their involvement, and participation by women and across castes was strongly encouraged (Heller et al., 2007).

The People's Campaign resulted in widespread changes. Local expenditure continued and was expanded, participation was considerable (1.8 million people were estimated to attend local forums on priorities) and relatively inclusive and, most importantly, it created opportunities for participation where none had existed before (Heller et al., 2007). A number of tangible outcomes have been evidenced in various evaluations, for example that there was significant extension of public health facilities such as the provision of safe drinking water (Elamon et al., 2004). As might be expected with such widespread change, there were also administrative issues, financial concerns and issues of corruption along the way.

Some see the Kerala example as a result of unique circumstances, whereby the history, cultural conventions, high literacy and life expectancy rates, alongside changes to national policy (the Indian government introduced constitutional changes which ultimately allowed this approach in the first instance) collided to make deliberative democracy particularly fruitful; however, its significant outcomes also led it to be a widely cited example of local deliberation in action.

One important reason for noting these broader political trends, and deliberation that is occurring around a wide variety of social, environmental and scientific issues, is to recognise that calls for research to feature, influence and respond to public questions reflects research (as well as other political matters) infringing on both public and private settings. A move to deliberative engagement and participation has occurred in many geographical areas of the world including the United Kingdom, United States, Australia, Canada and Brazil, and whilst it might be typified by its use in existing democratic countries, the United Nations is recommending the enhancement of associated deliberation mechanisms particularly in the western Asian region (this includes countries like Libya, Iraq, Saudi Arabia and Egypt), where it is seen to be essential in efforts to restore trust amongst citizens in new states that are emerging (United Nations, 2013). Although engagement has a strong European history, particularly in Scandinavia, Belgium and Switzerland, there are also European countries with very low public participation, such as Cyprus, Hungary and Bulgaria (European Commission, 2012). In the countries where they are used, participatory and deliberative approaches are widespread across many different types of subject matter, including sustainable development, healthcare and environmental decision making to name but a few, as well as within different types of constituencies such as children and young people (Percy-Smith and Thomas, 2010), both within and outside political structures. Though governments and large political infrastructures have not completely embedded deliberation in their governance structures, and its fundamental influence on broad political institutions has not been absolute (O'Mahony, 2013), deliberative mechanisms are pervasive, particularly around specific policy goals and initiatives (Sheedy, 2008), and are thus important for researchers to be aware of. Next it is important, then, to consider why this is seen to be useful and how we engage in practice.

Engagement

Engagement can occur in many ways associated with the research process, including within policymaking, within individual disciplines and as part of the research process itself. Before explaining this further it is worth unpicking in a little more detail what we mean by engagement, and how it relates to deliberation and participation.

Defining 'engagement' is problematic, despite the fact that it has been broadly accepted as a concept within policy and public engagement communities (Schäfer, 2009; Trench, 2008). The lack of a more fixed definition has led to some criticism that it allows for interpretations which effectively permit public relations in disguise (Powell and Colin, 2009), or do not reflect a more multifarious process which can be occurring, especially around complex areas of policymaking that relate to emerging areas of research (Irwin, 2009; Irwin and Michael, 2003).

In the context of research and engagement within policy or political settings, there are a number of definitions which have come to be influential. These include definitions that are occurring at international, national and local levels. A number of these definitions are provided in Table 8.1. It is important to bear in mind when considering these definitions that differing terminologies are in operation, in terms of whether such approaches are referred to as 'citizen' or 'public' engagement and participation.

From an academic perspective the work of Rowe and Frewer (2005) has come to hold considerable influence. From their perspective, engagement encompasses a variety of differing approaches, of which participatory approaches are just one type. They define three types of public engagement, dependent on the flow on information. These are public communication, consultation and participation within the context of engagement. The International Association of Public Participation (IAP2) (2007) has further built on this work, creating a spectrum of

Table 8.1 International definitions of public/citizen engagement and participation

United Nations Department of Economic and Social Affairs/ Division for Public Administration and Development Management	[Citizen engagement] The involvement of citizens in the decision-making process of the State through measures and/or institutional arrangements so as to increase their influence on public policies and programmes, ensuring a more positive impact on their social and economic lives.
European Commission Horizon 2020 The EU Framework Programme for Research and Innovation	Public engagement (PE) in Responsible Research and Innovation (RRI) is about co-creating the future with citizens and civil society organisations, and also bringing on board the widest possible diversity of actors that would not normally interact with each other, on matters of science and technology. PE implies: – the establishment of iterative and inclusive participatory multi-actor dialogues between researchers, policymakers, industry and civil society organisations, NGOs and citizens;

Table 8.1 (cont.)

	– to foster mutual understanding and co-create research and innovation outcomes and policy agendas effective in tackling societal challenges; – fostering wider acceptability of results.
The International Association for Public Participation (IAP2)	'Public participation' means to involve those who are affected by a decision in the decision-making process. It promotes sustainable decisions by providing participants with the information they need to be involved in a meaningful way, and it communicates to participants how their input affects the decision.
The National Coalition for Dialogue and Deliberation (United States)	Various forms of highly inclusive public dialogue and deliberation that are critical steps towards policy development, collaborative civic action, and other forms of public problem solving. Often used interchangeably with the term 'civic engagement' (to many, incorrectly) public engagement generally involves a mutually beneficial partnership between the public and an entity perceived as having power (government, a university, a corporation, etc.). Many use 'public engagement' as a general term for a broad range of methods through which members of the public become more informed about and/or influence public decisions.
Canadian Policy Research Networks (Canada)	Citizen engagement values the right of citizens to have an informed say in the decisions that affect their lives ... Citizen engagement emphasizes the sharing of power, information, and a mutual respect between government and citizens.

Table 8.1 (cont.)

IBM Center for the Business of Government (United States)	Citizen engagement is part of a family of democratic reform ideas that includes public participation, public involvement, participatory democracy, deliberative democracy, and collaborative governance. When used in relation to the online environment, a new vocabulary is evoked, which includes e-democracy, digital democracy, e-government, and electronic governance. What is important to know about these terms is that, while they all make distinctions around the purpose, breadth, and techniques of participation, at base they recognize and build upon a fundamental right of all citizens to have a say in the decisions that affect their lives. Citizen participation policies and programs reflect a basic adoption of this principle and extend a 'standing invitation' to citizens to engage in policy development and decision-making activities.
Research Councils UK (United Kingdom)	The Research Councils use Public Engagement as an umbrella term for any activity that engages the public with research, from science communication in science centres or festivals, to consultation, to public dialogue. Any good engagement activity should involve two-way aspects of listening and interaction.

public participation which reflects an increasing level of public impact over five stages from 'inform', 'consult', 'involve' through to 'collaborate' and, finally, 'empower'.

In addition, it is vital to stress that some see there being important differences between participation, which perhaps implies a level of involvement alone, and engagement, which suggests a more empowered role (Lukensmeyer and Hasselblad Torres, 2006). This is particularly defined by the United Nations, which identifies the key difference between participation and engagement as being about the way that it is instigated and structured and its expected outcomes. The United Nations (2011) conceptualises engagement to be that which is conducted by government authorities, is institutionalised, with impacts on public services, policies or development. In contrast, participation is seen to be on the initiative of citizens, informal, and to deliberate, assess and propose improvements (United Nations, 2011). As such, participation, whilst of intrinsic value, is not seen to give publics the same share in decision making (United Nations, 2011).

Approaches which seek to engage citizens, rather than simply communicate to them, have come to hold considerable influence amongst policymakers, researchers and learned institutions that seek to communicate and engage with members of the public around research issues (Felt and Fochler, 2008). Beyond the political context and alignment with democratic principles, a number of different reasons for public engagement have resonance with diverse areas of policymaking and research; however the key broad drivers include:

- Provides insights into public attitudes and concerns before an area of research is investigated or applied.
- Creates socially robust knowledge, with an opportunity for public contributions and insights.
- Has potential to inform or justify the investment of taxes in publicly funded research.
- Reduces potential for polarisation of perspectives, with a greater understanding of common ground.
- Recognises that in some contexts people do not work from a deficit and have other contributions to offer.

As outlined in Chapter 3, the point around deficit is an important one. Rather than assume that people are working from a position of ignorance, engaged and participatory approaches recognise that people have contributions to make to research processes but this too can be a controversial view, as we will see later in this chapter.

Within policy settings, deliberative, participatory and engagement approaches are occurring in a variety of locations as outlined in the previous section. Outside of the policymaking context many researchers are now engaging in public and citizen engagement experiences as they relate to their individual disciplines and surrounding communication. Learned societies, research funders and other stakeholders now commonly 'engage' around pertinent research issues where at one time it may have been common simply to communicate about them. For example, research funders might involve the public in deciding which areas of work should be funded, what questions form priorities and how they might take up that research in their own lives or contexts. Some research organisations and funders are also slowly considering when in the research process engagement should occur, seeking to embed engagement 'upstream'. This relates to claims made by some academics and other interested parties (Wilsdon and Willis, 2004) that the ideal scenario for engagement with research is not at the stage of outcomes, but far earlier in the process, when the purpose, principles and priorities of research are being debated and before significant funding commitments have been made. In addition, for many researchers, approaches to engagement may already be intrinsic to the long-established methods which they themselves use in their research processes. Here engagement is not a separate part of the research process, nor simply an outcome, it is part and parcel of the data that they need to explore, analyse and consider within their research questions. This is perhaps sometimes overlooked by the engagement community, who tend to think about engagement as occurring separately from the process of research.

It is important to stress that the drive for increased engagement does not mean that every area of research requires a significant level of deliberation and questioning (Korthals, 2013), but that for some topical, significant, consequential research such opportunities for engagement can be productive in increasing awareness, knowledge, opinions or the variety of other goals that a researcher, participant or stakeholder may have in mind in any one engagement setting.

Designing engagement

Developing activities to facilitate these loose framings of public engagement is not without practical challenges. Engagement can be time-consuming, expensive and require commitment on the part of researchers, as well as other participants. However, as more and more engagement work has occurred, there have been increasing efforts to share and communicate effective approaches to engagement alongside the learning and evaluation surrounding individual projects that have worked effectively.

Engagement activities vary considerably in terms of aims, scope and method; there is not a 'one-size-fits-all approach' (Sheedy, 2008), but there is certainly a wide variety of information available which can assist in designing engagement of value to your work, as well as for those that have contributed to it. Box 8.1 provides information on a series of guidelines, handbooks and instructional texts which it might be useful to consult.

When viewing these guidance documents it is important to remember that not all have been designed with researchers in mind; some, for

---

Box 8.1 Resources providing guidance on public engagement

Guidelines on Citizens' Engagement for Development Management and Public Governance by the United Nations Department of Economic and Social Affairs (2011). These guidelines provide information on definitions and concepts, the benefits of engagement, practice and conditions for effective engagement, as well as evaluation: http://unpan1.un.org/intradoc/groups/public/documents/un-dpadm/unpan045265.pdf.

Handbook on Citizen Engagement: Beyond Consultation by Amanda Sheedy (2008). Published by the Canadian Policy Research Networks, this handbook provides content on the purpose, preparation, design and implementation of citizen engagement, as well as a range of examples: www.cprn.org/doc.cfm?doc=1857&l=en.

Public Deliberation: A Manager's Guide to Citizen Engagement by Carolyn Lukensmeyer and Lars Hasselblad Torres (2006) at the IBM Center for the Business of Government. The guide explores the purpose and practice of both face-to-face and online deliberation: http://transformgov.org/en/knowledge_network/documents/kn/Document/305430/Public_Deliberation_A_Managers_Guide_to_Citizen_Engagement.

Resource Guide on Public Engagement by the National Coalition for Dialogue and Deliberation. Covers the goals, resources and collaboration required for engagement, in addition to online engagement and examples: http://ncdd.org/rc/pe-resource-guide.

National Coordinating Centre for Public Engagement The website of this United Kingdom-based organisation provides a number of resources focused on engagement, including a section on how to do it: www.publicengagement.ac.uk/how.

The Best of Sciencewise Reflections on Public Dialogue contains an overview and key lessons on pivotal issues in public dialogue, based on Sciencewise's ten years of experience in dialogue on policy issues: www.sciencewise-erc.org.uk/cms/assets/Uploads/Best-ofFINAL.pdf.

---

example, are aimed at policymakers seeking to design engagement, the private sector or non-governmental organisations. What do the guidelines have in common, that you as a researcher might be able to utilise? Box 8.2 encompasses a number of the main recommendations from these sources.

The key point to remember is that whilst an engagement approach might be new to you, many have now been used extensively and effectively, and so doing your research on which approach is best, how it might work and what its potential outcomes are will assist you in designing the most effective process.

Box 8.2 Tips for designing engagement

---

1 Plan what the engagement sets out to achieve (e.g. consensus, reform, enhanced well-being, specific outcomes etc.).

2 Consider when engagement is best placed to occur (e.g. before, during or after a project, policy or piece of research).

3 Engage others in the process (e.g. ensure the purpose and commitment to engagement are shared with others in the team, consider joining a public engagement network).

4 Examine who should be engaged in the process (e.g. inclusiveness of participants, relevance of other stakeholders).

5 Consider any key challenges that might occur (e.g. the context of the engagement, people are unprepared, have expectations that are not met etc.).

6 Plan which would be the most appropriate approach to undertake (e.g. inform, consult, involve, collaborate, empower etc.).

7 Decide which engagement method will be used (e.g. dialogue, citizen juries, polling, online etc.).

8 Assess what information will be needed by participants (e.g. objective and appropriate guidance or materials).

9 Consider the resource requirements (e.g. time, logistics, facilitation or moderation support, room hire and refreshments).

10 Design engagement to be transparent and accountable (e.g. record or transcribe activities, account for outcomes and actions).

11 Design effective reporting (e.g. final reports, reporting back to participants).

12 Plan how the engagement will be monitored or evaluated (e.g. qualitative and/or quantitative evaluation).

Engagement and the citizen

Citizen engagement is premised on the belief that people should have and want to have a say in the decisions that affect their lives. While some may claim that voting and consultation processes achieve this, it is clear that citizens are increasingly frustrated with these democratic mechanisms. They feel that their voices are not being heard and that decisions made by elites do not necessarily reflect their values. Citizen engagement provides a vision for a way forward – a way of reinvigorating current democratic practices and institutions, bringing meaning to people's participation and fostering a two way dialogue between citizens and governments. (Sheedy, 2008: 1)

As Sheedy (2008) states above, citizen engagement is based on the belief that people should and want to have a say in decisions which have the potential to have an impact on them. However, where research is concerned we know there can be all sorts of factors that make this assumption more complex.

In fact we know relatively little about the views of citizens where public engagement with research is concerned. We know a lot about the specific subjects, perspectives and opinions they generate within engagement activities but we rarely extend those questions to the experience of engagement itself, beyond practical considerations (Lehr *et al.*, 2007). This might include how people conceive of their responsibilities, their desire to engage, definitions of engagement, relationships with expertise, as well as more straightforward aspects such as whether they even have the time to be involved (Pouliot, 2011; Hornig Priest, 2009; Michael, 2009; Kerr *et al.*, 2007; Irwin, 2001). In addition, very little is known about how that wider group of citizens regards and views outcomes of engagement, and whether they simply accept the decisions of a citizens jury, for example, due to the credibility and currency of such framings (Gastil and Richards, 2013).

The small amount of work which has been done suggests that public engagement can attract involvement amongst those who are disengaged with traditional forms of civic engagement (John *et al.*, 2011), and that citizens recognise some value in such processes (Wilkinson *et al.*, 2011a; Burall and Shahrokh, 2010). For instance, 39 percent of Eurobarometer survey respondents agreed that citizens should be consulted and their opinions considered when making decisions about science and technology, and over half (55 percent) think that public dialogue is required (European Commission, 2013). That being said, 31 percent are happy to simply be informed and there are some regional variations, for example much higher interest in dialogue is recorded in countries like Denmark, Sweden and Germany, as compared with areas in Eastern Europe (European Commission, 2013). Those with a higher level of education and greater interest in research are also shown to have more positive views towards engaging (European Commission, 2013).

More detailed consideration and research on public participant perspectives would be insightful. In particular, it would help to alleviate some of the concerns around how people may or may not become involved. Korthals (2013: 105) summarises that 'not everyone wants to deliberate all the time', many people are happy with typical decision making, but others lack capacity, fear their input may not be recognised or are worried about 'power relations' at play. Korthals (2013) recommends that greater transparency would prevent deliberative opportunities from becoming restricted to those who are confident or educated.

We can see some resonance in between public concerns about 'power' and some of the critical academic voices which have been raised regarding the appropriateness of certain public engagement approaches. Plato, for example, was scathing about the democratic principle of equality, treating all 'men' as equal, whether they are equal or not; and thus, how experience and knowledge relate to a right to decision making is historically contentious (Held, 2006: 23). From a researcher's perspective the idea that someone may generate valid questions or perspectives or seek to influence the impacts of your research can be unsettling.

> In sum, since the middle of the twentieth century, science has been slipping from the high peak it once occupied and the citizen's relationship to science has changed. Citizens feel less intimidated when it comes to science and technology. Scientists have become less remote ... A new term is needed to describe this sense of empowerment – the sense that every citizen is part of the ball game of science and technology because there is no difference between us and the official ball players ... Default expertise is the expertise – or, at least, right to judge that ordinary citizens feel they possess because science and technology are so fallible. (Collins, 2014: 15)

Collins and Evans (2002, 2007) have particularly taken up this point in the context of science and technology. To simplify, they argue that uncertainty can be revealed to the public before sufficient discussion or understanding amongst the 'core-set' of researchers and, rather than define people as expert or publics, with equally valid contributions to make, they suggest further distinction is necessary, recognising that some people will have expertise based on their networks, contributions or other understandings but that these contributions may not be equally valid (Collins and Evans, 2002).

In summary, from both a participant's perspective and that of the researcher, there are likely to be reasons why engagement may not always be achieved or desirable. Participants are driven by their own needs and priorities, which may or may not include participation in such activities. The need for engagement can be overstated; 'deliberations do not need to be organised in all situations ... they are not always necessary – nobody is saying this', particularly where existing democratic processes are sufficient (Korthals, 2013: 103). Researchers may not feel it is appropriate for their research to be opened up in such ways, or it may simply not be required, but it is also important to remember that participation has its uses and it is unusual for researchers to be overrun by public comment.

Problematising engagement

Providing opportunities for people to engage with research, particularly research which may overlap with political issues, is thus seen to hold many potential benefits. For instance, it can potentially improve the quality of research, increase public trust and awareness in the types of research that are funded, and involvement in such approaches may improve people's capacity to engage with other issues in future. However, there are also significant criticisms that have been raised and of which it is important to be aware.

As definitions of engagement have some flexibility there has been concern that this can mean that the two-way context of such approaches is easily ignored; an activity may be far more akin to informing and communicating to publics, than to engaging or deliberating with them (Thorpe and Gregory, 2010; Chilvers, 2008; Kerr *et al.*, 2007). For researchers familiar with a sense of low public awareness, literacy or understanding of their topic areas, participatory engagement activities can be subject to notions of public understanding which assume that people lack knowledge (Wilkinson *et al.*, 2011b; Davies *et al.*, 2009; Davies, 2008; Irwin, 2006; Cook *et al.*, 2004), and the expectation of an 'ignorant' public to be educated can remain beneath the rhetoric of engagement (Featherstone, Wilkinson and Bultitude, 2009; Burningham *et al.*, 2007; Michael and Brown, 2005; Kerr, 2003; Alsop and Watts, 1997). To provide one example, the HapMap community engagement project in Japan, which sought to develop a culturally sensitive understanding of people's perspectives on issues associated to the human genome, faced constraints due to a widespread assumption that its role was to establish public acceptance (Suda *et al.*, 2009). Equally without a clear understanding as to what engagement can comprise, researchers may not feel fully prepared for it, allow appropriate time, or provide opportunities for listening and interaction (Wilkinson *et al.*, 2011b; RCUK, 2009). Assuming that engagement is akin to a teaching or educational experience, whether conscious or not (Holliman and Jensen, 2009), can lead to engagement approaches that rely on teaching rather than collaboration (Wilkinson *et al.*, 2011b).

Increasing understanding of your subject matter is not necessarily a problem; in fact, as a number of the examples in other chapters attest, there is still a role for communication and educational approaches, but if engagement activities remain more analogous to public relations or 'window dressing', then they can lead to disappointment on the part of citizens who are involved in such processes, as they may not feel an engagement activity has met their expectations or led to the types of outcomes they would have anticipated (United Nations, 2011: 10; Gaventa and Barrett, 2010; Thorpe and Gregory, 2010; Horst, 2008). A common criticism of engagement is that typically, very few processes allow the citizens to set the agenda, and associated with this there can be variations in how much real debate is apparent (Gastil and Richards, 2013; Thorpe and Gregory, 2010). Complex areas of research are likely to have shades of uncertainty (Korthals, 2013), meaning that it can be challenging to frame the issues without having preconceived ideas (and therefore it might more often be framed on the part of the experts involved) as to the scenarios most likely to occur. Those using such approaches to base decisions may also have an expectation that consensus is a desirable or possible outcome. Whether consensus is necessary is open to interpretation (Korthals, 2013), and for some issues, for instance of a moral or ethical flavour, it has been highlighted that consensus is an unreasonable goal, therefore the expectation that engagement will provide answers or decisions may not be realistic in practice.

Concerns are often raised regarding how representative the views expressed are, when, in the majority of circumstances, it is necessary to define some kind of representative sample for a wider group of citizens. Engagement is often searching for ideal types, participants without a view, opinion or bias, which might defeat the object of consulting in the first place (Thorpe and Gregory, 2010). Where disagreements do occur, publics can easily be depicted as 'resistors', labelling 'anti' publics and 'pro' experts, whereby good engagement has too easily become associated with the absence of conflict and appearance of agreement (Thorpe and Gregory, 2010). It has also been suggested that some participants are influenced by the presentation of researchers (Falk *et al.*, 2007; Rennie and Williams, 2006; Falk *et al.*, 1998;), and over the duration of an engagement process people can become less questioning, sympathising with the perspectives of decision makers to the extent that they lose their identity as lay people (Kerr *et al.*, 2007; Davies, 2006).

Whilst the United Nations is keen to stress that engagement should result in impacts on decision making, in fact we still know relatively little about how many engagement processes 'translate' into policy decisions (John, *et al.*, 2011; Davies *et al.*, 2009; Horlick-Jones *et al.*, 2007; Hagendijk and Irwin, 2006; Irwin, 2006). Few engagement activities provide an opportunity to allow citizens to make the final choice or decision, often they are simply able to prioritise or to offer opinions on a range of outcomes (Gastil and Richards, 2013). The impact of engagement has been less well considered than the practical approaches that can be taken and is often restricted to isolated examples and projects. One study which sought to address this gap involved analysis of one hundred research studies of citizen engagement, from over twenty countries, in settings which included local associations, social movements and campaigns as well as within formal governance spaces (Gaventa and Barrett, 2010). The study observed over eight hundred effects from citizen participation, of which 75 percent were seen to be 'positive' effects. These impacts included greater awareness of civic networks amongst participants, as well as changes in tangible skills like increases in knowledge, organisational skills and awareness of possible actions and rights (Gaventa and Barrett, 2010). Thorpe and Gregory (2010: 285) suggest that the oversight where concrete outcomes are concerned may be a discreet indication of the ways that policymakers perceive engagement; '[f]or policymakers, public participation has value merely by generating social-psychological cohesion and a feeling of responsibility, quite apart from whether it devolves real power'.

Therefore, whilst engagement now provides greater opportunities for a range of participatory approaches to occur around research it still has weaknesses, including how it is defined, designed, facilitated and evaluated. An awareness of these in preparing for engagement, as well as reflexive consideration of them during and at the end of an engagement process, can assist in making sure that at least some of the pitfalls are minimised.

The policymaking process

As we have already outlined, engagement with research occurs in a political context, and many of the engagement approaches researchers take have been influenced by political fashions. However, there are also other means through which researchers' work may have policy outcomes and we will now explore perspectives regarding how research can influence policymaking.

Starting from the assumption that many researchers will be involved in the collection of some type of evidence, it is useful to consider evidence-based policymaking as an opening perspective. Evidence-based policymaking seems like a logical approach; indeed for those who are less familiar with policymaking communities, the idea of needing to highlight the use of evidence in policymaking might raise the question 'What would otherwise be used?' However, it is well recognised that in reality a 'chasm' often exists between the production of knowledge and how that knowledge is used by governments (Bogenschneider and Corbett, 2010). Evidence-based policymaking has represented a concerted effort in the last decades of the twentieth century to create policymaking climates which are more securely based in evidence than in political ideology, personal values, manifestos or economic consideration. In the context of the United Kingdom, such an approach strongly came to favour in the late 1990s when the *Modernising Government* White Paper (Cabinet Office, 1999: 7) committed to forward-looking policy-making which would 'involve and meet the needs of all different groups in society'. Whilst use of evidence-based policymaking in a formal sense varies internationally, countries including America (Bogenschneider and Corbett, 2010), where drives for increased research-based policy have been apparent since the 1960s, as well as a number of countries in developing areas of the world (Sutcliffe and Court, 2006) have also turned their attention to the principles of evidence-based policymaking. At a European level, strengthening the dialogue between researchers and policymakers has been a major concern, to the extent that European-funded project coordinators have been 'encouraged to put the policy-usefulness of their research findings to the forefront of their objectives and their work programmes' (European Commission, 2008: 7).

Although evidence-based policymaking flags the involvement of different types of users, it is strongly rooted in the idea that systems can be created which will allow policymakers to systematically identify the best available evidence, drawing on high-quality research in order to produce the best outcomes. There are varying interpretations as to what 'evidence' might involve, and so it has been argued that 'research-shaped decision making' (Bogenschneider and Corbett, 2010: 4) or 'evidence informed policy' (Pawson, 2006) might provide alternative descriptions. Regardless of the semantics, such an approach aligns well with the view that such evidence is likely to be informed by academic experts and communities, and this, therefore, is likely to present communication opportunities for the now far-reaching research community. However, it is this academic extensiveness that creates one of the first issues where policymaking is concerned, as Bogenschneider and Corbett (2010: 3) comment:

> It is hard to shake the impression that we may be functioning in a policy environment that operates, ironically enough, according to an inverse relationship between science and politics – the more and better research we produce – the less effect it has on the policymaking process. With increasing amounts of data and analysis emerging from our universities and research/evaluation firms, the likelihood that even the most studious of public officials can sort through and make sense of the science available to them is not very high.

Whilst evidence is useful for policymakers for a variety of reasons, including to improve the quality of decisions, to demonstrate their knowledge and to counteract evidence raised by their constituencies who are increasingly information rich (Bogenschneider and Corbett, 2010), drives for evidence have created additional infrastructures and agencies to monitor and regulate evidence, and this has increased pressure on academic representatives to provide evidence beyond professional judgement or insight (Pawson, 2006). Evidence-based policymaking is not, then, without its issues, as summarised in Table 8.2, central to which are aspects of the research context, evidence, the nature of policy problems and the structures of politics and policymaking.

Evidence-based policymaking has created clear opportunities for researchers to engage more in policy processes, but it also raises questions about how frequently evidence is able to influence decisions when in reality political and economic motivations do exist in such decision making, as do other constituents, stakeholders, pressure groups and party politics.

From the researcher's perspective there is also likely to be some

Table 8.2 Problems in evidence-based policymaking

Research context	– Time lag between a policymaker's need for information and the timelines of research.
	– Processes such as peer review (essential for credibility) can delay evidence reaching policymakers.
	– Researchers are most familiar with communicating to other researchers, policymakers have differing demands.
	– Researchers become used to ambiguity, which can clash with the need for certainty.
	– Researchers are often cynical of the political process.
	– Lack of awareness/training around how to communicate with policymakers.
Evidence	– Varying definitions as to what counts as 'evidence'.
	– Hierarchies of evidence at play (preference for empirical).
	– Bias towards evidence provided by reputable organisations.
	– Bias towards evidence that is most generalisable.
	– Bias towards evidence that is most timely.
	– Bias towards evidence that is easiest to access.

Table 8.2 (cont.)

	– Evidence can be most relevant to different policy stages (e.g. evidence relevant to agenda setting might be irrelevant to implementation).
	– Evidence can be reduced to a 'bullet point', distorting its meaning.
Nature of policy problems	– Real-world problems often demand urgent answers.
	– Drive for generalisable evidence can conflict with local conditions for policymaking.
	– Policy problems can involve values, moral or ethical concerns which do not always align easily with data.
	– Policy problems can elude consensus, even when evidence is apparent.
	– Problems can require multi-disciplinary responses which do not always align with how the research has been gathered.
Policymaking	– Runs to its own timetable.
	– Lack of transparency as to how policymakers can be reached.
	– Lack of transparency around how decisions are made.
	– Unrealistic expectations of researchers/evidence.
	– Interested in questions that can be impossible to answer in the current research context.
	– Variations in policymakers' experience and use of research (e.g. those with less experience tend to utilise formulaic processes more).
Politics	– Influence of other factors (resources, ideologies, practical considerations).
	– Politicians seen to pay 'lip-service' to research.
	– Politics becoming more polarised in some countries and less distinctive in others.
	– Connection back to evidence may not be clear when communicating decisions that have been taken.

Sources: Bogenschneider and Corbett (2010: 7–8); Sutcliffe and Court (2005: 3–9); Pawson (2006).

disciplinary variation in how your research might influence policy. Researchers are sometimes criticised in policy circles for maintaining an unrealistic perception of objectivity; however, many will have genuine questions and concerns as to how their role as a source of information for policymakers could compromise their integrity and politicise their work (Steel *et al.*, 2004; Cortner, 2000).

For example, social science, whilst perhaps an obvious contender for policy-linked activities, can be open to more visible uncertainty than some other disciplines; 'people talk back, they [people] change the "laws" which govern their behaviour and generally act in a way which creates difficulties from a research point of view' (Gustavsen, 1986: 153). Social scientists are often cautious, then, of their predictive power, which can mean clear solutions to a policymaker's problem are not always obvious. Openness to a policy role can also vary; though the historical roots of the social sciences are deeply linked to social problems, the principle that social research should be usable and with benefit to society has long been an area of contention (Turner, 2007; Heller, 1986). Social scientists' quest for purity in 'clean, well controlled and unprejudiced settings' (Levy-Leboyer, 1986: 33) would call into question, for some, the appropriateness of political influence as a social scientist (Hammersley, 2004) and the implied requirement to resolve significant social problems (Lauder *et al.*, 2004).

Regardless of disciplinary background, researchers may prefer to remain outside of the policy limelight; some have reported experiencing considerable political pressure in such roles: 'attacks', 'bullying' and 'vilification' when findings do not support a government agenda (Davies and Hosein, 2006). However, there are also some specific disciplines which are seen to be particularly allied to policymakers' needs; for example, economics proves amenable to evidence-based policymaking (Keith, 2008; McLaughlin and Turcotte, 2007; Sharpe, 1975).

Just as we might expect in a book focused on communication, there are, then, problems around differing needs in such a process, and a process which is still very much in its infancy: 'Evidence-based policy is much like all trysts, in which hope springs eternal and often outweighs expectancy, and for which the future is uncertain as we wait to know whether the partnership will flower or pass as an infatuation' (Pawson, 2006: 1).

Nevertheless it is clear that, despite these issues, many researchers today will be working in areas of policy relevance, be it issues associated with the economy, environment or culture which may require them to consider how they could communicate in such settings. How can such researchers go about this?

Communicating with policymakers

Communication is perceived to play a crucial role in setting policy-makers' agendas. For members of the research community, building a professional reputation, publishing in high-profile journals or creating 'knowledge brokerage' opportunities have all been identified as ways via which policymakers may be accessed. However, the communication trail is far from straightforward and the expectation of a linear or transmission model from researcher to policymaker has long been rejected (Lövbrand, 2007), just as it has with regard to members of the public.

Some of the problems researchers face when seeking to communicate with policymakers can include identifying which policymakers might be interested in their research and how to access them. Integration within a policymaking framework can result in researchers requiring new communication skills and approaches, in addition to opening them up to differing types of public scrutiny (Steel *et al.*, 2004). It is also of course important that you are confident in the evidence you have. From the policymakers' perspective it can be challenging to identify relevant research amongst the wealth of literature of relevance to their interests, or to recognise the most pertinent points amongst academic articles or conference presentations which may have a more traditional academic audience in mind (Sardo and Weitkamp, 2012). Just as researchers may struggle to identify and access policymakers, so too can policymakers find it challenging to identify and reach research expertise, often in timeframes which require prompt responses and timely, reliable information.

Some universities and research institutions have clear opportunities to engage with policy processes, for example in the United States what is known as the Wisconsin Idea, the principle that universities should reach beyond the classroom and provide knowledge and expertise of value to policymakers, government and society, seeks to foster university partnerships which align research and other activities to public policy needs (Bogenschneider and Corbett, 2010). There are also a number of other examples of organisations which are seen to directly align with policy-associated needs, for example, Science Shops and knowledge exchange offices, as well as research agencies, policy-focused units and research centres with specialist expertises which all provide clearer routes to academic expertise (see also Chapter 9). Think-tanks and advocacy groups also provide an opportunity to link to the world of policy, although it is important to bear in mind that such groups often have a far clearer political agenda, which may or may not be something you see as desirable. These types of opportunities have increased over time, as knowledge-broker roles have progressively been recognised. Knowledge brokers who manage, link, capacity build, facilitate, translate, network and communicate appear to be increasing as the amount of information we can access at our finger tips continues to escalate (Meyer, 2010).

Bogenschneider and Corbett (2010) provide a series of practical tips for researchers interested in these types of opportunities, including:

1   Ask the research questions in which policymakers are interested.
2   Appreciate that policymakers have different roles and decision making occurs at different levels. Some policymakers may need a quite general level of information, others will be more specialist and familiar with the specifics of your area of expertise.
3   Be aware that policymakers may have alternative responses to your research; your interpretation of evidence or data may not be the same as a policymaker's.
4   Remember that no one interaction with a policymaker will be the same, nor will experiences necessarily be built on or communication consistent.

Case study 8.2 Science for Environment Policy

Science for Environment Policy (SfEP) is a free news and information service which is tailored to help policymakers keep up to date with the latest environmental research. Ruth Larbey, Editor of SfEP, sums up the service as having two key purposes: 'To communicate the latest, rigorous, relevant scientific research on environmental topics in a quick, accessible and, importantly, free format every week. We want to feed good-quality evidence into environmental decisions made at regional, national and local levels, and especially into policies which affect lives, health and livelihoods in Europe and beyond.' Over 19,000 users subscribe to the service's weekly News Alert, which drops summaries of peer-reviewed environmental research and findings right into policymakers' inboxes. Managed by the Science Communication Unit at the University of the West of England, Bristol since 2006, the service is funded by the European Commission.

Crucially, the service deals with some of the main problems policymakers face in dealing with research, as Ruth describes. 'The primary problem – as with many of us – seems to be lack of time.' A related problem, says Ruth, 'is too much noise: finding effective ways of filtering the vast amount of information out there. Uncovering potential biases and investments, which could render conclusions unacceptable, can take a lot of time and effort as well. Policymakers may struggle to incorporate information from outside the walls of their particular "silo" – not only because of quantity, but because of incomparable methods, metrics or assumptions.' Ruth describes how the service is able to factor out some of these issues, as well as giving access to information from journals that can be prohibitively expensive for some policymakers.

Content for the service is judged on the basis of traditional news values, including the research's relevance to the audience, the quality and likely impact of the research, whether it is good or bad news, and also whether it reveals anything unexpected. Importantly, as Ruth shares, it mediates between the policymaker and scientist: 'the process of producing our publications is itself another way that the scientific evidence comes into contact with policymakers. In checking facts, statistics and methodologies, the SfEP team facilitates a conversation between researchers and policymakers, which sometimes makes evident differences of attitude or interpretation – which we try to discuss openly.'

SfEP has expanded from an emailed news alert, and policymakers can now follow the latest stories through the service's Twitter feed, access Thematic Issues and In-depth Reports focusing on specific policy topics or explore a Future Brief examining emerging environmental issues. Formal evaluations of the SfEP products suggest that it certainly meets policymakers' needs; it assists policymakers in using science in policymaking, helps them to understand science and to keep track of the latest research. A survey of researchers suggests that they also see benefits in their research being featured by the service: it brings their research to the attention of those in important organisations, people outside of their countries, and reaches policymakers as well as members of the public (Wilkinson and Weitkamp, 2013).

For other researchers interested in connecting with policymakers, Ruth shares some tips. She suggests that researchers should include a budget for communication at the inception of a research project, think about the needs of policymakers and be 'contactable, open to conversations and feedback, and keep your methods straightforward and understandable'. Whilst being published 'by a traditional scholarly outlet still seems to provide research with a veneer of authority', Ruth says newspapers, opinion pieces, policy journals, online blogs and discussions could also prove to be good routes of access and recommends a 'two-pronged approach'; 'get both an "authoritative" version, and short, accessible versions of your conclusions out there … and don't be too reticent about putting forward your interpretation'. As Ruth points out, 'policymakers are dealing with great uncertainty anyway – and they may prefer to hear an argument for a point of view than something presented as absolutely objective and stripped of meaning. Equally, don't try to market a self-sealed product that accounts for every policy nuance: let policymakers bring this knowledge and context to the table.'

Bogenschneider and Corbett's (2010) studies suggest that policymakers make judgements beyond evidence; they build relationships based on trust and common sense. So, whilst no one interaction may be repeated in future, it is worth remembering that if you do have a constructive relationship with a policymaker or group you may want to maintain that relationship. Benyon and David's (2008) interviews with government policymakers, research funders and commercial research organisations suggested that they often relied on known individuals or research centres when requiring academic advice or input. This tendency to

> **Box 8.3 Tips for communicating with policymakers**
>
> ---
>
> – Undertake training specifically on communicating with policymakers. Training that includes policymakers as speakers, or within the timetable, is particularly valuable.
>
> – Frame communication to raise awareness of issues, highlight policy implications and assumptions that policymakers might make.
>
> – Investigate policymakers who might be particularly relevant or interested in your work, consider how you can tailor your communications to them.
>
> – Speak to research managers or support organisations, to assist you in facilitating contact with networks and groups to which they may have access or of which they may be aware.
>
> *Source:* Based on Weitkamp (2012).

draw on individuals who are trusted and represent a similar perspective to political representatives or policymakers has been noted elsewhere (Sharpe, 1975).

Perhaps, then, a happy compromise is for researchers to be aware of the opportunities to reach policy circles, with a heavy dose of caution regarding how their research may or may not influence policy. Box 8.3 provides some final pointers for researchers looking to advance their communications in this way.

Summary

There will always be discussion around how, who and why people can participate and engage in political decision making and, as research touches on many peoples' lives, both publicly and privately, the twenty-first century has witnessed an increase in approaches for people to deliberate, participate and engage around such decisions. Opening up conversation in this way is not relevant to all research, nor would this necessarily be practically viable. It does not mean that any action or outcome will necessarily follow, as critiques of the process attest. Neither does it mean that knowledge and expertise are unimportant. Deliberation can have educational effects on both researchers and participating publics, increasing 'knowledge and understanding of the consequences of their actions … a strong motivation to constrain self-interest and to consider the public good' (John *et al.*, 2011: 11). Citizen participation is about creating a 'safe haven' (John *et al.*, 2011: 18).

Recognising and extending research to others through such processes values a potential contribution, but it may not be something all citizens deem as being without risk or as relevant to them.

Ironically, the rise in research, information, issues and agendas may in itself be part of the reason why people are now questioning the policymaking process, particularly where new and emerging areas of research are involved. We are reliant on layers and layers of people to make decisions on our behalf, with layers and layers of evidence and expertise. Policymakers attempt to draw on the best evidence, but the process from research to policy is complex and multifaceted, and it may not be a maze that all researchers are inclined to explore. Many of the tensions around public engagement and communication with policymakers (such as how it is defined, what is the purpose, and what outcomes it can have) exist because it is within a context which has fundamentally different drivers. Policymakers must consult and deliberate with both public and academic perspectives, but also incentivise and shelter research that will have economic benefit. Thorpe and Gregory (2010: 281) posit that engagement as an instrumental mechanism, a technique to increase public trust and confidence, reflects the elites' preference for public engagement, 'as a tool for producing societal conditions (e.g. public confidence) for innovation and post-industrial economic competition'. Thus, whilst political engagement with publics and policymakers has potential opportunities for researchers, it also has its weaknesses, and an awareness of this as a researcher helps to identify its appropriateness for you.

Further reading

Bogenschneider, K. and Corbett, T., *Evidence-Based Policymaking: Insights from Policy-Minded Researchers and Research-Minded Policymakers* (New York: Routledge, 2010).

9

Crowd-sourced research

This chapter explores opportunities for publics to participate in the research process (as researchers rather than as the subjects of research or in the governance of research). The chapter examines the growing field of what is sometimes described as citizen science, but also called crowd-sourced research, amongst other terms. Because the terms citizen science and DIY science have become current, they are used here, but the approaches should not be seen as exclusive to the natural sciences (see, for example, Dufau *et al.*, 2011 and Dunn and Hedges, 2013). These types of projects are applicable across a range of disciplines, including social sciences and the humanities. The chapter considers the ways in which non-experts and researchers might collaborate, including approaches like the Science Shops movement, as well as projects driven by individuals' interests, like hackspaces and the maker movement. Some of these might not, at first look, appear fruitful areas for research communication, but there are opportunities to tap into the existing interests and needs of people that also provide avenues for communication and engagement.

In this chapter, the term crowd-sourced research is used when referring to both top-down (research-led) and bottom-up (community-led) projects. Although citizen science projects can be community led, the chapter makes a distinction between these two approaches, using the term citizen science for those projects primarily designed to contribute to wider research agendas, and community-initiated research for projects primarily aimed at addressing community needs. DIY science is used when referring to projects that are less about scientific research than about catering to an individual's interests. This includes projects where individuals undertake research (or reprocess publicly available data) using the same methods as traditional research institutions, but without the traditional infrastructure, as well as projects aimed more at leisure interests, such as hackspace projects and the maker movement. Necessarily, people involved in DIY science have particular interests in the field of study, either personally or through a community need, and some will already have considerable research or technical skills and expertise, so it is important not to make assumptions about background or expertise.

Key to what differentiates crowd-sourced research, and particularly citizen science, from other forms of public engagement, is the intention to 'produce sound science. Citizen science projects, for example, usually incorporate means of assuring the quality of the research activities according to accepted scientific norms' (Wiggins and Crowston, 2015: np). Judging the projects by scientific standards has raised questions from the research community about the quality of the data, though the large data sets collected can offset these concerns, especially when supported by clear and well-designed research protocols (Grand *et al.*, 2014).

Who participates?

Some research has begun to emerge regarding the likely participants in crowd-sourced research. In the citizen science realm, the creators of Galaxy Zoo, a long-running project that has citizens classifying galaxies, have explored why people participate in the project (Raddick *et al.*, 2013; Raddick *et al.*, 2010). Galaxy Zoo attracts more male (80 percent) than female participants, which is also reflected in participation in amateur astronomy projects in general, so the demographic bias is likely related to the subject rather than to participation in citizen science projects more generally. Although responses to the Galaxy Zoo survey were received from participants in 118 countries, there was a strong bias towards participants from the United States and United Kingdom. While it is possible to reach international audiences with internet-based citizen science projects, attracting these audiences is challenging. The Galaxy Zoo team (which is based in the United States) note that they had large increases in volunteers signing up from the UK following a BBC report on the project, highlighting the importance of publicity for recruitment internationally.

In terms of motivations to participate in citizen science projects, Dunn and Hedges (2013), exploring humanities research, noted personal and altruistic, as well as intrinsic and extrinsic, motivations for participation. Raddick *et al.* (2013) found that identification with the project goals and interest in scientific content were the primary motives for participation, while learning and participating in a social community were less frequently cited as reasons. They also noted differences between men and women in the responses, with women more motivated by the beauty of galaxies and the fun of classification and men more motivated by an interest in the science. However, the most common primary motivation was to contribute to scientific research, which suggests that there are many potential volunteers who would value the opportunity to contribute to research studies.

Dougherty (2014) explored the identities of attendees at the Lisbon Maker Faire, described as a show-and-tell for people to demonstrate what they are making, and show what they are learning (Maker Faires are discussed below in the section on DIY science). The majority of attendees used the terms hobbyist, tinkerer, builder and engineer to identify themselves. Half of makers responding to the survey indicated that making is a social endeavour, though these collaborations may be conducted via the internet rather than face-to-face. The social aspect of participation in hackspaces, which are effectively community workshops and are also discussed in more detail below, was also identified by Charter and Keiller (2014). However, environmental motivations dominated amongst repair café participants, with volunteers indicating a desire to help others live more sustainably, to provide a service to the community or to extend the life of products as primary motivations (Charter and Keiller, 2014). Altruistic motivations have also been associated with citizen science projects (Dunn and Hedges, 2013, Bonney *et al.*, 2009). Respondents to Dougherty's survey at the Lisbon Maker Faire were overwhelmingly male (81 percent) and had postgraduate qualifications (80 percent), making them a highly educated group. Charter and Keiller (2014) found a similar gender and educational balance in hackspaces (90 percent male, 70 percent with bachelor's or postgraduate qualification). Although more women participated in repair cafés (Charter and Keiller, 2014), this was still primarily a male endeavour (60 percent men, 40 percent women). As with hackspaces, 70 percent of participants in repair cafés have a bachelor's or postgraduate degree.

Riesch and Potter (2014: 117) point to the need for the public to gain something from participation: interviewees and project managers involved in citizen science projects both 'consistently stressed that the public need to get something tangible for themselves in return for participating, and this is something we feel needs to be made explicit in the design of future CS [citizen science] projects, especially those that may not be particularly focussed on public engagement and therefore would need to find value for participants through other ways'. Dunn and Hedges (2013: 153) argue that participation in such projects may offer a range of benefits to participants, including 'the fulfilment of an interest in the subject; personal gains such as skills, experience or knowledge;

some form of status; or a feeling of gratification'. They also observe that project-related social networking tools may foster a sense of community amongst participants that can extend beyond the life of the project.

Citizen science

In many respects citizen science is not new; bird counts, for example, have been taking place for over a hundred years in the United States with the annual Christmas bird count. Archaeology, astronomy and natural history have strong traditions of involving volunteers in research and/or existing communities with significant interests and research skills – communities which have sometimes been termed 'amateur' scientists. However, the value of citizen contributions to formal research is increasingly recognised, and a large number of projects are springing up around the world that include contributions from interested amateurs and local communities, often but not always under the umbrella of 'citizen science'. 'Today, most citizen scientists work with professional counterparts on projects that have been specifically designed or adapted to give amateurs a role, either for the educational benefit of the volunteers themselves or for the benefit of the project. The best examples benefit both' (Silvertown, 2009: 467). The explosion in the popularity of citizen science projects is at least partly a result of widely available digital tools that facilitate participation in data collection and processing. Whether it is classifying galaxies for Galaxyzoo.org, submitting your Nature Watch observations by email or using your mobile phone to submit animal and bird pictures to the South African Virtual Museum project,[1] there are now many opportunities for the public to contribute to research projects.

While citizen science may not be new, changes in technology, particularly the growth in handheld or mobile technologies, makes it far easier for public participants to collect and submit data to researchers, essentially acting as human 'sensors' (see Case study 9.1, on citizen journalism). Equally, digital technologies, such as gaming platforms, mean that it is now easier to design data processing approaches that appeal to the public, who may 'play the game' while also valuing the feeling that they are contributing to scientific research (see Chapter 6). Involvement in projects which bring publics together with researchers may, therefore, enable research issues or data processing problems to be treated using novel approaches, potentially bringing researchers, data and publics together in new ways. In this section we use the distinction proposed by Nascimento, Guimaraes Pereira and Ghezzi (2014), that citizen science projects can be distinguished from other types of grassroots initiatives because they are institutionally led.

Case study 9.1 Citizen journalists contributing to public health

Professor Pascale Allotey, Professor of Public Health at Monash University Malaysia, is combining citizen science and citizen journalism in a new project that is designed to build skills within local communities while at the same time involving them in identifying health priorities. The project will train local community members in science reporting, sharing with them public health research findings from Monash University. Once trained, the reporters will explore public health needs and priorities with local community members, feeding information back to the public health team through their journalism. 'The project will build the capacity of members of the community as trained citizen science reporters to write articles from their perspectives,' Pascale said.

Established as a research platform by an international partnership of universities, South East Asia Community Observatory (SEACO) is a generic research platform capable of supporting a wide range of multidisciplinary and interdisciplinary research in the clinical and biomedical sciences, the social sciences, economics, education and environmental sciences. Pascale is using the platform for longitudinal life-course monitoring of health and well-being at a population level. She feels that traditional methods of collecting data, which typically involve interviews at specific points in time, would offer a limited perspective, since interviewees often focus on issues of immediate interest. Instead, she wanted to create 'a process through which there could be continuous engagement between SEACO and the community so that they could actively participate in a dynamic research process, with an understanding that the research that we undertook was collaborative.'

She believes this type of approach offers three key benefits to local communities: first, it empowers the community to identify their own health priorities and enables them to advocate for change. Second, it facilitates a participatory process for public engagement in health research. And third, it enables the development of strategies for the communication of health research to communities by communities.

The approach is not without challenges, however. Citizen journalism projects generally need a strong focus on ethics and understanding of privacy as part of the training. 'We would, for instance, discourage a "name and shame" approach to identifying problems in the community,' Pascale explains. In some countries, there are also restrictions on internet content which could present challenges to this type of approach.

SEACO has already recruited 40,000 ethnically Malay, Chinese and Indian people in five sub-districts in Segamat, Johor, Malaysia. The Citizen Science Reporters project also involves an NGO that specialises in citizen journalism to train members of the general public from all age groups to enable them to report news and current events from around Malaysia via professionally edited video footage filmed using smartphones. 'As part of the training, reporters learn how to set up their own YouTube channel to publish their stories and SEACO only picks up these stories with permission from the citizen reporter,' said Pascale. The content will focus on a range of age-appropriate population science topics, with citizen reporters compiling human-interest stories about population health issues within their communities.

The work aims to help identify new population health priority areas from the community's perspective and to report on the community's perceptions of their involvement in research. It also offers an opportunity, through regular workshops, for participants to learn about SEACO research and how the citizen involvement is informing the SEACO research agenda. Pascale highlights that this approach 'needs to include opportunities for participants to be comfortable with and understand smartphone technology, as well as to recognise the quality of different types of journalistic pieces (e.g. news formats vs documentaries)'. Citizen journalists may also need training to recognise the needs of their audience.

Bonney *et al.* (2009: 10) define three types of citizen science projects based on the level of public involvement:

> *Contributory projects*, which are generally designed by scientists and for which members of the public primarily contribute data; *Collaborative projects*, which are generally designed by scientists and for which members of the public contribute data but also may help to refine project design, analyze data, or disseminate findings; *Co-created projects*, which are designed by scientists and members of the public working together and for which at least some of the public participants are actively involved in most or all steps of the scientific process.

It is worth noting that all three levels of public involvement described by Bonney *et al.* (2009) highlight the involvement of professional scientists and scientific institutions as either directing or having equal ownership of the research question. These differing levels of participation can also affect community-initiated projects and approaches designed to enable citizen access to scientific resources (e.g. through Science Shops), though the fact that the problem is owned by the community or individuals suggests that most will be classed as co-created projects and the differing levels of involvement affect individual participants more than the project as a whole.

Levels of participation are likely to vary, and projects may be designed to enable citizens to choose an appropriate level of participation for them. Citizen science projects also typically involve at least a little interaction between researchers and the public; some projects involve substantial interaction for some members of the public, as citizens may be involved in project design and work together with scientists to create robust research protocols. However, there are plenty of examples of citizen science projects that offer little scope for interaction for the majority of the public, and some public participants may want only limited involvement, so it is important to consider at the start of any project involving citizens in research the extent to which you and they are seeking interaction.

Smartphones and mobile computing offer unprecedented opportunities to collect and verify data on a variety of research topics and to involve citizens in the process of data collection, but not all citizens who might engage with these projects necessarily want to use these tools. So another factor to consider at the design stage is the tools your participants are willing to use, highlighting the need to involve potential participants early in the design process. As Graham *et al.* (2011: 315) point out in relation to mobile technology, 'the need to constantly evaluate, revise, and refine mobile tools based on what users are willing to do, what they can do with confidence, and what they expect in return, while also meeting the data requirements of the scientific community, makes developing mobile apps for citizen science projects an interesting challenge'. These same issues apply to many other aspects of citizen science projects: you have to have a very clear idea of what your potential participants are willing to do and the types of technologies with which they will engage. Table 9.1 outlines a process that should help you design an effective and satisfying project, ensuring that you consider both the research needs and public participants' desires.

Questions remain about citizen science and the benefits that may accrue to research and participants alike. For example, questions arise about the ways in which lay people are involved in research projects, with some arguing that many citizen science projects offer only very limited opportunities for public involvement (see, for example, Nascimento, Guimaraes Pereira and Ghezzi, 2014) and others questioning whether the public should be seen as a 'free resource'. Even in situations where the researchers involved in a citizen science project see potential wider benefits of the approach for lay participants, tensions arise regarding the roles that researchers play. As Riesch *et al.* (2013: 15) report in relation to the OPAL project, a citizen science project on exploring the local environment:

> Performing hybrid research and communication roles left people feeling often unable to give both sides of CS [citizen science] the attention they deserve without having to work extra hours, and possibly damaging future academic careers. Separating research from communication roles however removes the advantage for the public of interacting with genuine scientists. Again, because research and PE [public engagement] are intimately intertwined, this is a more intractable problem for CS

Table 9.1 Key planning steps for citizen science projects

Stage 1: Project initiation	Assemble project team. Ideally, team should comprise scientific experts, citizens, data analysis experts.
	Set clear research question/s.
	Consider duration and longevity of programme.
Stage 2: Design project	Set clear aims for the project.
	Provide definitions for scientific terms and any other necessary materials.
	Consider how participants will be recruited (e.g. is there an existing organisation through which you might recruit participants?).
	Develop methods to assess and monitor project, provide feedback to participants.
Stage 3: Design data collection tools	Develop a clear, easy-to-use protocol.
	Determine how data are to be collected (e.g. paper, email, app). Ensure these are appropriate to the skills and resources of likely participants.
	Consider cost to participants (e.g. submission via app may be expensive).
	Consider validation and verification of data.
	Devise data analysis methods.
	Consider data display and opportunities to share findings with participants.
	Test methods and refine.
Stage 4: Initiate project	Recruit participants and provide necessary training.
	Collect and analyse data.
	Disseminate results, including to participants.

Source: Adapted from Donnelly *et al.* (2014)

because it is not possible to separate communication from science activities, and scientists are therefore not in a position to back out of their communication activities: A scientist can cancel a public lecture or say no to appearing on radio if they felt they need to concentrate on their science, but no is not an option when the science itself relies on the performance of effective communication activities.

But perhaps the strongest concerns have been raised by those studying citizen science projects from the participants' perspectives. Good-quality citizen science projects do provide interesting and engaging opportunities for participation in and learning about research. However, there is a danger that researchers looking to ride on the coat tails of the latest trendy public engagement tool will create projects that fall short of

citizens' expectations, tarnishing a concept which has offered many interesting insights and opportunities for the public to learn about and engage
with research. Concerns have also been raised that some researchers now
view the public as a free resource to help further their research, raising
questions about the way that the public are involved and the credit
they may share in the discoveries they make (there are examples, which
are perhaps becoming more common, of members of the public being
credited or even given authorship on papers to emerge from their work).
Interestingly, in the case of humanities research, Dunn and Hedges (2013:
165) argue 'that most humanities scholars that have used crowd-sourcing
as part of some research activity agree that it is not simply a form of
"cheap labour" for mass digitisation or resource enhancement; indeed,
in a narrowly cost-benefit sense it does not always compare well with
more conventional mechanisms of digitisation'. Instead, they suggest that
'creativity, enthusiasm and alternative foci that communities outside that
academy can bring to academic research is a resource that is now ripe for
tapping into' (Dunn and Hedges, 2013: 165).

The growing popularity of citizen science projects (and perhaps the
somewhat misleading name) has also led to the emergence of projects
that lack involvement from researchers. These citizen-driven projects
can be valuable, but, as mentioned before, there are concerns about the
quality of data produced and, without expert verification, the potential
scientific value of the data collected may be questioned (Grand *et al.*,
2014) – an issue which may also affect DIY science projects. Projects
that lack expert involvement in at least one stage may struggle to make
a clear contribution from a research (or legal) perspective, though there
may well be benefits to participants from the perspective of engagement,
or educational benefits.

Community-initiated research

A few projects have emerged which seek to provide communities with
access to research support and skills, notably the Science Shops and open
source movements. These initiatives recognise that communities face
problems, such as environmental pollution, but may not have the skills
or resources to gather evidence that would allow them to address the
issues. In some cases, communities are able to locate researchers willing
to explore citizen science-oriented approaches, as discussed above. But
there are other ways to facilitate community access to research, and
to enable public participation in the creation, collection and analysis
of data. Through such participation, projects such as the online open
source project Public Lab (see Case study 9.2) seek to enable individuals
and communities to advocate for change.

Approaches such as the Public Lab draw on two framings of citizen science proposed independently by Irwin (1995) and Bonney *et al.* (2009). Alan Irwin (1995) describes citizen science as combining the concepts of science as assisting citizens to address their needs with the notion that citizens have important contributions to make to science through, for example, contextualising knowledge. Bonney *et al.* (2009) use the term Citizen Science to describe projects which involve lay publics in some (or all) stages of the research process, also sometimes referred to as public participation in research; this definition is more closely aligned to the definition which has been used in the preceding section. Irwin's work highlights important aspects of community-oriented research: that communities may face specific problems which are not addressed by institutional science (perhaps because they are small or local, or well known in other contexts) and that communities may apply their local knowledge and perspectives to shed new light on old problems.

Case study 9.2 Public Lab: supporting communities to tackle environmental concerns

In the aftermath of the BP oil spill in the Gulf of Mexico in 2010, Shannon Dosemagen, now Executive Director of Public Lab, discovered how difficult it can be for local communities to get information about the scale and likely impacts of an ongoing environmental disaster. As Shannon explains, she and several other people who later became co-founders of Public Lab 'started launching balloons and kites about 2,500 feet in the air and capturing images. We did this both as a means of capturing information and also as a way to engage people that were in the Gulf coastal region who wanted to participate in clean-up efforts but didn't have that opportunity.' The balloon and kite project ultimately involved around 250 people and collected hundreds of thousands of images over a five-month period.

This project got the organisers thinking about the need for a platform that would help communities and individuals who wanted to investigate local environmental concerns. When Shannon started looking at the tools available for environmental monitoring, she discovered that, while they were available, their cost meant that in reality they were accessible only to corporations, research institutions and government agencies. Public Lab was founded to see if they could change that dynamic by creating low-cost tools and embedding them in a social methodology that enabled everyday citizens to access and use them.

A key part of the Public Lab approach is valuing the expertise of local communities. As Shannon explains, 'We wanted to create a space where different types of expertise could collaborate on the same plane. When you look at citizen science, many times you'll see a researcher posing a problem and asking people to give them information or data points that they can use for their research. But for us we wanted to rethink that model and recognise that of course there is scientific expertise but there is also local expertise.'

Staff at Public Lab, which is a not-for-profit organisation, also bring a wide range of expertise, from technical skills to design, education and also staff with specific skills in community organisation. Staff are distributed in local chapters within North America and work directly with communities there, but Public Lab also works with local organisers (unpaid) around the world who use the Public Lab tools and methods to support local projects. There is also a broader community of around 5,500 who use Public Lab resources (available through the website, http://publiclab.org/) and tools, such as a spectrometer, to address specific interests.

But Public Lab provides more than technology. The Community Development team works closely with communities. 'We work with people to develop a research question, to help them think through the hardware tools they need and work with them on a software analysis platform, so that there is a cohesive place for data to be stored and accessed, and help them do the data analysis. We also have a person who works on the tail end, helping communities to use data for action,' Shannon said.

Public Lab focuses on environmental pollution, but the resources it provides and the wider community tackle a broader range of issues. As Shannon sees it, 'We're providing infrastructure, the website where people can post research notes, host place pages and set up a listserv for their area.'

As Public Lab has developed, so has interest in projects and platforms that facilitate community access to research skills and knowledge. Reflecting on the increased attention to this area, Shannon urges others interested in enabling community research to be 'cautious about just creating technology for the sake of creating technology and not thinking about the reasons why people might want to be involved and the social methods that are embedded in the work you are doing. I feel disappointed when I see one-off technology projects that are not supported by broader social methods of engagement.'

D'Ignazio *et al.* (2014) argue the case for 'small data' (as opposed to 'big data'), which are owned by the communities that collect the data and which allow them to investigate and address local environmental (and other) risks. They argue that while some organisations are providing access to data (usually large datasets), 'for such "open data" to empower the public to make informed decisions, vote wisely, or wisely engage in collective action, more must be achieved: the data must be rendered legible, and meaningful, for the various public audiences' (D'Ignazio *et al.*, 2014: 117). Community ownership of the whole research process requires the communication aspects to be considered at the outset in 'small data' projects, as well as issues of access and ownership of the data, making community-initiated research approaches closer to Irwin's definition of citizen science.

University College London refers to such a bottom-up approach as 'extreme citizen science', defining it as a 'situated, bottom-up practice that takes into account local needs, practices and culture and works with broad networks of people to design and build new devices and knowledge creation processes that can transform the world' (Anon, nd: np). Using an interdisciplinary approach, the UCL 'extreme citizen science' group seeks to design technologies that enable local people to understand their local environment. Similar to Public Lab, this group helps communities to engage with scientific methodologies to address specific environmental issues. Its Intelligent Maps project is being tested in the Republic of the Congo as a means of helping communities develop 'Community Memories' that explore the state of their local environment, their relationship with that environment, and identify and address environmental threats. For example, in one project under the 'extreme citizen science' banner, Mbendjele hunter gatherers are combining their detailed environmental knowledge with data collected using smartphones to 'improve the control of commercial hunters and diminish the harassment they [Mbendjele hunter gatherers] often experience at the hands of "eco-guards" who enforce hunting regulations' (Vitos *et al.*, 2013: 1).

Science Shops

Science Shops also enable community-initiated research. However, unlike the approach of projects like Public Lab, which draws on principles from the open source software movement, Science Shops are local by nature, giving communities in the areas surrounding a participating university or research centre access to their skills and expertise. Science Shops are usually, but not always, linked to a university or research centre and the services are often provided by students (DeBok and Steinhaus, 2008). Thus, Science Shops act as a bridge, or way in, for local communities to access local research expertise. Emerging in the Netherlands in the 1970s (Watchelder, 2003), Science Shops carry out research on behalf of the local community and individuals. Although Science Shops are diverse, and provide access to a wide range of research disciplines, they do have two key elements in common: they serve the local community and they are not-for-profit enterprises (European Commission, 2015). In their original conception, Dutch Science Shops offered access to a wide range of research skills and disciplines, not limited to the natural sciences but including humanities and social science research methodologies and expertise (Watchelder, 2003).

The original non-profit structure has continued, with some Science

Shops operated by students outside of the university administration, but other models have also emerged, including consultancy-based approaches where community (and sometimes commercial) organisations pay for services provided by skilled, professional researchers, and university-operated shops where students largely do the research (which is supervised by faculty) and which aim to demonstrate the value of the university to society at large (Watchelder, 2003). These university-operated shops may provide services both with and without charge to clients. Examples of Science Shops have elaborated on these ways of working, adapting them to new contexts. Most draw on the original principles of providing community groups with access to research expertise, often with the explicit intention to value community expertise and therefore additionally offering opportunities for community involvement throughout the process (Tryon and Ross, 2012). As such, Science Shops are 'an important instrument that helps NGOs and local communities to participate in decision-making procedures' (DeBok and Steinhaus, 2008: 167).

DIY science

DIY may be associated with poorly constructed cabinets and faulty wiring, but DIY science is something else entirely (though it may involve both poor and faulty workmanship). Nor is the DIY science discussed in this chapter in the realms of projects to do with kids in the kitchen, though DIY science may indeed involve the kitchen. Instead, in this chapter, DIY science takes us into the realms of hackspaces and garden laboratories; it's about people conducting research or creating knowledge outside traditional research institutions. DIY science draws on the 'open source everything' paradigm proposed by Steele (2012) and is perhaps most obvious in the computer science and electronics fields. However, the free format of DIY science means it has potential in a wide range of research domains (not all of which might be classically thought of as science). The more individual forms of DIY science should, perhaps, also come with a health warning, as practitioners can land themselves in jail, as Richard Handl, from Ångleholm in Sweden, discovered when he attempted to split the atom (yes, nuclear fission) in his kitchen.[2]

There have probably always been maverick researchers, some of whom, now lost in the depths of history, may well have invented the marvellous tools we take for granted today, such as the wheel. Certainly, until relatively recently, most research was conducted outside of the institutions we now associate with research endeavour (Chapter 2 touches on this in the context of communication with the public); as we saw in the preceding sections of this chapter, keen amateurs and those with particular interests are contributing to research carried out under the auspices of formal institutions. But there are also ways for researchers to engage interested 'amateurs' outside these formal research spaces, including makerspaces, hackspaces and FabLabs (fabrication laboratories). 'The DIY scientist appears as someone who tinkers, hacks, fixes, recreates and assembles objects and systems in creative and unexpected directions, usually using open-source tools and adhering to open paradigms to share knowledge and outputs with others' (Nascimento, Guimaraes Pereira and Ghezzi, 2014: 30). The distinction made in this chapter between community-initiated research and DIY science is one of scale and purpose: we define DIY science as small group or individuals pursuing projects through personal interest. These are, by definition, 'interested' publics.

Makerspaces, hackspaces and FabLabs are workshops and spaces that allow members to access tools and work independently or collaboratively. FabLabs, for example, 'provide widespread access to modern means for invention. They began as an outreach project from MIT's Center for Bits and Atoms (CBA), and became a collaborative and global network' (www.fabfoundation.org). Like hackspaces, the FabLab network is global, and the foundation runs a Fab Academy that trains those wishing to start their own FabLab. There are even programmes designed to support these engaged individuals to undertake their own research, such as SpaceGAMBIT, which launched an open funding call for projects in 2013. SpaceGAMBIT aims to democratise space research, and by working 'with partners and the maker movement to find out what's keeping us stuck on Earth, engage the crowd to find solutions, and share the results with the world'.

How can the research communicator engage with individuals using such spaces? First is to identify which of the variety of DIY science initiatives most suits your own research area. Sources such as Dougherty's (2014) study of attendees at the Lisbon Maker Faire provide insights into the motivations of participants at particular types of projects (see also Charter and Keiller, 2014 for a study on repair cafés and hackspaces). Second, it might be helpful to keep an open mind regarding what you might offer. Maker Faires provide a platform for speakers, so may provide a suitable venue for a public lecture, provided it is practical in nature (speakers are typically makers, but there is no reason why a researcher could not also submit a proposal). Local hackspaces may also offer such opportunities, such as the Kiberpipa in Ljubljana, Slovenia, which focuses on open source computing, or the Dublin Music Hackspace, which provides a space for musicians to collaborate on DIY projects.

Equally, these open source communities can be places for the creation of collaborative projects that provide an opportunity for discussion of technologies or issues arising from your research: the collaborative project might directly relate to your research, or it might be that the collaborative project provides an opening for discussion of issues faced by the community and on which your research sheds light, such as internet security. The Slovenian NanoSmano project, for example, brings artists, scientists and hackers together for participatory workshops which are designed to allow interactions between different forms of knowledge with a view to democratising nanotechnology research (Kera, 2012). Similar projects, such as the Science Hack Day (which is actually forty-eight hours), also bring together special interest groups and researchers. The Smart Citizen Project, which started with a collaboration between FabLab Barcelona and the Institute for Advanced Architecture of Catalonia, seeks to enable lay people to participate in local decisions, using open source technologies. The project taps into the interests and expertise of the Institute for Advanced Architecture of Catalonia in the areas of architecture and technology and how these affect human habitation and has created a platform that allows individuals to monitor their local environment: it has sensors to measure air composition, temperature, light intensity, sound levels and humidity. These are just a few examples of the ways that researchers might engage interested publics through DIY initiatives such as hackspaces, Maker Faires and FabLabs. These are technology-driven enterprises and, as such, it is likely you will be able to use the internet to identify local or subject-specific interest groups that you might approach with an idea for a lecture or other type of research communication project.

Summary

Interest from the research community in crowd-sourced research approaches has increased, with examples of projects spanning the humanities and natural sciences. While many crowd-sourced research approaches are led from the research community, there are a number of examples of projects that build on the open science/open source movement to provide communities and individuals with access to research tools and expertise, with a view to enabling them to tackle local issues more effectively and from a sound research base.

These platforms offer new ways for researchers to engage with the public. Citizen science approaches enable research that would otherwise be difficult to carry out, while at the same time offering lay people insights into the research process and community. These approaches are not unproblematic, as citizen scientists may be seen as a free resource, who receive little reward for their efforts. Equally, the use of 'free' citizen labour may be at the expense of providing career opportunities for skilled researchers. At the other end of the spectrum are projects that tap into the particular interests of specific communities, such as maker and hacker communities. While some examples of this type of approach are discussed here, the opportunities are limited only by your own creativity in project design.

Notes

1 The Animal Demography Unit of the University of Cape Town has a number of projects involving citizens in mapping the animal and birdlife of South Africa. See: http://vmus.adu.org.za/.
2 www.theguardian.com/science/2012/feb/03/jon-ronson-diy-science-experiments.

Recommended reading

Dunn, S. and Hedges, M., 'Crowd-sourcing as a component of humanities research infrastructures', *International Journal of Humanities and Arts Computing* 7.1–2 (2013): 147–69.
Irwin, A., *Citizen Science* (London: Routledge, 1995).
Nascimento, S., Guimaraes Pereira, A., Ghezzi, A. *From Citizen Science to Do It Yourself Science: An Annotated Account of an Ongoing Movement* (Ispra, Italy: European Commission, 2014).

PART III

Conclusion

10

Impact

The word 'impact' is a real buzz word in academic fields, to the extent that we questioned whether it was risky to title a chapter 'impact'. The danger with popular terminology is that as swiftly as it comes into fashion, so too can it be disowned, but it is important to recognise that many of the issues bound up in 'impact' are not new to research communication. What does impact mean? If we start simply, the *Oxford English Dictionary* defines impact as 'the effective action of one thing or person upon another; the effect of such action; influence; impression'. However, as we will come to later in this chapter, impact also has other important connotations that it is useful to consider. Impact and evaluation can be interlinked, but they have subtly different implications. Evaluation is frequently focused on the outcomes of an activity, which can often be obvious and immediate, whereas impact would imply there has been some longer-term influence or change. In research communication we have an interest both in how evaluation can be designed to factor in outcomes and impacts, and also in how the evaluation of research communication activities can itself support evidence of the impact of research.

This chapter will start with an overview of why and how to evaluate communication and engagement projects, including discussion of different types of evaluation such as formative, process and summative which you might think about in relation to communication activities. This will include consideration of the approaches you might use, such as document analysis, questionnaires, observations, interviewing or focus groups. We will also think about creative evaluation techniques: are there ways that evaluation can be more creative, valuable or novel? What benefits and risks might this bring to evaluation? If you are new to evaluation methods we will also briefly consider how you would analyse such data, for example via qualitative or quantitative analysis techniques, as well as provide some tips on key computer packages and programmes in the area to assist researchers.

Finally, returning to the matter of the emphasis on impact, we will also consider how communication and engagement activities can influence your research profile. The contemporary focus on outcomes and impact through communication will be outlined, including discussion as to whether only positive outcomes are a sign of good engagement. We will complete the chapter with a discussion of the impact agenda and how communication and engagement is increasingly coming to be framed as 'research impact', and the implications of this for researchers, PhD students and undergraduates.

Why evaluate?

Evaluation approaches have a long history and are used across a variety of settings. In the broadest sense, 'evaluation includes all efforts to place value on events, things, processes, or people', although, more tightly defined, evaluation is commonly found in the fields of health and social intervention programmes, as well as in settings as diverse as advertising, political campaigning, human resources, commercial and industrial contexts (DePoy and Gilson, 2008; Rossi, Freeman and Lipsey, 1999: 4). The utilisation of social science research methods within evaluation has been commonplace since the 1930s, influenced by the increased availability of such research within universities, as well as by the rise in social programmes and interventions across many countries in Asia, Africa and Latin America, as well as in the United States and Europe (Rossi *et al.*, 1999). Around the same time, specific locations for research communication, such as museums, also began to pay increased attention to reliable research on the character, needs and habits of visitors. The fascination with evaluation has steadily grown as drivers towards the evidence of benefits and outcomes from social and cultural practices have increased, influenced by a climate of competition, economic sensitivity and performance management (Hoggarth and Comfort, 2010; DePoy and Gilson, 2008), which encourages practitioners to evidence the outcomes and impacts of their work. As Hoggarth and Comfort (2010: 26) state, the ability to evidence outcomes 'has become an essential skill simply for survival in the modern context', as so few services and organisations now have permanent funding.

In terms of research communication, an emphasis on including evaluation within activities developed in parallel with increased dedicated funding opportunities for research communication activities through the latter half of the twentieth century. Funders have multiple reasons for encouraging evaluation within projects: it allows them to monitor that aims have been achieved; the success and pitfalls of particular approaches, opportunities or collaborations; and provides scope to consider the broader field of activities which they might be supporting. Unfortunately, the encouragement amongst funders to embed evaluation in communication projects may, at times, drive researchers to see funders' requirements as the ultimate purpose for evaluation, rendering invisible some of its other important benefits.

For instance, an evaluation might help a researcher to identify problems in a project which they can then rectify and it also allows them to share that learning with others, which can prevent others repeating mistakes in future projects. An evaluation, depending on its quantity and quality, may in itself form an opportunity for dissemination if, for example, it is written up for academic publication or reporting. However, perhaps most importantly, evaluation has important benefits for participants in projects; it drives improvements in quality, provides transparency and openness, and encourages participants to 'speak up' about their experience of a project or event. It can also promote innovation, particularly when working with inventive techniques or participants who may not typically be seen as responsive to research communication. From a participant's perspective, an evaluation might help them to see what they have achieved or taken from their involvement, as well as bring closure to their participation (Hoggarth and Comfort, 2010).

Returning to the idea that we are encouraged by many research communication funders to evaluate a project, this can create one of the first sticking points in evaluation design; all too often we might associate evaluation with the end point of our project, the final reporting about its accomplishments that we will complete, distracting us from the multiple purposes and contributions that evaluation can offer. Instead it is sensible to think about evaluation at three key stages: formative, process and summative.

Formative, process and summative evaluation

Before discussing these three types of evaluation in detail it is helpful to define some other terms you will come into contact with when evaluating. First, you might have your 'activity', for instance a public talk which you have created; next you would have your 'output' – this might be the number of times you give that talk, and this may then have an 'outcome', perhaps an immediate raised awareness of your research, followed by an 'impact', perhaps some kind of policy attention or change based on your data or ideas (Owl Re, 2008: 1). Outcomes and impacts are sometimes confused or used interchangeably; impact would typically imply a longer-term rather than short-term outcome (Hoggarth and Comfort, 2010).

Formative work occurs before a communication activity has occurred and can provide vital information regarding how you might design or develop your efforts. It is something with which most researchers will be familiar, as typically research design includes a feasibility or pilot stage. However, often we can forget about the importance of testing things out where communication is concerned; applying the same principles provides almost exactly the same benefits. Formative evaluation might include trying out tools or techniques, collecting some data on participants' wants or needs, or doing some detailed preliminary research on similar activities or projects. The scale of a formative evaluation is likely to vary, depending on the magnitude of the communication efforts planned, and whilst it sounds obvious that you should 'do your research' on what you envisage carrying out, it's surprising how often researchers forget this when facing a substantial communication effort for the first time. For a small project, designed, say, for schools, formative work might involve simply speaking to a teacher to find out a bit more about the needs and context; for a larger project it might be that a pilot activity with a whole student group is indispensable. If you are using a method that is already well tried and tested in research communication, then formative evaluation may not necessarily be needed (RCUK, 2011); instead, you might draw on examples of some other projects as 'proof of concept'. Not only does formative evaluation help to design the best content possible, but it also allows us to iron out issues before they occur, and funders like to see an awareness of this. Presenting some data (even if relatively informal) from a formative evaluation in a funding application reduces the uncertainty around ideas or plans.

Next comes process evaluation, and again, this might be something you habitually do as a researcher, though perhaps do not think about in the context of your evaluation design. Once a communication activity is up and running, particularly if there are multiple people involved, it's likely that you will be talking, discussing and conversing on what is happening in the project. Process evaluation captures this; it might include things like minutes or notes from meetings, reflective diaries on the project or some basic analysis of summative evaluation data that are being collected. Like formative evaluation, process evaluation reduces the risks around a project; if things aren't going as planned, there is time to learn from that and make changes, or to seek support and advice. When working with collaborators, perhaps from different perspectives or disciplines, process evaluation is a good way to capture multiple learning and insights. Process evaluation is particularly helpful to include when working with participants over extended periods; often such participants are giving up more, be it time, ideas or contributions, to such activities, and so having an up-front method to capture their experiences throughout can encourage a greater sense of inclusiveness around a project.

Finally, we have summative evaluation, and this tends to be the stage of evaluation with which most researchers will feel fairly comfortable. Summative evaluation tends to focus on the conclusion of a project: what are its outcomes and impacts? There are numerous routes to collect data for this stage, as we will come to later in this chapter, but the most important thing is that it is planned early on, in any activities. Although it is summative, thinking about evaluation at a late stage as a cumulative end point can mean that we don't leave much time for the design or analysis of data collection methods. There are also often important things to consider which might need to be embedded earlier in the project; to again take the example of a schools-based project, it might be important to collect some evaluation data before a project intervention, particularly if there are plans to consider any type of direct outcome or change. It's also worth bearing in mind that if an activity might develop further, perhaps applying for more funding or changing it to a different subject matter or participant, the summative evaluation stage could provide formative evaluation for that new project (Gammon and Burch, 2006) and is one way to build efficiencies into evaluation design.

Whether all three stages of evaluation are appropriate for a project and what scale of evaluation is necessary depends on a variety of factors, including the activity's purpose, the evaluators' skills, the time and funding available for the project and whether it is externally funded, with evaluation expectations in place. This brings us to the starting point for evaluation, which relates to the aims and goals of an activity and how to consult stakeholders.

Case study 10.1 The Centre for Appearance Research and Dove Self-Esteem Project

The Centre for Appearance Research (CAR), based at the University of the West of England, Bristol, aims to make tangible differences in the lives of those who experience appearance-related concerns around the globe (www1.uwe. ac.uk/hls/research/appearanceresearch). The Centre's psychologists conduct interdisciplinary research on appearance, visual difference and body image, and aspire to keep end-users at the centre of their work. In doing so, CAR collaborates with a number of organisations, including charities and associations that promote positive body image. We spoke to Phillippa Diedrichs about one such collaboration, that with the multinational consumer brand Dove.

Dove is a personal care brand producing a variety of skin, body and hair-care products, but it also has a strong sense of social responsibility, encapsulated in the Dove Self-Esteem Project (selfesteem.dove.com), which seeks to improve the body image and self-esteem of young people through body-confidence educational tools delivered in schools, online and in community settings. Phillippa's research is interested in exploring how young people can have a positive body image, and collaborating with Dove has allowed Phillippa to consider the impact of research in new ways. As she says, 'Working with a multinational company has inspired me to think about effecting change through research on a much larger scale that I ever did before, which is incredibly exciting.' To date, Dove has reached over 14 million girls with its educational tools. Collaborating with the Dove Self-Esteem Project also meant that Phillippa became much more conscious about the strengths and limitations of her field of research: 'The key challenge for me in communicating research in a corporate environment is that it has forced me to critically and carefully assess the depths *and* limits of the existing research in this area.' How academic research is used in a corporate context can be tricky, as she continued: 'While we have made great progress in the field of body image research, there are still lots of things we don't know and one research question can take several years to answer. Therefore, it's been challenging at times to be guided by the evidence base while also fostering innovation and growth.'

Phillippa and her colleagues were able to identify the styles of interventions in schools that could work most effectively in promoting a positive body image with adolescents, and recommend scientifically proven programmes and strategies to Dove to implement on a global scale. Phillippa has found the collaboration with the corporate sector to be very stimulating, as she explained: 'The Dove Self-Esteem Project is always looking to innovate and improve its body image education programmes to be in line with the fast-changing media and visual landscapes that young people live in and the fast-paced corporate environment, which requires ongoing creativity and originality.' Learning more about marketing and communication techniques used by Dove has, according to Phillippa, 'allowed me to be much more strategic and creative with the way I seek to influence other stakeholders to adopt evidence-based approaches to improving body image'.

Whilst the collaboration has encouraged Phillippa to think creatively about her research communication, it has also influenced how Phillippa thinks about tracking her own research impact: 'The Dove Self-Esteem Project has carefully designed monitoring and evaluation systems to track the dissemination and reach of its educational tools.' Phillippa highlights then that collaboration can allow researchers to monitor their impact through the work of others: 'I recommend speaking to collaborators about the systems they have in place and how you can use them to track the impact of your research.'

Her involvement with government and policy advisory groups means that Phillippa's work has also been discussed and utilised as evidence in parliamentary settings; but, thinking back to CAR's agenda around direct influences it has also had significant impacts from a more practical standpoint. Phillippa's work has contributed to the Dove Self-Esteem Project, using her research within its global body image programmes which are carried out in schools and through organisations like the World Association of Girl Guides and Girl Scouts. As Phillippa describes, 'The primary benefit of communicating my research with the Dove Self-Esteem Project is that it has led to tangible improvements in the quality of body image programmes delivered to girls on a global scale. Body image programmes that are scientifically shown to improve girls' body image are now being delivered to girls in 112 countries around the world as a result of our research partnership. This is the largest dissemination of evidence-based body image programmes to date, and it is incredibly rewarding.'

Phillippa's research has clearly had resonance with a contemporary global campaign and, as she says, has allowed her to think about research impact in new and more extensive ways, but that doesn't mean to say there aren't tips that other researchers can take from it. Perhaps crucially, Phillippa says, 'It's important to have a strategy for tracking the dissemination and implementation of your research from the start of a project.' So, thinking about how you can do this for any research communication, at a local, national or global level, is something all research communicators can keep in mind.

Questions, aims and objectives

When we design the aims for a project it can be tempting to think about the grandest and most impressive expectations. Researchers are used to pushing the boundaries of knowledge, demonstrating originality and seeking to exhibit real advances in their respective fields. Of course the same should apply to communication, but an eye on the pragmatic, where aims or questions for evaluation are concerned, can both make an activity more achievable and realistic as well as allow the design of evaluation to be embedded in a project from day one. A communication project may not necessarily involve research questions, but evaluation, particularly that influenced by social research design, is often guided by a set of specific questions. In some areas, like health and education, evaluation activities may embed an expectation for change or action, whereby the questions may evolve or adjust as the evaluation continues. Rossi *et al.* (1999) suggest that you consider two key points in designing good evaluation questions. Firstly, they must be reasonable and appropriate, avoid grandiose goals and keep an eye on the pragmatics of what a project can realistically deliver. Secondly, they must be answerable by the likely observables or evidence you will be able collect. For some research communication projects a question might be less appropriate. In such cases it is common to use aims and objectives instead. Aims are broad statements about what a project aspires to achieve, whereas objectives are the steps that will be put in place to achieve them. It is important to avoid ambiguities and it can be helpful to double-check that aims or questions are still achievable once the evaluation methods and approach have been finalised. Despite both aims and questions being widely used within research, many people remain confused about how to design them. The resources in Box 10.1 provide some helpful ideas.

Box *10.1* Resources for designing aims, questions and objectives

---

SMART

The principle of SMART objectives (that objectives should be specific, measurable, attainable, relevant and time bound) has been widely used in project management since the 1980s. You can find resources on SMART at a wide number of online project management websites simply by using SMART as a search term.

SMARTER

SMARTER takes the principle of SMART a couple of steps further, the 'E' and 'R' can be applied in different ways, but typically include wording such as 'extending', 'evaluating' and 'recognised', 'rewarding' or 'revisiting', thus implying an appreciation of outcomes and impacts which might arise. Again, resources on SMARTER can be found at a number of project management websites.

Prince2 Plans

Prince2 is a method of project management estimated to be used in over 20,000 organisations, encouraging users to design processes for effective project management. The 'plans' stage of the Prince2 principles sets out how, when and by whom a specific target or set of targets will be achieved; this can include products, timescales, costs, quality and benefits (TSO, 2009). The Prince2 website provides some resources to get started with: www.prince2.com/how-plan-project-o.

Generic Learning Outcomes

The Museums, Libraries and Archives Council's Generic Learning Outcomes (GLOs) focus on a broad and inclusive conception of learning, and particularly the benefits people may experience when interacting with locations like museums and libraries. Although focused on learning primarily, they can be used to think broadly about the possible objectives of a research communication activity:

www.inspiringlearningforall.gov.uk/toolstemplates/genericlearning/

Why is it helpful to think about aims in the design process? Many evaluations implicitly expect to consider some kind of change, influence, outcome or impact that an activity has had on participants. Being realistic about whom it will affect, what that effect might be, when it could potentially happen, why it will occur and how, can facilitate the process of thinking about how to measure, capture or assess the potential impacts before reaching the stage of designing the specifics of the evaluation. That is not to say that you should design the purpose of a project purely to make life simple from an evaluation perspective, but often there are small tweaks which might be made to an aim which make the project more achievable in both its delivery and evaluation. Gammon and Burch (2006) recommend taking particular care in designing summative evaluation of long-term impacts. Though not impossible, the resources, planning, time and interpretation required to measure long-term impacts may mean that it is more achievable to focus on reliable data about immediate impact when evaluating smaller projects (Gammon and Burch, 2006).

Many research communication projects also have stakeholders, the most obvious one being an external funder, but other partners (perhaps other academics, organisations or practitioners) can also be involved, as well as potential participants. Where participants are concerned formative evaluation plans can include some consultation with them, perhaps around the more practical aspects of the project (for example if they would enjoy an approach or design), but it is also important to explore their expectations of the project. For example, we might anticipate that people attending a public talk would want to spend most of their time hearing from a speaker, only to find that they would like some extra time to socialise with fellow participants. Evaluation is often critiqued for neglecting participants' perspectives within the design (Kushner, 2000); remember, they may have motivations, perspectives, views and expectations which are unknown or unexpected amongst those that are designing or funding it.

There is also much to be gleaned from other types of stakeholders. Funders are looking for an effective activity and an evaluation which is fit for purpose in terms of their requirements. Funders report that some communicators see evaluation as a trick or a threat, but they are not looking to catch people out (RCUK, 2011). Application guidelines, funders' websites, example end-of-award reports, telephone calls to the individual responsible for the scheme, will all provide useful information on the shape, style and extent of evaluation that is expected. Talking to other partners is also important in designing an evaluation of value to all. If you are collaborating with individuals who perhaps have more interest in the medium you are using (maybe an artist, game designer or journalist) they might be interested in different outcomes than those which interest you; likewise any partner organisations, perhaps a museum, venue or school, will also have goals that they want to achieve. We have had experience of working with partners who had entirely different expectations of what a project aimed to achieve, as well as those who see no purpose at all in evaluating. An open conversation about the evaluation and the differing 'values' in operation amongst stakeholders (DePoy and Gilson, 2008), when discussing the aims of a project, will help to design an evaluation which is effective for all involved and might flag interesting points or considerations which you may not have thought about before. Research communication can encourage such a variety of outcomes: educational, artistic, participatory, pragmatic and behavioural, to name but a few, and this presents a vast array of opportunities for evaluation.

Evaluation is not a neutral process (Hoggarth and Comfort, 2010), and DePoy and Gilson (2008) highlight that all evaluation is 'value based', that beliefs and opinions about what is 'good', 'desirable', 'important' and 'correct' should be acknowledged in evaluation design. From a practical perspective, evaluation can infringe on the experience of others within the activity, be it asking them to contribute their views, or the time that they might have to spend on an activity. Developing the evaluation more collaboratively can increase a sense of buy-in amongst those who will later contribute (Rossi *et al.*, 1999) and also acknowledge any of the values which are influencing those differing individuals.

Methods

Before we begin to identify methods for evaluation it is worth mentioning that some of the most straightforward data to collect, things like audience numbers, frequency of events, number of downloads, are considered to be outputs, rather than evaluation. This type of information is monitoring data (RCUK, 2011) focused on what the project produced. These data may well feature as part of the context of an evaluation report, but generally won't provide the depth needed for a detailed evaluation which also considers outcomes and impacts. Box 10.2 has some novel examples of outputs from one museum. In most contexts, evidence of effectiveness is now favoured over the evidence of outputs (Hoggarth and Comfort, 2010). That being said, for some small-scale activities monitoring data can be enough; it might be all the funder is expecting, or the only information that can be realistically collected. However, for more sophisticated or extensive activities there are a variety of options available.

Box 10.2 **Unusual public engagement outputs**

---

13 open rehearsals from orchestra-in-residence wild Up, in preparation for its critically-acclaimed Hammer performances

73 sequin-emblazoned blazers, worn by security guards, for Lisa Anne Auerbach's **United We Stand**

76 houseplants in repose, thanks to Machine Project's **Houseplant Vacation**

116 radio shows produced by KCHUNG Radio during its public engagement residency last fall

205 books donated by Hammer staff to Libros Schmibros, lending library-in-residence, Libros Schmibros

566 visitor portraits taken for Harrell Fletcher's and Adam Moser's **Yearbook**

600 blindfolds purchased for the Institute for Art and Olfaction's scent concert, a **Trip to Japan in 16 Minutes, Revisited**

750 magnolia leaves stamped with art-viewing prompts for Charles Long's **Seeing Green**

Source: Adapted from Agsten (2014)

There are lots of methods which researchers might use to measure the outcomes and impact of their communication efforts. Many of these are likely to be familiar to some researchers based on their own disciplinary interests but others may be new, or not something previously considered in the context of research communication activities. Remember that although an evaluation may have differing pressures, timings and purposes than a traditional research project there is still much to be gained from being organised and prepared. DePoy and Gilson (2008) highlight that frequently the need to review information and other literature (such as evaluation reports from similar projects) is a step which is ignored within evaluation design. Examining how others have run similar activities, or best practice from the literature, can help to validate or suggest methods to use in evaluation or identify existing data that are available (DePoy and Gilson, 2008).

In terms of selecting methods for evaluation, a variety of evaluation guidelines provide an overview of key methods that can be used, as Table 10.1 illustrates. Evaluation of research communication activities has had a tendency to rely on quantitative survey approaches, and often in rather quick and simple ways. This might be because many research communicators are most familiar with quantitative methods; or it may reflect the level of priority that is sometimes given to evaluation within projects: it can easily become the last thing on the list, and so capturing snapshot quantitative information can be a relatively straightforward thing to do. Unfortunately, this can neglect the complexity of designing a good evaluation; 'getting evaluation right demands as much careful thinking as designing an event or activity in the first place, and the two really go together' (Gammon and Burch, 2006: 80).

Table 10.1 Evaluation methods

Method	Strength	Weaknesses	Creative adaptations
Question-naires	– Evaluation can be captured at participants' convenience or during set times in activity – Large sample sizes – Simple, quick and cheap – Anonymous – Familiar to participants	– Completion rates can be low – Questions need careful design – Lack depth – Require a certain level of literacy	A simple questionnaire can easily be adapted to use physical props in response to answers or to have specific questions embedded within an activity, taking care to remember any influence there might be on responses, or ethical considerations in rendering these visible.
Online question naires	– As above – Can reach larger sample sizes – Can be designed for efficient analysis without additional data entry	– As above – Require reliable internet access – Data protection needs careful consideration	Online questionnaires are easy to set up and it is easy to embed images or interesting question styles within them. They are also amenable to use with response pads or buttons, or with tablets, which can encourage quick completion.

Table 10.1 (cont.)

Method	Strength	Weaknesses	Creative adaptations
Interviews	– Focus on issues of relevance, whilst allowing unexpected issues to arise – Private and confidential – Participants voice issues authentically	– Requires appropriate interviewer skills – Tendency for smaller sample sizes – Time needed to collect data, transcribe and analyse – Care needed around interviewer influence	Peer-to-peer interviewing might engage participants in a conversation and the sharing of information with each other. Remember to design any interview questions appropriately and support participants through the process. Care needed if sensitive issues are under discussion.
Case studies	– Provide in-depth detail on small number of cases – Focus on issues of relevance, whilst allowing unexpected issues to arise – Create a cohesive picture of experience of an activity or project	– Can require more than one to account for differing experiences – Can be superficial, with lack of depth – Can be challenging to report appropriately	Rather than seek out cases, examine if you could encourage cases to self-select. Consider creative approaches that you might use to create a narrative of cases, for instance by incorporating digital diaries or images.
Focus groups	– Focus on issues of relevance, whilst allowing unexpected issues to arise – Can provide positive and supportive atmosphere – Participants voice issues authentically	– Require appropriate facilitation – Time to collect data, transcribe and analyse – Can create challenging, alignment and differences in views	Consider if participants might design or run their own focus group, engaging them as 'evaluators' in the design and running of the data collection, with appropriate support. Think about interesting prompts or activities to break up a more traditional

Table 10.1 (cont.)

Method	Strength	Weaknesses	Creative adaptations
	– Can create challenging, alignment and differences in views	– Can be intimidating – Require appropriate recording equipment	focus group. Care needed if sensitive issues are under discussion.
Obser-vations	– Can be structured to focus on issues of relevance – Reveal variety of aspects that can impact on activity beyond those visible to participants – Helpful for examination of routine or habitual aspects of behaviour	– Time needed to collect and analyse data – Can be influenced by observer's assumptions – Can be intrusive, consent may be required – Challenging for large activities or participant numbers without a structure – Can assume influences only on basis of what has been observed	Investigate if video or audio recording would allow for observation, with appropriate consent procedures in place. Think about other mechanisms through which you might observe a participant's journey, for example check-in points as they move around at a festival or drawings of the map that they took in a museum visit.
Document analysis	– Draws data from contextual documentation – Efficient in using existing materials – Reveals variety of aspects that can have an impact on activity beyond those visible to participants	– Context of documents can be lost – Availability of data can be overwhelming – Access to some documentation may not be permitted	Consider using approaches like Wordle to identify keywords and trends. Utilise computer programmes (see Box 10.4) to generate themes, connections and maps over the data.
Partici-patory evaluation	– Novel and enjoyable – Increases sense of participation – Can provide positive atmosphere – Can raise unexpected issues	– Requires appropriate facilitation – Influence of other comments – Can generate wide-ranging data/data of less relevance – Can be intimidating	Examine materials and props you might use in support, images, cut-outs, craft or mini-drama, which would allow participants to express perspectives in different formats and increase novelty.

Table 10.1 (cont.)

Method	Strength	Weaknesses	Creative adaptations
Comment/ guest books and boxes	– Simple, quick and cheap – Anonymous – Can raise unexpected issues	– Requires a certain level of literacy – Can generate wide-ranging data/data of less relevance	Think about being a guest at a wedding, create an area for the materials which is attractive, appealing and may have other information or small gifts of interest to people.
Drawings, charts, mindmaps and diagrams	– Simple and quick to create – Less reliance on literacy – Novelty encourages participation – Can raise unexpected issues – Good for comparing 'before' and 'after'	– Challenging to analyse/interpret – Can require additional 'labelling' when reporting – Can intimidate participants – Provides limited insights	Source attractive and enjoyable materials for people to illustrate with (pens, crayons, modelling clay, collage cut-ups); consider using the format of a game to create a 'Pictionary' of responses.
Graffiti walls	– Simple, cheap, novel – Informal – Evaluation can be captured at participants' convenience	– Can generate wide-ranging data/data of less relevance – Challenging to transcribe/analyse/ interpret – Influence of other comments – Requires a certain level of literacy	Appraise the space you are in; 'graffiti' can be applied to no end of materials, from notebooks to doors, walls and physical objects. Consider digital graffiti, for instance around a hashtag.
Social media and online materials	– Availability of data – Helpful for regular evaluation (e.g. process) – Encourages participation amongst regular online users – Sense of anonymity	– Availability of data can be overwhelming – Can be intrusive and consent may be required – Requires reliable internet access – Anonymity/social media culture may influence comments	Create spaces for social media interaction within an activity. Consider extending and prompting interaction before and after, for instance by asking people to connect with a group or hashtag which then includes prompts and reminders.

Table 10.1 *(cont.)*

Method	Strength	Weaknesses	Creative adaptations
Images, photography and video	– Evaluation can be captured at participants' convenience – Simple, cheap, novel – Informal – No reliance on literacy – Interesting examples for evaluation reports	– Can generate wide-ranging data/data of less relevance – Challenging to analyse/interpret – Consent for use of images/videos may be required – Participants need access to digital photography, recording or materials – Editing and 'performance' elements could create less-authentic data	Consider layering evaluation (Boyd Davies, 2009); images or recordings can be reviewed and examined by participants, in groups or individually, after their completion as an opportunity to consider shared responses as well as differences. Integrate social media, for example by the use of collage apps to allow participants to form connections between images. Facilitate the creation of 'mood boards' to capture a range of images (also applicable to drawings etc.).
Diaries	– Focus on issues of relevance, whilst allowing unexpected issues to arise – Private and confidential – Participants voice issues authentically – Novel – Provide chronological experience	– Participants voice issues for the 'reader/evaluator' – Can be viewed as 'private' – Requires a certain level of literacy – Can generate wide-ranging data/data of less relevance – Challenging to analyse/interpret – Participants may lose interest/fail to complete	Diaries can be extended to the project team behind a communication or engagement activity; what thoughts, processes, changes and responses did you have along the way? Diaries may continue beyond the activity's primary interaction, to capture continued reaction, reflection and use of an activity or project.

Source: Hoggarth and Comfort (2010); Woolf (2004)

Considering the specific aims of a project, and the best method to assess these, is the most reliable way to select methods – it shouldn't just be down to what is easiest. A wider consideration of methods reduces the tendency to have one method in mind which is then squeezed into a project, regardless as to whether it is appropriate. For example, you might design a detailed questionnaire for a small-scale festival activity, when actually a few minutes spent interviewing your participants would garner more detailed data. Plans should also be considered from a practical perspective: what time, costs and resources will be required? Do you or the team you are working with have the experience or expertise to deliver the method (Hoggarth and Comfort, 2010)? When thinking about methods, consider if the data needed (or those through which you can access it) will be accessible to you, the reliability of that data and also any ethical considerations there might be in collecting it (see Chapter 11 for advice on this). It's important in evaluation design not to include too many methods for the sake of it, and to carefully think about exactly which data need to be provided. Popping in the odd extra question can be tempting but may add to aspects like transcription and analysis time.

There is some interest in whether evaluations should follow standardised procedures or frameworks for evaluation; this would allow evaluations to be compared more readily, by funders for example. Box 10.3 provides examples of frameworks and practical guides to evaluation that may be useful at the design stage.

The creation of such frameworks or benchmarks often reflects the need for those working at strategic organisational levels to have better ways to extrapolate findings beyond individual projects or to justify wider resources and support for particular initiatives or disciplinary communities, for example through synthesis exercises or some kind of meta-evaluation; but they also reflect drivers to increase the standards and quality of evaluation across research communications. Whilst these frameworks have very useful prompts regarding the variety of potential outcomes from research communication efforts, and are particularly helpful when evaluating for the first time, it is also worth acknowledging that amongst the broader field of evaluation the requirement for more 'theory', 'rules' or 'principles' for evaluation design has been well rehearsed. Evaluation often requires a flexible and creative approach, as Rossi *et al.* (1999: 33) point out, 'we must acknowledge that evaluation is at least as much art as science, and perhaps should be and always will be. Inevitably, the evaluator's task is to creatively weave together many competing concerns and objectives into a tapestry in which different viewers can find different messages'.

Evaluation does not operate as 'one size fits all' (Rossi *et al.*, 1999),

---

Box 10.3 Selected frameworks and guidance for evaluation design

---

Empowering Evaluation: Evaluating Empowerment
This report encourages you to think about designing evaluation approaches which can be empowering for both you as an evaluator and your participants. Although the report has fewer practical elements than some other guides, it provokes consideration and reflection in your evaluation design. www.iacdglobal.org/files/empowering_evaluation.pdf

Framework for Evaluating Impacts of Informal Science Education Projects
Published by the US National Science Foundation, this guide provides a framework and advice for those evaluating informal STEM projects and activities. http://informalscience.org/documents/Eval_Framework.pdf

Friendly Evaluation Toolkit
Designed by the National Trust, this readable guide covers all of the basics of a good evaluation design. http://abcofworkingwithschools.files.wordpress.com/2010/08/friendly-evaluation-toolkit-national-trust.pdf

Making a Difference: A Guide to Evaluating Public Participation in Central Government
This guide is framed to be most relevant to those using public engagement for policy purposes; however, it comprises useful sections on all stages of the evaluation process. www.involve.org.uk/evaluation-guide/index.shtml

Partnerships for Learning: A Guide to Evaluating Arts Education Projects
Partnerships for Learning is a flexible framework which seeks to recognise there are different ways to approach evaluation. It is particularly relevant if you are trying to evaluate the creative process. www.artscouncil.org.uk/media/uploads/documents/publications/phpLYOoMa.pdf

Public Engagement Evaluation Guide
This 'hands-on' practical guide provides support and advice for organisations that were supported by Beacon for Public Engagement funding. www.manchesterbeacon.org/files/manchester-beacon-pe-evaluation-guide.pdf

The Evaluator's Cookbook
This lovely guide considers evaluation exercises as 'starters, main courses and puddings', providing a range of participatory evaluation approaches that are particularly suited to working with young people. http://cms.nottinghamshire.gov.uk/theevaluatorscookbook.pdf

User-Friendly Handbook for Project Evaluation
This handbook provides guidance for National Science Foundation-supported projects to design appropriate evaluations. Although with a slight educational focus, it provides a range of generic advice on evaluation. http://informalscience.org/documents/TheUserFriendlyGuide.pdf

and there can be tensions between those working in evaluation practice, who often recognise a pluralism of approaches to gather data, and the needs of those who scrutinise the results of evaluation and increased needs for accountability (DePoy and Gilson, 2008), including within research communication. Thus, whilst frameworks can be helpful in reminding us of the data or approach that can be used in evaluation design, there might be more fluid approaches which are better suited to an individual project and context which would be unrecognised in the use of a standard model alone.

In terms of being creative about the methods chosen for evaluation, there are a lot of options. It's important to remember that whilst there are few radically new approaches to evaluating an activity, there are creative ways to use existing methods so that the evaluation does not appear to be typical, yet it draws on the same strengths as its 'parent' approach. For instance, there are now all sorts of ways that we can capture images; participants may regularly use sites like Instagram or Pinterest, or take 'selfies' on a smartphone (as suggested by one group of MSc students with which we were working). Rather than collect written or verbal materials, images could be one form of data collected during an activity, to which more traditional image-based analysis techniques can be applied. Table 10.1 provides some further examples.

Creative techniques have their benefits – they can be novel, encourage participation and reflect participants' interests or needs – but also weaknesses – analysis might take more time, the data can be overwhelming or unreliable. As with any method, it's important to consider methods carefully and not become too carried away if an approach is particularly exciting or appealing. When using a more creative approach, trying it out on a small-scale activity or project would allow any issues to be resolved before developing it further or employing it in a large-scale project.

It's also worth spending some time thinking creatively about any sources for evaluation data which might already exist. In the data-rich world in which we now live perhaps data are already being collected which could be utilised? The appropriateness of this from an ethical standpoint should be considered; for example, some ethics committees would require information on consent procedures for data that has been collected by others, but it might also be the case that there is quite generic information to be accessed that would provide answers to some of the evaluation questions, like data on visitor numbers or school subject uptake.

Some research communication activities will employ a third party to carry out evaluation. Depending on the scale of the research communication activity, an evaluation might be carried out by a member of the project team, or through an external evaluator contracted by the funder. Regardless of the approach taken, applying a systematic approach to the evaluation, and keeping in mind the importance of 'objectivity', 'neutrality' and 'open-mindedness', can assist in creating a professional evaluation design (Hoggarth and Comfort, 2010: 82; DePoy and Gilson, 2008). It can be difficult if you have a stake in that which you are evaluating. Saville Kushner (2000: 108–9) puts this well in the context of the many evaluations he has carried out on programmes associated with music:

> I'm not crazy about music…. I think this is something significant to say because I encounter so many people engaged in evaluating music who do so from a firm basis of uncritical admiration for the stuff. I don't mean admiration for particular forms of music but, rather, an unswerving belief that music is a 'good' or 'inherently uplifting' or 'wholesome' thing. Most people I encounter in music fields are, to some degree or another, 'in love' with music. I am not – I care more about my evaluation. It is healthier for me as a professional evaluator to have some emotional and cognitive affinity with the practice of evaluation than with the field being evaluated.

Thus, whilst you may have some affinity for those subjects which you are communicating or evaluating, and it would be difficult to suddenly disregard that, keeping this in mind and structuring your evaluation professionally and transparently is important.

Evaluation analysis and reporting

One of the most important things to remember with regard to analysis is to allocate some time for it! Analysis can be one of the most challenging and frustrating stages, and if it is rushed there is the real danger that mistakes might creep into data and reporting, which might call into question the whole purpose of an activity.

Research communicators who are based at a university or other type of research organisation are likely to have access to some form of quantitative or qualitative computer programme. However, others may find that they don't have access to these types of programmes; this is not necessarily problematic, as more basic computer programmes like Microsoft Excel will often allow sufficient analysis for a reliable evaluation. Adopting the principles of organisation which qualitative programmes use will easily allow a consistent analysis of any qualitative data, as the basic functions of most qualitative programmes involve highlighting, cutting out and relocating text, and there is nothing to stop people doing this with a basic computer programme, or even a pen, paper and scissors.

Increasingly there are online tools which fill the gap between purchasing computer programmes and DIY approaches and some examples of these are provided in Box 10.4. If you are based in an organisation with computer software available, investigate access to subscription programs such as SPSS, Minitab, STATA, NVivo or Atlas.ti. Some programs also offer trial or limited access to parts of the package and this can also be helpful for small-scale or short-term evaluations.

Regardless of which computer package is used, analysis is not an autonomous process, and returning to project aims or questions should direct the analysis. Many quantitative analysis texts, as well as online

---

Box 10.4 Free online analysis programmes

CAT
This free coding-analysis toolkit allows you to code, add memos, export and collaboratively examine qualitative data. http://cat.ucsur.pitt.edu/

ELAN
Allows qualitative researchers to note and analyse video and audio data. www.lat-mpi.eu/tools/tools/elan

OpenStat
Designed with social science quantitative data in mind, OpenStat also has accompanying teaching and user guides. http://statpages.info/miller/OpenStatMain.htm

QDA Miner Lite
This qualitative package has functions including coding using tree structures, the ability to add comments and notes, as well as representation of code frequency. http://provalisresearch.com/products/qualitative-data-analysis-software/freeware/

R Project for Statistical Computing
R provides downloadable software for data manipulation, calculation and graphical display. www.r-project.org/

SOFA
SOFA (Statistics Open for All) focuses on a user-friendly quantitative package, allowing you to carry out basic statistical tests and reporting. www.sofastatistics.com/home.php

Wordle
Wordle creates word clouds which give greatest prominence to the most frequently used words in a text, and can be used for documents, transcripts or other written materials. www.wordle.net/

resources, talk the reader through the process of analysis, which may be helpful for those unfamiliar with quantitative techniques. Identify what is most appropriate for the aims, level of measurement, information obtained and sampling as the first steps in analysis (DePoy and Gilson, 2008). Remember that the level of analysis, whether descriptive, inferential or associational statistics is appropriate, will vary depending on the scale of the evaluation and its aims. The variety of techniques possible within a computer package and outlined within research methods texts can be overwhelming, so a firm eye on what is necessary is helpful, remembering that relatively simple descriptive data are often needed by a reader in order to understand the more complex aspects of an analysis. Finally, even when an analysis approach has been planned it can occasionally be necessary to backtrack, issues in how data have been entered can come to light, or certain approaches may not prove useful. Keeping a 'clean' version of a dataset is helpful.

Qualitative data analysis involves interview transcripts, observations or focus group documents; it can be difficult to see how to fairly and appropriately reflect data. A broad variety of analysis approaches are available for qualitative data; DePoy and Gilson (2008) helpfully identify the three most common: thematic, taxonomic and grounded theory. Thematic analysis approaches explore data as a whole for themes and patterns, linking indicative sections of data to them. Taxonomic analysis takes this a stage further, representing the relationships between themes through visual representations and written discussion. A grounded-theory approach also generates key themes and categories into which data are coded, but through an iterative process based on the data, which allows for new and revised codes to be generated. In other words the codes originate from the data themselves. Such analysis strategies assist in identifying dominant trends in qualitative data, as well as those which might be less noticeable but are still relevant.

Qualitative data can be easily manipulated, and some may question its value. Hoggarth and Comfort (2010) suggest being cautious about making claims that qualitative data are fully representative. It is also important not to ignore sections of data or take quotes out of context when handling data of this type. As with quantitative data, the complexity of analysis can vary depending on the requirements of the evaluation, and though applying codes and categories can make visible patterns in data, it is important not to overly quantify extracts that are being presented. An important asset of qualitative data is its illustrative, complex and unexpected qualities, often conceptualised in a participant's own words – meaning that care should also be taken to reflect those insights within an evaluation report.

At the end of an evaluation things may not have turned out quite as expected. It might be the case that a project did not quite reach its goals, that something went wrong which it wasn't practical to resolve or that an unexpected outcome occurred. There are transparent ways to present such situations and those who have a stake or interest in a project will often appreciate the honesty or insight this presents. From an evaluation perspective, at times we may need to sensitively write an account of aspects which others may find uncomfortable; having a good working relationship with stakeholders from the outset can help to smooth out any such issues that arise. Chapter 12 provides further advice on sharing evaluation findings.

Similarly, evaluation does not always occur quite as planned; for example, we've had students whose entire data-collection intentions have been sent off course by a very rainy summer. Again, any such problems can be discussed within reporting. Rossi *et al.* (1999) make a helpful point here, stressing that sometimes in an evaluation context compromises and adaptations have to be made with regard to methodological quality and standards to create an evaluation which is 'as good as possible' within a context which is likely to be responding to many different factors and people. There might be weaknesses in an evaluation, as evaluation can be 'messy' (Kushner, 2000); acknowledging this is important.

Research impact

From a researcher's perspective, impact might relate to both the influence of your research communication and how that research communication forms part of your research impact. There is the question of whether your communication activity has had an impact and what that is, which links back to a variety of aspects we have discussed in the context of evaluation, but there is also the question of how public engagement and communication can be an indicator of the wider impact of your research, and the issues this can highlight.

The need for measures of research impact has moved up the agendas of funders and stakeholders in recent years, though from an evaluation perspective the question of measuring and assessing longer-term and more challenging impacts has often been apparent (Hoggarth and Comfort, 2010; Anderson, 2003; Scott, 2003; Falk, 2000), as Gammon and Burch discuss:

> There is often pressure to evaluate the long-term impact yet there are severe practical problems to overcome. How will you maintain contact with a reliable sample of participants to conduct this research? How will

you ensure that you are not altering participants' opinions and behaviour by maintaining this contact? Do you have the resources to conduct long-term studies lasting months or even years? How will you ensure that what you are measuring is truly the impact of your event and not of a multitude of different experiences that a participant may have had in the meantime? (Gammon and Burch, 2006: 81)

A key implication of these questions in relation to research communication is a tendency to rely on the types of outcomes and impact (whether short or long term) which are most straightforward to map. Scott (2003), in writing about the drive for museums to better account for their impact, discusses the need to 'articulate' not only economic influences but also the role of museums in social, environmental and cultural settings; however, she highlights a lack of agreed indicators on how to demonstrate this, which makes this articulation difficult. The difficulty in generating such indicators is particularly well illustrated in the arts (McMaster, 2008; Holden, 2006; Furedi, 2004), and Chapter 5 provides more context on this. The arts' contribution to the economy via creative industries is a frequently postulated measure of impact, although within the disciplines the 'transformative' aspect of the arts amongst individuals and communities and its role in cultural identity is often more highly regarded (Belfiore and Bennett, 2008; Holden, 2006). This neglect of the role of 'transformation' is due to the complexity of evidencing it, influenced by its subjective nature, the variety of influences which are likely to have an impact on an individual's or group's 'transformation' and the difficulty to therefore define clear measures (Belfiore and Bennett, 2008). Instead a raft of impact indicators seek to illustrate the impact of the arts on exports, tourism, urban renewal, health, communities and so forth, but these have been criticised for relying on instrumental economic and social indicators at the cost of the aesthetic or intrinsic values of artistic endeavours (Belfiore and Bennett, 2008).

There can also be an assumption within such indicators of impact that a need for 'change', be it in behaviour, learning, attitude or awareness, or even transformation as discussed previously, is an implicit goal. The foundations of the field of evaluation within programmes of social change or action and the expectation for 'improvement' (Kushner, 2000; Rossi *et al.*, 1999), as well as the historical framing of research communication as an asset of cultural enhancement, may both tend to suggest that we look for beneficial impacts. However, many research communication activities sit in a space between leisure and education (Falk, 2000), where their 'worth' might be defined in other ways. Participants' motivations may not always include an expectation of 'benefit', whilst the goals of some research communication activities may not always include an expectation of 'change' amongst participants. A narrow focus on beneficial impact, an assumption that participants require some sense of improvement or rectification, may neglect broader conceptions of engagement, including the varied and mutual outcomes that engagement can have on the part of both the researcher and participant.

From a research communication perspective, it may be important to keep some flexibility in mind regarding the types of impacts that might arise and whether these are always 'positive'. An emphasis on benefit can 'gloss over' the negatives (Hoggarth and Comfort, 2010). For instance, your research might be controversial, suggest rather negative implications, be debated and questioned; is this still an impact? We would argue 'yes', although the framing of that impact might be more complex to present. Thinking about the variety of impacts which might result from an activity across all stakeholders is important; don't forget that there might be important influences on you as a researcher or on the framing of your research which it is important to capture. However, when designing your evaluation it can be easy to step into 'advocacy' mode, whereby you seek to strongly justify your activity, approach or even discipline.

Drawing on the second point, it is now commonplace to see research communication and engagement activities feature as one type of impact within a wider analysis of research impact. Research impact is subject to discussion in many individual countries, including Australia (Australian Research Council, 2014), Ireland (Science Foundation Ireland, 2012), the Netherlands, the United States (Grant *et al.*, 2010) and the United Kingdom, whilst long-standing academic conventions, like assessment of journal impact factors and citation counts, have been used as measures of the impact of research on the academic community for many years.

From a research communication perspective a broadening of the concept of impact is bringing renewed emphasis to ways that researchers might apply, bridge and integrate their work across disciplines, as well as communicate to non-academics and organisations the lessons and knowledge they have generated (Bastow *et al.*, 2014). It may be argued from a functional perspective that the drive to measure the impact of research is increasing the awareness and changing the cultural and institutional context for public engagement. However, it also raises some problematic issues.

Where public engagement is concerned, a greater emphasis on its inclusion within research assessment has led to concerns that there could be an increase in tokenistic efforts. It has increased conversations about the preparedness of some researchers to engage, as well as the support available to them. There are also challenges when much research communication is fairly broad and non-specialist, whilst assessment mechanisms of impact can require an association to specific individuals, projects, research or case studies. For researchers who have previously undertaken communication activities based on more personal motivations, or for social and democratic reasons, such as to share academic research with publics who have implicitly contributed, a neo-liberal monitoring of certain types of 'impact' which is dismissive of the role of more traditional academic work, like teaching, can create a sense of distaste (Maile, 2014). Certain subjects are also seen to have advantages in demonstrating impacts (for instance STEM is already an area where there are widespread industry links and frequent newsworthy stories for the media), as compared with those where impacts may be more obscure or harder to demonstrate.

For example, where the social sciences are concerned there have been concerns that these disciplines lag behind the 'prestige' of the physical sciences and the relationship this has to inherent aspects of such disciplines.

> Every social science focuses on constantly shifting human behaviours; conscious that humans have an innate and un-erodible capacity to change what we do in response to being told why we act as we do, or how we are expected to act in future. No social science produces immutable laws that once established last unchanged ... every social science has a research process that is cumulative, largely missing the 'breakthrough' discoveries or 'lone genius' insights on which public images of the physical sciences and technological disciplines still focus. (Bastow *et al.*, 2014: xii–xiii)

Although it may be argued that the lone genius is increasingly less commonplace in all 'big' sciences nowadays, these authors raise an important point around the difficulty of restrictive definitions of impact. Bastow *et al.* (2014: 289) emphasise that the influence of social science research is widely under-recognised; without the billions of dollars invested in STEM subjects (their data suggest that the median share of twenty-seven key countries' research and development spending on social science and humanities funding is just under 8 percent), they have not undergone the same careful monitoring of the economic benefits which are secured, nor does simply applying these same measures work for the social sciences. Bastow *et al.*'s (2014) three-year study highlights that the social sciences tend to be collective in character, create products of ideas and information which cannot be copyrighted or patented, rarely reduce impact to single research projects in isolation and can be challenging to 'profit maximise', with many of their innovations easily taken up by intermediary organisations like consultancies and think-tanks (Bastow *et al.*, 2014). However, notwithstanding these issues, their detailed study highlights a variety of ways in which the social science community has an impact on business, policymakers, the media, civil society, as well as the workforce, whilst also cautioning that the pathway to that impact can be complex, variable and poorly understood.

Bastow *et al.* (2014) warn that an approach to knowledge generation which focuses only on that which is applied and contemporary has the potential to reduce the generation of new, multifaceted, dynamic and failed knowledge from which we also learn. Furthermore, creating a strengthened sense of publics as the recipients of research potentially places the public not in dialogue but as a consumer, as Holmwood (2014) articulates. He states that although the impact agenda implies a sense of co-production, 'research *with* rather than *about*',

> [t]his agenda can appear sympathetic and persuasive, but once we think about who it is we are asked to carry out research with – business and policymakers – the absorption of research to the interests of power becomes evident ... The impact agenda is not about making the research process more democratic but is a re-drawing and tightening of the hierarchy of credibility. (Holmwood, 2014: 20–1)

Thus, whilst the drive for research impact may increase potential opportunities to communicate and engage around your work, it may also be important to remind yourself of the purposes and principles of engagement and the 'social good' (Maile, 2014). Inevitably some aspects of research are likely to have more appeal, resonance or ease for communication activities, or to more readily illustrate an impact; but just as the impact agenda may come to influence the research we carry out, so too may it influence that which we seek to communicate, and this needs sustained examination and reflection over future years.

Case study 10.2 The Thrill Engineer

When your work is influenced by the arts, engineering, the latest psychological and criminological experiments, not to mention horror films and rollercoaster rides, how on earth do you start to think about its impact? Dizziness or screams might be a novel way to measure the impact your research is having on participants, and it's one which potentially Professor Brendan Walker (www.aerial.fm/docs/home.php) could use.

Brendan Walker's research encompasses arts, design, engineering and psychology. Brendan is a Senior Research Fellow in the Department of Computer Science at the University of Nottingham, and Professor of Creative Industries at Middlesex University, and also runs his own design practice. Brendan's experimental work hinges around interests in aeronautical engineering, industrial design and bio-sensing technologies, to name just a few of its facets. His work frequently includes the use of heart-rate monitors, accelerometers and video-recording equipment to assess people's physiological and psychological experience in a range of different settings. For instance, in one project horror film viewers were assessed for the effects of panic and fear on the human respiratory system. Professor Walker's work has been funded across the arts and sciences. 'I see my work as a continuum,' says Brendan, 'a patchwork of interests that I have across the arts and sciences, a duality.'

Brendan is popularly described as a 'Thrill Engineer', in fact the 'world's only thrill engineer', reflecting the popular interest his work has created in the media and creative industries. Taking his scientific experiments into the public eye, Brendan has created a range of performances for diverse locations including Tate Modern, the Science Museum, the Museum of Modern Art in New York, and you can also expect to see him appearing as 'The Thrill Engineer', equipped with his trademark red boiler suit, at a variety of exhibitions and festivals. What is quite unique about this work is its combination of experiment and display – for instance the data which are being collected as a viewer watches a horror film or reacts to a theme park ride also forms part of the performance itself, as experimentation in real time.

Harking back to the nineteenth century, when the latest research was performed in public, Brendan aims to 'expose science to become part of entertainment'. Recognising that science can leave people feeling uncertain, concerned or dissatisfied, Brendan seeks to create a sense of public resonance, to produce 'real, long-lasting relationships between science and the arts', as well as to understand 'the emotional responses people have to my work'. Brendan talks about the example of the Coney Island Baby Incubator exhibit in the early twentieth century. The exhibit was an example of medicine in action, as the public filed past while doctors and nurses tended babies in incubators. Entry fees to the exhibit funded the project, saving thousands of new-born babies – all at a time before the use of incubators was accepted by the medical establishment. Brendan similarly combines experimentation with public fascination, and although not as ethically challenging as the Coney Island work would be today, it can still throw up issues for ethics committees used to dealing with more routine research.

Behind the novel performances Brendan develops all sorts of theorising, experimentation and 'making'. One output, *Punters: Auto-Portraits of Fairground Thrill,* involved monitoring data on arousal as people experience a fairground ride, resulting in a rating scale based on the dynamics of euphoria, which he reported in *The Taxonomy of Thrill*. He describes himself as having a 'role as a commentator … a fresh perspective, to be able to communicate the effect of fairground rides'.

And others began to take notice. Brendan's research has influenced constituencies from advertising agencies, using his principles to market their latest thrilling car, to food companies, establishing the most exhilarating flavours, or the creative industries, designing theme park experiences that will maximise excitement. His work has even been used by contraceptive companies providing tips on maximising pleasure. These projects have led to opportunities for presenting TV programmes aimed at all sorts of age groups, including slots on *Blue Peter* a popular British children's TV programme. Perhaps unsurprisingly, then, Brendan says there are lots of ways that his research can show impact, from commercial through to public engagement.

But behind it all sits the research, and that is important. The impact of Brendan's work has a path back to the participants wired up to the latest adventure ride, or the infant sampling fruit on the look-out for the most tantalising taste. It follows a journey through datasets of biosensor data to award-winning conference papers and publications. Finally, this can all be evidenced by TV broadcasts, advertising campaigns, new theme park experiences and festival visitor data for which Brendan has been able to provide written evidence of 'impact'. Whilst not many researchers will have this level of impact at the start of their careers, there are perhaps things to take on board from Brendan's experience. Creating a 'brand', whether intentionally or through a series of events, capturing how that brand is received and continuing to build networks around it, can be one way to think about the visibility of your research.

Summary

There are of course many strengths in thinking about the outcomes and impacts of research communication. It can influence quality, improve activities and increase an awareness and inclusion of evaluation, but there is also the potential to suppress innovation or smaller-scale activities with less clear evidence, or to create a target culture and distort or emphasise particular findings (Hoggarth and Comfort, 2010). As research communicators, we all have a role in creating pieces of the 'impact' jigsaw and recognising that the shapes of those pieces will be many and varied. At present there are strong drivers around assessing particular types of impacts, which might influence not only the way we evaluate our work but also how it is culturally recognised and supported. 'Social and economic "impact" are moving targets and the best we can ever hope for is a series of snapshots, a series of investigations that capture critical junctures in an ever-changing and dynamic system' (Falk, 2000: 6). Thus, arguably, research communicators also play a role in continuing to influence both how research communication is evaluated and the types of activities that are then encouraged and recognised.

The impact agenda may well encourage more widespread take-up and opportunities for research communication, but at the same time there are dangers, should these become tokenistic or driven only by extrinsic incentives. Many researchers feel a moral responsibility to engage around their work, or to see research being applied or influential; others prefer to generate different types of impact or to operate in research areas which are necessarily more basic or 'blue sky' in nature. Just as there is no 'one size fits all' for evaluation or epistemology, nor is there a 'one size fits all' in research terms; rather, there is a complex ecology of ontological positionings. As a research communicator it is important for you to be aware of broader trends and influences where evaluation and impact are concerned, not least because resources such as funders' guidance and frameworks can be practically helpful. However, at the same time it is important to remember the role of the individual within such processes, as Boyd Davies (2009: 133) summarises: 'all artists, designers or makers engage in evaluation of some kind: it is fundamental to what they do. It is hardly possible for someone holding a pencil to make a simple drawing if they are not constantly assessing the degree to which they are making productive marks.' Creative approaches to capturing outputs and impacts are an opportunity to develop in oneself, as well as with others, an opportunity to shape the 'value' of one's work, not only its quantity or measure.

Further reading

RCUK, *Evaluation Practical Guidelines: A Guide for Evaluating Public Engagement Activities* (Swindon: RCUK, 2011).

I I

Ethics

This chapter will focus on ethics from a broad perspective, considering two main approaches. Firstly, the chapter will consider ethics from a communication and engagement standpoint, how to engage with participants ethically, incorporate informed consent procedures, consider any data that are collected, used and stored, give participants access to further information and follow any relevant ethical guidelines. Secondly, the chapter will explore wider questions regarding the ethics of communication and participation. Is communication about research just about generating publicity? What new ethical questions are emerging with communication and engagement approaches? Does research communication need its own code of practice?

Ethics and research communication

As previous chapters of this book have demonstrated, many research communication activities involve people, and this chapter will begin by considering how you can engage people in your activities in an ethical way. The research that you are communicating may already have undergone some form of ethical review process or risk assessment, and researchers who carry out a lot of research with people or sensitive materials, for instance, are already likely to be very familiar with ethical processes. However, for some it might be the first time that you have thought about ethics; for instance, your research may relate to desk-, field- or lab-based activities that simply do not generate ethical issues, and therefore it can occasionally come as a surprise that there might be some ethical considerations to take into account when communicating with people. Alternatively, you may be based in an organisation which does not have an ethical framework or approval process and therefore have simply not been prompted previously to think about these issues. Either way, it's important to consider the ethical principles associated with your research communication activities, particularly if you intend to evaluate your activity and therefore will be collecting data from the people who are participating.

The importance of ethics

Regardless of your prior experience where ethics is concerned, ethical considerations of research are well established, meaning that there are a wide range of sources to consult in the design of an ethically sound communication project. Even if you are based in an organisation which does not have an ethical process or applies it only to mainstream research activities, thinking through the ethical aspects of research communication is important.

Ethics 'is sometimes used to refer to the set of rules, principles or ways of thinking that guide or claim authority to guide, the actions of a particular group' (Singer, 1994: 4), and although at times the terms are used interchangeably it is subtly different from morality, which involves a judgement on the part of the individual as to what is the appropriate moral behaviour (Wiles, 2013). Whether ethics should be applied or a matter for philosophical debate has not always been agreed upon; however, in the twentieth century increased ethical debate around topics such as war, women's rights, environmental and medical issues saw a resurgence of applied ethical thinking (Attfield, 2012), demanding ethical practice beyond consideration of ethical issues alone. Alongside this, increased research, particularly associated with medical and health settings, resulted in growing attention to the role and treatment of people within the research process.

Codes of professional ethics first appeared in the medical community during the nineteenth century, with the American Medical Association producing the first code of medical ethics in 1848 (Attfield, 2012). However, a number of the most significant ethical developments emerged following experimentation that occurred during the Second World War (Smith Iltis, 2006). One of the most significant codes, the Nuremberg Code of 1949, set out that human experimentation should adhere to ten points, including the need for voluntary and informed consent, clear justification for the research, appropriate training of those leading the research and the avoidance of mental and physical suffering (Wiles, 2013; Agar, 2012; Attfield, 2012; Smith Iltis, 2006). The Declaration of Helsinki followed in 1964, and it, as well as its subsequent revisions, added to the principles of the Nuremberg Code, with further stipulations including that research involving human subjects should undergo review processes (Wiles, 2013; Smith Iltis, 2006).

Such codes largely pertain to research activities and, as DuBois (2006) highlights, there can sometimes be confusion as to what actually constitutes 'research'. For instance, data collection carried out for educational or journalistic purposes, or for studies with no intentions to publish or disseminate data, sometimes avoid ethical review. However, regardless of the organisational definitions and requirements for engagement with such an ethics process, we would argue that considering ethical principles within the design of a research communication activity, even if certain aspects become irrelevant, can be helpful and is an important part of being an effective researcher. There have been drives to enhance researchers' 'ethical literacy', which means more than simply ticking the boxes to achieve ethics approval, and seeing ethics as part of the full research process (Wiles, 2013). From our perspective researchers are as likely to confront ethical questions when engaging in their research as at other stages of the research process.

Ethical principles

The key underlying principle of research ethics is that no one should be harmed in the process of research or evaluation (Hoggarth and Comfort, 2010). The word 'harm' needs to be considered at a broad level. It can of course include physical harm which might occur, particularly in medical or health-related settings, but it also includes psychological harm, for instance in social research if someone is revisiting a particular experience or memory. Furthermore, there might be social harm caused by your project; perhaps your evaluation might reveal information that could be damaging to participants if their identity was obvious or revealed, and this could even result in legal harm for you or for those with whom you are working. Thus it is important not to be dismissive of the potential ramifications of activities and to think realistically about any potential harm that might arise.

Sometimes we might be involved in an activity where there are potential ethical risks; for instance, you may be a researcher with an interest in teen eating disorders who plans to use social media to engage around a particular activity. It's likely that the interaction could be planned to have a whole range of benefits for participants, perhaps in talking about their views, finding out more about the research or being located in an information-rich environment. However, there could also be significant risks that participants feel under pressure to participate, that discussions have a negative impact on their experience or become emotionally challenging. In such cases it's important to carefully consider how those risks could be minimised, perhaps by having a set of agreed ground rules, working with users to design an experience which is most appropriate to them and having sources of support for people to call on if they need it. Some projects are situated in ethically challenging areas. That doesn't necessarily mean that they shouldn't happen but, rather, that time should be taken to very carefully plan and think about the process from the participants' perspective; 'ethics are not an exact science' (Hoggarth and Comfort, 2010: 86).

In addition to the need to minimise harm, there are a number of key ethical principles to consider. Hoggarth and Comfort (2010) designate informed consent, voluntary participation, anonymity and confidentiality as key, but we would also add to these principles the need for reciprocal communication and social awareness.

Informed consent

Informed consent can be a very challenging concept where research is concerned. The principle of informed consent means that individuals do not only consent for their (or those they are responsible for) participation in an activity, but are also informed of key information that might influence that consent. This can be extremely challenging when working at the frontiers of research, where the implications of the research or how it could be used may be hard to predict. In research communication it can be a little more straightforward. Key information might include aspects such as the purpose, the funder, what it will involve, with whom participants will be communicating, what data they will provide (if an activity is also being evaluated) and how those data will be presented in things like reports and publications. It might also include some practical information, such as how long the participation will take (Hoggarth and Comfort, 2010). Informed consent is thus most challenging when the information on how the data could potentially be used is not yet definite, for instance when there might be one purpose for data now, but potentially many more in the future. The participants' consent might be recorded on a consent form which they complete, or the agreement could be a spoken one if you are carrying out something like a short, snapshot interview. In some cases you may require 'implied consent' (DuBois, 2006), for example a statement at the outset of a questionnaire, or signs that clearly indicate a location which is being observed; people who do not want to participate will inform you of this by simply not becoming involved or not completing the questionnaire.

It's particularly important that in giving consent people are aware of any 'exits' in the process if they change their mind. For a one-off communication event which isn't being evaluated it might not be feasible to allow people to opt out after the fact. However, if you recorded and plan to transcribe the event for your website, or had participants complete an evaluation questionnaire, providing details on how to have their data removed and a feasible date (for them and for you) by when they can do so is something you can easily incorporate.

Voluntary participation

The consent procedures above are one way to ensure that your participants are engaged voluntarily, but there are also some additional factors to consider in this regard. It's important to think about any pressures that might influence participants. These might be a pressure to participate, pressure around what that participation might result in or an expectation that they should participate in a particular way (for example, in evaluation, give the 'right answers'). Even if you give participants the option not be involved there can be subtle ways that you make that more difficult, for instance by cajoling people into involvement, by making it very obvious to others if they are not participating or by overly emphasising the positive influence of their involvement (Hoggarth and Comfort, 2010). In this regard it's particularly important to think not only about the design of an activity or of data collection tools, but also about the supplementary information, like posters or invitations to participate, that are provided.

Case study 11.1 **Ethically impossible**

Between 1946 and 1948 the US Public Health Service carried out a series of sexually transmitted disease experiments on an estimated 1,308 prisoners, soldiers and psychiatric patients in Guatemala, none of whom had given their consent. Not only is this a fascinating and troubling case study from an ethical perspective, but the reaction of the commission which investigated the situation 60 years later is also of interest. Rather than hide away from an example of ethically questionable research practice, the panel decided to explicitly utilise it as a case study for communication and education: 'The best thing we can do as a country when faced with a dark chapter is to bring it to light,' stated the report's authors (Gutmann and Wagner, 2011: v). In this case the information previously shrouded in darkness emerged in response to a request from the president, Barack Obama, to investigate what had happened in Guatemala and to ensure that current rules (both national and international) would avoid such unethical treatment occurring again. Therefore it forms a novel case study not only in how ethical mistreatment can occur within research processes, but also in how communication and this specific example are being used to prevent such situations happening again in future research.

The nine-month investigation on the basis of the president's request found there had been a 'gross violation of ethics' as compared to the standards of today (Gutmann and Wagner, 2011: v). In the two-year period between 1946 and 1948, prisoners, psychiatric patients, soldiers and sex workers were deliberately infected with a range of sexually transmitted infections including gonorrhoea and syphilis. The sex workers were able to further transmit the disease. Of those infected in the original research population, the commission was able to find a record of treatment for just over half (678) of the research subjects. The experiments expanded to over 5,000 subjects, including children from rural locations, orphanages and state schools, as well as leprosy patients. Many experienced traumatic diagnostic work, including lumbar and cisternal punctures, through to the early 1950s.

Access to such individuals without their consent could not have happened without the involvement of others, and it is perhaps here where some of the most concerning elements of this example emerge. The commission found widespread involvement amongst US and Guatemalan officials, including senior medical directors and personnel, institutional leaders and government directors, as well as leading academic scientists and researchers. Although the report high-lights that some ethical conventions were not in place at that time, those that did already exist were neglected; '[i]n the commission's view, the Guatemala experiments involved unconscionable violations of ethics, even as judged against the researchers' own understanding of the practices and requirements of medical ethics of the day' (Gutmann and Wagner, 2011: 92). Evidence was found that many of those involved in the work actively shrouded it in secret, aware of the ethical concerns it could generate. And whilst findings from the research were reported, this was often through a complex web of unofficial publication or citation, whereby detailed peer review of the actual research context was left unexplored.

In the commission's view, these ethical misdemeanours were rendered even more shocking due to the medical context in which they occurred. The research ignored key ethical principles, including protection of the vulnerable, the need for informed consent, scientific justification and protection of privacy and confidentiality, as well as any form of ethical review before the work began. 'Careful consideration of the ways these actions violated ethical principles both honors the memory of these victims and helps ensure that society learns from these offenses' (Gutmann and Wagner, 2011: 94).

In this context, the commission created a study guide (http://bioethics.gov/node/778) to communicate about the episode and provoke ethical reflection. The free guide was intended to be used by those teaching ethics in schools, colleges and universities, as well as by members of the public in settings such as book clubs, to 'get us all talking about ethics' (Presidential Commission for the Study of Bioethical Issues, 2015: np). The depth of evidence the commission was able to gather creates an ideal resource for people to consider the ethical quandaries involved in a real case study, and provides facts and information, discussion prompts and questions, as well as links to further resources.

The commission sees the guide as fulfilling an important role, particularly for those students and researchers who may not have access to any ethics training or advice: 'One lesson of the Guatemala experiments, never to take ethics for granted, let alone confuse ethical principles with burdensome obstacles to be overcome or evaded, is a sobering one for our own and all subsequent generations' (Gutmann and Wagner, 2011: 94).

Confidentiality and anonymity

Once people have decided to participate, it's important to consider confidentiality and anonymity. These can become confused but there are important differences where research communication is concerned. Confidentiality means that the data or information provided by participants will be kept with the researcher or team, whilst anonymity means any reported data would not relate back to them as an individual (Hoggarth and Comfort, 2010). Where confidentiality is concerned it is particularly important to consider how data will be collected and stored. Data protection is key, and many organisations will have data protection procedures that must be followed, including how data should be stored, protected, maintained and destroyed. There are also legal requirements around certain personal data which it is important to investigate and adhere to.

Take particular care that you do not accidentally reveal your participants through subtle identifying features or because the participant's community is so small that their participation is obvious. For instance, if you were carrying out an evaluation within museums it might be the case that the museum or even the individuals working in it could be identified by others very easily; in such cases it might be better to have consent, in advance, not to anonymise the data. Applying pseudonyms is one approach to providing anonymity, but care is needed to ensure that the names used are also appropriately broad and don't inadvertently identify an individual because they are used only in certain groups. Whilst pseudonyms can usefully be used to anonymise people or organisations, be aware in choosing pseudonyms not to apply names which could be stereotypical as well as discreetly revealing. You should also take care not to reveal data by accident (Hoggarth and Comfort, 2010). For instance, participants will sometimes informally ask who else is involved; this information should not be mentioned unless participants have agreed. If you are involved in electronic communications with participants, remember how often contact details are accidentally shared through being inadvertently copied on an email.

Reciprocal communication

Participants often play a considerable role in both evaluation and research communication activities, so reciprocal communication is also important to consider. Depending on the length of engagement you have with people, it's possible that they may have questions, queries or information they would like to share beyond the constraints of an activity or interaction. Providing appropriate contact details for people on an information sheet or considering some format for continued communication, perhaps through social media, could be appropriate. Similarly, people may like to know what happened at the end of an activity, for instance by being provided with an evaluation summary or some form of update on the outcomes. This can either be an 'opt in' mechanism or include all participants, but people often like to see the value or outcome when they have given time, perspectives or ideas. The important thing is that whatever a researcher commits to they must be able to do, so don't suggest that you will provide something which in practice it would be difficult to deliver. Finally, at some stage you may move on to other things, and so it is important to think about how you withdraw from a situation. You might create the conditions for this in advance, for example by providing a timeline for the activity at its outset, or plan a polite exit when things draw to a natural close. Either way, it's important to thank participants for their involvement and consider the closure they may need around an activity, in addition to your own.

Social awareness

During a research communication activity we interact with people from different backgrounds and social situations and with varying needs and requirements. These can impinge not only on the wider considerations of how to design an activity but also on the practical considerations that might be made within it. Discrimination can occur on a variety of bases, but the key issues that may impinge on a research context are perhaps those based on disability, race, religion, sex and age. Discrimination does not always occur on purpose, and in a research communication context you should be most cautious about any indirect or subtle arrangements that you put in place which could disadvantage a particular individual or group. This might include all sorts of things, such as having an unsuitable venue, poor design of text-based materials or selecting a date which conflicts with a religious holiday. Whilst it's impossible to account for the needs of every possible participant in designing a research communication activity, especially if you are catering for a general audience, there are choices which you might make, like the time of day it is scheduled, that ultimately result in an activity being as inclusive and welcoming as possible.

It is also important to consider any other issues of equality that you may need to take into account when deciding with whom you plan to communicate. A number of these issues are discussed in Chapter 3. Your communication efforts may be targeted at people who have particular characteristics (such as gender, ethnicity or religion), or equally it may be that a particular group justify more specific attention in terms of their experience (Hoggarth and Comfort, 2010). You should consider whether targeting specific participant groups is right for your activity, but also avoid assumptions in working with them. If your work impinges on a particular issue or condition, such as a disability, there are a variety of charities and organisations which can provide advice, style guides and information on how best to work with individuals and groups.

In addition to all of the above, when working with some participants there might be further factors to consider. For example, if you are working with children and young people, investigate any permissions, criminal record checks or qualifications you may need. The United Kingdom has a Disclosure and Barring Service (DBS) check, while there is a Certified Criminal Record Check in Canada and a Police Certificate in Japan, so check your local requirements. In some settings it may be the case that you are told that a person with appropriate responsibility, like a teacher, will also be present, meaning that you don't have to undergo one of these types of check. If that is what you have been told, make sure that it happens. It's easy for people to forget and slip out to catch up on email or make a quick phone call. Speak up if this happens, to protect both yourself and your participants.

Furthermore, those you are working with may not be able to provide consent for themselves – for example, if they are deemed vulnerable in some way (DuBois, 2006). In such cases consent from a parent, teacher or caregiver, effectively acting as a 'gatekeeper', may be needed. This can mean that you need to communicate regularly with a support service, community group, charity or school to broker contact and you need to provide some extra information for their use. For example, they may want a letter to send out to all consent providers on your behalf, an insert for a newsletter or similar, and you may need to build extra time into your activity to allow for this extra layer of consent. In general, those who are working with groups which may be deemed 'vulnerable' will be able to provide you with some advice on what would work most appropriately for them, but such individuals can be time poor, so do prepare what you can in advance and think sensitively about their expectations and needs.

Gaining consent from another party should not stop you from still explaining the information around the project to the participants (Hoggarth and Comfort, 2010). Whilst a consent form provides written evidence of consent, you should allow time for people to ask questions and discuss the form or information sheet with you (Smith Iltis, 2006) so that they have an opportunity to fully understand their participation.

Case study 11.2 Ethics and older people

Helena Wythe experienced some challenges when working with a vulnerable group as part of her PhD research based in the Science Communication Unit at the University of the West of England, Bristol. Not only was she researching a sensitive topic, food preparation and hygiene, but she also wanted to gather the views of a group that was potentially challenging to reach, older people, including the oldest 'old', aged 85 and over. Along the way she drew some important insights about working with a generation with a great deal to share. 'I found it fascinating; older people have this wealth of accumulated experience, whether they have had a fairly conventional and happy life, or have had to deal with quite tragic circumstances,' said Helena, reflecting on the experience.

Helena's research started from a perspective of 'value', as she was interested in the 'assets' older people have when it comes to their food preparation. That might be informal lessons from their family, knowledge from school or the years of practice older people have had in storing, preparing and consuming their meals. As Helena explained, focusing on a group deemed 'vulnerable' was important. 'Vulnerable groups need to be included in research to redress the social inequalities they may (or may not) have … I think that it's imperative that research with vulnerable groups continues to be a priority.'

Finding older people to talk to was something about which she had to think creatively. By using a network of community groups and 'lunch clubs', Helena was able to get to know her participants long before she asked them for their views. Helena talked about her research interests from the outset, shared meals and developed trust with her participants, whilst at the same time making it very clear that they were under no pressure to participate in her later data collection.

When participants were then invited to become involved, they already knew a little about Helena and the research project. This was supported by large-type documentation and extended periods of time during which people could decide whether they wished to participate, as well as additional opt-out points in the process if they changed their mind. For instance, giving participants a quick phone call the day before the interview not only provided a reminder that Helena would be meeting them as arranged, but allowed participants an additional opportunity to decline or to ask further questions.

As interviews occurred, some older people decided to have family members or friends present, and were welcomed to do so. Helena also thought about helpful things she could do. For example, participants were asked to select a location for the interview and a seat of their choice, as poor eyesight was sometimes a problem and this meant they could be as comfortable as possible. It also meant that Helena had to allow a little more time for these interactions than might typically be the case. 'You have to step off your busy hectic life of deadlines and work and whatever else is going on to just slow down and *listen*,' explained Helena. 'Older people don't necessarily have the same time constraints and so everything needs to be done at their pace.'

As the process drew to a close, Helena had thought carefully about the needs of those who had participated. Information was available on aspects like bereavement support, as this sometimes came up in the course of the conversation. Rather than payment for time, Helena offered a gift as well as a thank you note and was happy to help out with small tasks – for instance, one participant asked her to walk to the shop for an ice cream.

In building trust, Helena was aware that it was important that she did not simply disappear from her participants' lives once her needs were met. She planned for her visits to gradually become slightly less regular, before a final visit during which she presented the community groups with a communal gift. By the end of the process the experience had also influenced Helena, as she explained. 'I visited the lunch clubs for quite a few months and you'd also see people deteriorate in that time … and that was difficult when you'd come to know them well.' However, in working with older people, Helena also kept in mind that 'they are the same as everyone else, with the same ranges of likes, dislikes and opinions and are as diverse a group as any other you'd encounter'; so, whilst additional ethical considerations are important, 'the same care and attention should really be given to whoever is taking part in your research as a matter of courtesy, you fit everything around them'.

Incorporating ethics

A range of ethical codes and guidelines exist for students, professionals and amateurs to draw on. A selection of generic sources are included in Box 11.1. Such guidelines tend to provide just that, a guideline, though in some cases non-adherence to them might mean a researcher is declined professional memberships and care should be taken around legal aspects which are incorporated within such advice. However, such guidance largely provides advice as a starting point, recognising that one size does not fit all (Eagle *et al.*, 2013; Wiles, 2013). Pimple (2002) suggests that simply 'following the rules' is not the same as being ethical, although it often overlaps. Considering ethics simply as something you must do may miss the point. At times you may need to do more than is recommended, or even run counter to a recommendation, in order to engage ethically (Pimple, 2002).

Aside from research contexts, journalism also has some useful professional codes on which to draw. Regardless of your view of journalists, these include well-established principles regarding integrity, objectivity and misrepresentation, which are also considerations within a research communication context (Dahlstrom and Ho, 2012). These are also indicated in Box 11.1.

As well as these specific sources of advice, the Health and Human Services Office for Human Research Protections (OHRP) in the United States of America maintains a guide to laws, regulations and guidelines on the protection of human subjects in over one hundred countries and from several international organisations. It is listed in Box 11.1 and provides an excellent link to guidance internationally, including throughout Europe, Asia, the Middle East, Africa, North America, Latin America and the Pacific; it is regularly kept up to date. Beyond the international guidance provided, if your activity has been funded by an external source it is important to consult its resources. Many research councils, charities and funding sources will have their own ethical guidelines. In addition, there are national associations and societies for particular disciplines, like market research, sociology and psychology. Although often targeted more at research, they will likely have some useful pointers to bear in mind.

The above codes and guidelines have numerous things in common around the principles of ethical conduct mentioned in the last section, but they also have some additional advice which can be helpful in some situations. For example, some provide guidance, should you witness behaviour that could be troubling or inappropriate, with advice on what to do in that situation. In some contexts there are legal and professional expectations around particular behaviour that you may have a responsibility to report. Although this is perhaps more rare in research communication contexts, some up-front consideration of such issues can be reassuring.

These guides also discuss issues such as 'deception', a process which might occur if data were being collected covertly, or if the true aims of an evaluation were in some way distorted. This again tends to be fairly unusual in research communication settings, but there are reasons why some researchers continue to use such approaches, as they are necessary for the knowledge that is required (DuBois, 2006). However, the potential implications of deception mean that if you are planning to take such an approach it is particularly important to pay careful attention to any relevant advice and guidance.

Box 11.1 International ethical codes and guidelines

African Evaluation Association
www.afrea.org/sites/default/files/resources/AfrEA%202007_guidelines%20standards%20%26%20onorms_EN.pdf

Association of Internet Researchers Ethics http://aoir.org/ethics/

Belmont Report www.hhs.gov/ohrp/archive/belmontArchive.html

European Federation of Psychologists' Associations, Meta-Code of Ethics www.efpa.eu/ethics

European Society for Opinion and Marketing Research, ICC/ESOMAR International Code on Market and Social Research www.esomar.org/index.php/professional-standards.html

EthicNet, Database for European Codes of Journalism Ethics http://ethicnet.uta.fi/

FERCAP, Forum for Ethical Review Committees in the Asian and Western Pacific Region www.fercap-sidcer.org/

FLACEIS Latin American Forum of Ethics Committees in Health Research www.flaceis.org/

Health and Human Services' Office for Human Research Protections (OHRP) www.hhs.gov/ohrp/international/index.html

International Communication Association Ethics Statement www.icahdq.org/about_ica/ethics.asp

International Council of Museums Code of Ethics http://icom.museum/the-vision/code-of-ethics/

International Sociological Association www.isa-sociology.org/about/isa_code_of_ethics.htm

International Statistical Institute www.isi-web.org/about-isi/professional-ethics

Management of Social Transformations (MOST) www.unesco.org/most/ethical.htm

Pew Research Journalism Project www.journalism.org/resources/ethics-codes/

RESPECT Code www.respectproject.org/code/

Universal Ethical Code for Scientists www.gov.uk/government/publications/universal-ethical-code-for-scientists

Visitor Studies Association Resources for Ethical Research http://visitorstudies.org/ethical-research

World Medical Association Declaration of Helsinki: Ethical Principles for Medical Research Involving Human Subjects www.wma.net/en/30publications/10policies/b3/

Finally, in addition to general ethical guidelines there is also a variety of specific advice which might be pertinent to a specific method you are using, for instance within an evaluation. A good example of this is observational approaches, for which there is a very extensive associated literature. Ethical guidance which is pertinent to specific methods is frequently updated as traditional research approaches are adapted to new and emerging contexts that raise new ethical questions, to this day. For example, online communication is of growing interest to communicators and researchers but raises significant ethical questions around privacy and consent (Wiles, 2013). Similarly the use of visual approaches, such as photographs and imagery, can also raise new questions, a fundamental one being how images of participants challenge principles of anonymity (Wiles, 2013). So, whilst there are extensive documents to which you can refer in considering ethical issues which might be relevant to your activities, and a growing literature around new and emerging techniques, it is also the case that at times creative communication approaches can raise new ethical quandaries about which you may need to take the time to think carefully or keep up to date.

Ethical questions

Moving from the practical standpoint regarding how ethics might be considered in your research communication activities, there are some broader ethical questions that research communicators ought to consider. As Peter Singer (1994: 3) states, 'ethics is about how we ought to live. What makes an action the right, rather than the wrong, thing to do? What should our goals be? These questions are so fundamental that they lead us on to further questions.'

In the space of a chapter it is difficult to consider all of the potential ethical questions that research communication might raise, but there are at least a few with which we might start, and perhaps these will come to be further considered in your own activities. Here we have chosen to focus on questions of *power*, *access*, *purpose* and *privacy*, but this is not an exhaustive list.

As a communicator there can be questions of *power* with regard to your interaction with participants. Hoggarth and Comfort (2010) discuss in the context of evaluation that generally an evaluator has, or will appear to have, more power, because ultimately they can influence the future of an activity or project. However, this often also applies in the context of individual communication activities. If you are representing yourself as a researcher, communicator or facilitator in an activity, even one which might be very strongly based on dialogue, there is a likelihood that other participants may feel they have less power than you. That may relate to quite simple things, for instance that you have the power to draw a discussion to a close, or to more challenging dimensions whereby participants may see your views as privileged or having more importance. It's very important to think about this in designing an activity because sometimes quite simple accidents, such as being seated in a privileged position or an off-the-cuff remark about something you may have read, can radically alter the power balance within an interaction.

As a researcher you will also have certain privileges of *access* to communication, and questions over access for other types of participants are of much interest amongst those in research communication. For instance, it is common for certain groups to be deemed 'hard to reach' or for research communicators to have an interest in how certain communities are excluded from research communication settings, such as museums (see Chapter 3 for more consideration of these issues). Since the outset of research communication activities, there has been the dilemma of whether to meet the needs of the specialist, particular groups of participants or to focus on the needs of all. O'Neill (2009) emphasises that from an ethical perspective communicative acts must be 'accessible', and to this end they must be both 'intelligible' and 'relevant' to their intended audience; transparency and freedom of information alone are not enough from an ethical standpoint. Thus, in this sense communicators, as well as those who mediate, have obligations in that role. Their communications should be appropriate and tailored, just as participants too have a responsibility to decipher, interpret and question that which they encounter (O'Neill, 2009). Equal consideration may not be the same as equal treatment, as people have different needs. Thus, often there may need to be some prioritising of those whose interests are seen to have greater value (Attfield, 2012; Singer, 1994). Consequently the main consideration from an ethical perspective might be to consider foremost for whom you are catering, and for what purpose, although perhaps there are also wider questions to consider amongst the research communication community at large regarding how certain groups of people have privileged access (Dawson, 2014b; Dickert and Sugarman, 2005) and/or whether a focus on communication for all, the public at large, is ethically appropriate.

Next, and linked to the above point, there can be ethical considerations around the *purpose* of research communication. Research communication is often driven from the perspective that participants will grow and benefit from the experience, whereby at times the responsibility of researchers to communicate their research for the benefit of people or the reduction of risk is in itself seen to be the ethical thing to do (Thompson, 2012; Garrett and Bird, 2000). From an ethical perspective there is seen to be an intrinsic value in developing one's human capacities. Attfield (2012: 56) provides the examples of 'the capacities for growth and self-motion; for perception; for linguistic communication; for practical reasoning; for self-determination; for understanding and theoretical reasoning; for taking responsibility for one's beliefs, attitudes and actions', and so forth. It is hard to argue against such motives; however, for you as a research communicator it is also important to consider that people have differing conceptions of 'value' and that what you value as an individual researcher in terms of growth may differ from what your participants value (DuBois, 2006).

Values are also not the same as 'needs'. A human need can be an instrumental need (for example, food and shelter for survival) or an intrinsic need (for example, well-being for human flourishing), and Attfield (2012) argues these are relatively universal. Thus, research communication also has an impact on our needs: participants may find out information which benefits their instrumental setting (for instance, how to better insulate their home) or that influences their intrinsic needs (for example, by conversing about a difficult issue which is of relevance to them). Whilst research communication may fulfil certain needs, again we may need to reflect on differences in views. What we see as valuable as a need may not be shared by participants, and they also have a role to play in determining their own needs (Attfield, 2012). The need for particular knowledge, or the need for young people to enter a particular career (Garrett and Bird, 2000), are often cited as key motivations for research communication, yet this may not fully recognise the role people play in defining their own needs. In research communication there can be a thin line between sharing research and 'advocacy' for your subject or discipline, and researchers have differing views on whether this is appropriate (Dahlstron and Ho, 2012; Meyer and Sandøe, 2012; Pimple, 2002), yet as research communicators we may rarely reflect on how we make assumptions around 'need' and how this influences our practices and activities.

Furthermore, in the context of both values and needs the move towards public engagement would suggest a wider appreciation of individuals' personal values and autonomy, but at times we may question whether this is truly put into practice in that which occurs (Dahlstron and Ho, 2012). The boundaries between public relations, publicity, advocacy and research communication are often unclear (Chalkstream Communications, 2014; Meyer and Sandøe, 2012). This may overlook the 'possible tensions between public good and public relations' (Chalkstream Communications, 2014: 7). Furthermore, as Dahlstron and Ho (2012) highlight, some research communication approaches, for instance use of the techniques of persuasion, are not only hidden from participants but also underexplored from an ethical perspective in research communication when compared with fields such as advertising, which has an extensive history of considering issues such as manipulation, rights to information and voluntary exposure. This suggests that much could be learned from effective public relations practice, were a wider appreciation of the commonalities between research communication and public relations considered. Though the motivations for public engagement have been questioned, particularly in the context of public engagement designed to reduce controversy (Stilgoe *et al.*, 2013; Dahlstron and Ho, 2012; Sutcliffe, 2011; Wilsdon and Willis, 2004), this has yet to be translated into the context of individual activities or a more widespread critical discussion of the ethical appropriateness of this type of activity.

Finally, research communication, particularly that which is occurring in an online context, is not excluded from discussions of *privacy*. An interesting example is that of communication around the use of data. As Wiles (2013) highlights, there has been a growing interest in the need to maximise the value of research by making data more readily usable amongst researchers' contemporaries, as well as by future researchers. There has also been a considerable expansion in online public engagement projects, such as citizen science activities or public consultation through social networking. In other words, there is now more research available for people to manipulate online and contribute to, should they so wish. However, data sharing raises ethical quandaries, for instance around the informed consent process, where it is now far more difficult to inform participants as to how their data might be used in future (Wiles, 2013). Online activities which require others to submit data they have collected, or are in some way assisting to analyse, can raise emerging questions around aspects such as authorship and ownership (Grand *et al.*, 2014). Open source software, customer-developed products and 'crowd funding' are putting people at the heart of some large companies' and organisations' research and development (Sutcliffe, 2011), but at times leaving ethical questions around this as an afterthought.

In themselves, these new approaches to research are occasionally opportunities for the embedding of engagement within an ethical conversation. For example, in the United Kingdom the Economic and Social Research Council (ESRC) and Office For National Statistics (ONS) carried out a Dialogue on Data comprising a series of fourteen workshops with over 130 members of the public and twenty experts to establish public understanding and perspectives on the use of administrative data for research. Although there were some expressions of concern, for instance around privacy and security, if certain conditions and restrictions were met people were also confident that such data could be used effectively (Cameron *et al.*, 2014). This is one example of where public engagement in itself could potentially have an influence on new ethical norms in the future. In contrast, the Care.data system, which plans to make better research use of National Health Service medical records, has experienced delays in the introduction of the system, due to calls for additional safeguards and strategies (for example, the introduction of an advisory group) and the need for an increase in accessible information about its plans. The introduction of Care.data met with considerable concerns amongst both patients and health professionals, in part due to a lack of communication around the plans (Torjesen, 2014).

Research communication can, then, comprise ethical issues as subject matter, be they questions of the environment, poverty, equity and justice, health or bioethics, animal rights or impacts on future generations (Attfield, 2012), and can contribute to their resolution via engagement, but research communication in its practice may also raise ethical considerations which it is important to consider.

An ethical code of practice?

Ethical considerations regarding communicating science and research have largely been overlooked, and can be found at the foundation of certain research controversies: 'it seems likely that at least some of the controversy surrounding many of our current science-related controversies is due to violation of some unarticulated ethical considerations' (Dahlstron and Ho, 2012: 610; Meyer and Sandøe, 2012). Whilst researchers are well versed in the practical ethical contexts associated with research, such as conflicts of interest, consent and data protection, there has been very little consideration of the ethical contexts of research communication techniques (Stilgoe *et al.*, 2013; Dahlstron and Ho, 2012; Thompson, 2012). In addition, not all those involved in research communication have professional affiliations; for instance, those in low-level support functions or 'public information officers ... are expected to promote their employer' (Chalkstream Communications, 2014; Dahlstron and Ho, 2012: 605) and so may have little opportunity to consider the ethical contexts of their communication activities. At present there is not an ethical code for research communication, although as discussed earlier in this chapter there are certainly multiple guidelines on which to draw. However, before we bring this chapter to a close there has been one development which it is worth considering in some detail, as it may present future opportunities not only to consider public engagement in new contexts but also to consider some of the broader ethical ramifications of both research and its communication.

Responsible Innovation is a framework which has emerged from a science and technology setting, and although it is influenced by a particular research context and funding setting, those involved in its development argue that it has potential for use in a wide variety of contexts (Stilgoe *et al.*, 2013). Discussions of the need for greater responsibility go beyond this particular framing, and the consideration of how research can better benefit and involve society, assess risk, be open and transparent, and adapt and respond, are also being debated under the guises of 'responsible research and innovation', 'responsible development' and 'social responsibility' (Italian Presidency of the Council of the European Union, 2014; Stilgoe *et al.*, 2013; Sutcliffe, 2011; Pimple, 2002). The Responsible Innovation framework, however, acknowledges that the responsibilities of the scientific community with regard to the knowledge it creates, and its social influences for both benefit and harm, are complex and contested. This is further complicated in areas of innovation where judgements of responsibility and risk, based on existing technologies or processes, are unavailable because the approach is so novel or new (Stilgoe *et al.*, 2013). Although participation in the governance of research has increased, there has been 'little scope for broad ethical reflection on the purposes of science or innovation' (Stilgoe *et al.*, 2013: 1569).

The framework thus encourages the adoption of four key dimensions, some of which overlap and relate, in addition to having flexibility in the methods through which they can be mobilised. Firstly, the framework encourages 'anticipation', that researchers should have the foresight to consider the 'what if?' questions associated to their research at an early enough stage for there to be some constructive influence. Secondly, it encourages 'reflexivity', whereby researchers reflect on their 'activities, commitments and assumptions' as well as their limits, and draw on appropriate professional codes, which may include ethical procedures (Stilgoe *et al.*, 2013:1571). Thirdly is 'inclusion', the creation of spaces for the public and stakeholders to question and participate through deliberative or dialogue-based activities. Finally comes 'responsiveness', an allowance that research can change or respond to circumstances as well as public and stakeholder values: 'responsiveness involves responding to new knowledge as this emerges and to emerging perspectives, views and norms' (Stilgoe *et al.*, 2013:1572). Although most obviously in relation to 'inclusion', for all of the four principles above, the framework is inclusive of a variety of techniques which are participatory, deliberative and/or engagement based.

One organisation which has taken up this approach in the United Kingdom is the Engineering and Physical Sciences Research Council (EPSRC), which has committed to the activities and research it funds aligning to principles of responsible innovation 'creating value for society in an ethical and responsible way' (EPSRC, 2014: np). It has an expectation that its researchers will 'anticipate, reflect, engage and act' when appropriate, with the purpose of 'engage' being to open up 'visions, impacts and questioning to broader deliberation, dialogue, engagement and debate in an inclusive way' (EPSRC, 2014: np). In addition, its framework explicitly states that it expects researchers to conduct their work ethically and legally, and to inform on any concerns and dilemmas. Whilst stating that the approach is not prescriptive, it also takes a share of the responsibilities, recognising that some of the responsibilities in hand sit not only with individual researchers but also amongst the wider professional community (EPSRC, 2014).

At present, discussion and use of the Responsible Innovation framework is at an early stage and those involved in its formulation are keen to see that it is implemented with care, over time, amongst conversations that are also occurring in other contexts regarding responsible research and innovation and responsible development (Italian Presidency of the Council of the European Union, 2014; Stilgoe *et al.*, 2013). There are emerging examples of projects seeking to put such principles into practice, such as the European Union-supported RRI Toolkit (http://www.rri-tools.eu/toolkit). However, from a research communication perspective it has two core points of interest. Firstly, these discussions are underpinned by the integration of public involvement (Sutcliffe, 2011). Secondly, from an ethical perspective we see an increased integration of ethics, engagement and the research process, providing greater reflection and responsiveness around questions of values.

Summary

Communication and ethics can be seen as 'separate entities', with the ethics of communicating research 'taken for granted' (Meyer and Sandøe, 2012); however, as we hope this chapter has demonstrated, consideration of ethics should not be constrained to a focus on traditional research techniques alone. Ethical considerations can impinge on research communication activities in both practical and applied ways, as well as having more reflexive influences. It is of benefit to the communicator to consider what is the appropriate level of ethical consideration for an activity, and to incorporate time into the planned activity to make such considerations. Whether a researcher is thinking about ethics for the first time, or for the first time in the context of their communication projects, there are a wide range of resources and materials available to support the evolution of an ethically sound activity. Informed consent, voluntary participation, anonymity, confidentiality, reciprocal communication and social awareness are relevant to research communication activities, and particularly so if you plan to incorporate any form of evaluation.

Ethical conduct is to some extent a craft, not simply a duty or a set of rules. Communication of research is in and of itself increasingly seen to be part of the ethical codes of research (Doubleday, 2009; Dickert and Sugarman, 2005), but the complexity of the relationship between ethics, trust and communication is worthy of a fuller exploration. This is particularly the case when some research ethics codes are embedding research communication in order to foster increased public trust, use and value of research within society; effectively, the wider public are an 'audience' for the ethical code (Doubleday, 2009), rather than a mutual beneficiary.

Similarly, a broader understanding of the relationship between public relations, research communication and advocacy is warranted not because public relations are negative – rather, there are some excellent examples of public relations that are effective, encouraging goodwill and mutual understanding (Chalkstream Communications, 2014) – but for reasons of critical reflection and consolidation of learning across the sectors, a more transparent relationship may be constructive. In this chapter we have raised just a few of the ethical quandaries that may exist around research communication, including how it relates to the role of researchers and research communication within society. Increasing discussions of frameworks, including but not limited to responsible innovation, may create a more concerted effort to consider the ethical contexts of research communication; ethics is therefore something which is important at the level of individual communicators as well as the community more broadly.

Further reading

Attfield, R., *Ethics: An Overview* (London: Continuum, 2012).

Doubleday, R. 'Ethical codes and scientific norms: the role of communication in maintaining the social contract for science', in Holliman, R., Thomas, J., Smidt, S., Scalon, E. and Whitelegg, E. (eds), *Practising Science Communication in the Information Age* (Oxford: Oxford University Press/The Open University, 2009) pp. 19–34.

12

Dissemination

Academics may be used to communicating their research findings to their peers, but when they become practitioners of communication and engagement they may not consider the need to communicate the success (or otherwise) of new or novel approaches to communication. Likewise, the practitioner community does not have the same drivers (publications are not metrics by which they are judged) to communicate findings from project evaluations or to synthesise best practice guidelines. As a result, the communication and engagement community are often criticised for failing to share their evaluation results and insights, and this has led to criticism of the community and individual projects for 'reinventing the wheel'. This chapter will highlight not only why it is important to share best practice with this community but also how readers might further disseminate their work. It also considers the 'conundrum' of communicating about research communication. The chapter finishes with a short summary of the key points of this book and what we hope are encouraging and motivational, confidence-building insights that will enable readers to make the best use of the approaches outlined.

Sharing research communication

It is somewhat ironic that many researchers and practitioners who are heavily involved in research communication are occasionally criticised for not having better mechanisms to share good practice and the results of their work. Sharing research communication helps us to learn from others, and having our work scrutinised ultimately improves its quality, bringing benefits to current and future research communication activities. There are also ethical incentives in appropriately sharing work to which others have contributed their time or ideas. However, there are multiple reasons why research communicators do not always share their work very effectively.

Firstly, communication between academics who have an interest in research communication and practitioner communities is challenging. Practitioners, such as those based in museums, galleries or science centres, as well as those who would identify themselves as professional communicators, journalists or mediators are often pressed for time, quickly progressing from one activity to the next. This can mean that practitioners do not read the academic literature or attend academic conferences that discuss research communication; making some of the more obvious places for communication less successful. Furthermore, practitioners are not always under the same institutional pressures or norms to communicate their findings, and they may not have the professional academic research and writing skills that are required for work to feature in academic journals. For those practitioners working in small companies or freelance, there may even be institutional barriers to dissemination (including a desire to manage their intellectual property and the need to move on to the next project, rather than spend unpaid time on communicating about the previous one).

Equally, academics who are communicating about their research may not see dissemination of these events as a priority, since they may not align with their primary research interests. Furthermore, academics with an interest in research communication are often critiqued for their lack of awareness of practitioner needs and realities, and can appear distant or unwelcoming to practitioner perspectives or simply fail to take into account the realities of working in other sectors. As people come to research communication from multiple backgrounds and interests, there are also a multitude of disciplinary perspectives within the field which lead to questions as to whether research communication is a discipline in itself and can further cloud the dissemination process (Pitrelli, 2010).

Secondly, traditional publishing routes are often fairly inaccessible. To take journal publications as one example, many people with interests in research communication may not have access to journal subscriptions, or may not consider how research communication activities might feature in such publications. Conferences can be expensive and time consuming to attend and, as mentioned previously, without one disciplinary identity, there are a variety of locations where, potentially, work can feature. Although academic publishing is striving to be more accessible and open, potentially meaning that there will be broader accessibility to publications at least, the costs are now often moving from the subscriber to the content provider, again a potential deterrent for those keen to share their work but based in settings where funding may be restricted.

Thirdly, budgets for research communication can often be relatively small and short term, failing to truly support researchers or practitioners who wish to disseminate the outcomes of that process. This may mean that some people do not see this as central to their role or as a valued aspect of the research communication process; it may be another job that falls to one's own time, meaning it fails to truly reach its potential.

And finally, there is perhaps the more fundamental issue of seeking to communicate about communication, or engaging about engagement; if the work itself is on the communicative process, you can become entangled in a kind of communication loop. However, there are numerous ways that you can consider sharing your research communication practices, as we will now explain.

Dissemination resources

At the end of many research communication projects it is common to create some kind of short report; in some cases this will form part of an evaluation, feedback to funders, or simply be for internal purposes as a record of the activity; how these might be better shared is worth consideration:

> There are many evaluation studies that have been completed, reported on, and then placed on a physical or virtual shelf, never to be seen again except perhaps in an academic journal article or website. We are not dismissing the critical importance of scholarly publication as one venue for dissemination … [however,] evaluation practice has failed unless the knowledge derived from the systematic inquiry is used for the purposes for which the thinking and action processes were intended: informing the improvement and/or status of professional activities and entities. (DePoy and Gilson, 2008: 196)

As DePoy and Gilson (2008) highlight, it is useful to think about stakeholders that might have an interest in your activity. In dissemination activities, principles apply that are similar those which will have guided your research communication efforts: bear in mind that different stakeholders have different conceptions of what constitutes evidence. 'Dissemination must be preceded by an understanding of what the audience will value as accessible, comprehensible and believable' (DePoy and Gilson, 2008: 197). Identifying whom you aim to reach in your dissemination and what their needs will be are important first steps. You might also extend this consideration to reflecting on whether your dissemination should be as open and accessible as possible, for instance making sure the format of a website allows for use by visitors with differing needs, or considering publications that allow for different formats of access (DePoy and Gilson, 2008). Below we consider some key dissemination routes. We have included reports, conferences and journal publications, although it is important to remember that many of the techniques for research communication – such as social and digital media – which we have discussed throughout this book can also be used for dissemination activity, if appropriate to the audience you are seeking to reach.

Reports

Reports are a fairly standard way to write up the results of research communication efforts, but how you share them is crucial to the potential influence they might have. You may decide to include them in an institutional website or research repository (this would apply to any type of research communication dissemination; you might also submit materials like plans for an activity, scripts or other outputs to this type of resource), but unless you have a troop of dedicated readers it may be unlikely that they will be regularly accessed. Box 12.1 contains some tips on how to make reports more usable.

Generally, reports tend to be more accessible than some other types of publication, as they are often fairly readily available; however,

---

Box 12.1 Making reports user friendly and accessible

- Carefully consider the title, make it catchy, accurate and clear to insure it is likely to appear under relevant keywords on search engines.

- If you are able to influence the website metadata associated with your file, then consider how this might be used to make it easier for search engines to find (use principles of search engine optimisation).

- Write an effective Executive Summary or Introduction, making sure key information on the activity stands out in the first pages.

- Format the document to contain key information for specific readers (if you plan multiple reports for different stakeholders) or to make relevant information obvious if there are multiple readers (e.g. have recommendations grouped by type of stakeholder).

- Use hyperlinks and additional resources to share other information of relevance and increase the likelihood that your report will feature highly on search engine results.

- Include details of the methods and tools used to collect data. If possible, include the original tools (e.g. questionnaires) in an appendix.

there are also a number of useful collections and websites to which you might add your report, as well as other research communication resources, which can help them to be located more easily. Databases like InformalScience.Org (http://informalscience.org/) and the Collective Memory (http://collectivememory.britishscienceassociation.org/) will allow you to add reports, whilst resources like the Out of School Time database (www.hfrp.org/out-of-school-time/ost-database-bibliography/database) and the World Bank Group (http://ieg.worldbankgroup.org/webpage/evaluations) have collections of reports (see Box 12.2 for other suggestions for locating and storing evaluation reports).

If you aren't able to submit your report to one of these types of site, then do consider how you can highlight its existence through other means, which might include lodging it on a project website. Once you have made your report available, talk about it on relevant social media and consider how your digital profile might link to it. You might also send out invitations to look at it to relevant individuals or contacts. Examine relevant mailing lists and networks that you might want to join (the PCST mailing list and Psci-Com mailing list are both good examples of science communication networks), as these can also be a good way to flag your work to others. People are more likely to find out

---

Box 12.2 Evaluation archives and databases

BiblioMap (health promotion) http://eppi.ioe.ac.uk/webdatabases/Intro.aspx?ID=7

Centers for Disease Control and Prevention (health promotion and social marketing) www.cdc.gov/HealthCommunication/Research/

Collective Memory (STEM) http://collectivememory.britishscienceassociation.org/

EPPI Centre Database of Education Research (education) http://eppi.ioe.ac.uk/webdatabases/Intro.aspx?ID=6

Exploratorium Evaluations (STEM) www.exploratorium.edu/vre/visitor_research/reports.php

Informal Science.org Evaluation Report Database (STEM) http://informalscience.org/evaluation/browse?type=evaluations

OERL Evaluation Reports Collection (STEM) http://oerl.sri.com/ccli.html

UNICEF Evaluation and Research Database (children's rights, education and humanitarian actions) www.unicef.org/evaldatabase/

about evaluation reports that are publicised, so this is an important step in dissemination.

Conferences

Conferences are a common way to share research communication projects, both as they develop and/or before other formal publication of results. They are also a great way to network and to meet others with similar interests. However, finding out about relevant conferences can be challenging and not all are entirely clear about how you submit a presentation, workshop or session to the programme. The first thing to do when you identify a conference of relevance is to explore the submission information. This can normally be accessed online; if that doesn't answer your questions, consider contacting a conference organiser. Conferences can be expensive, so it is worth considering whether attendance can be included within your research communication budget if one is available.

The next stage is to research what has been presented at the conference before. Many conferences have loyal attendees, so a bit of background research can shed light on topics and formats that will be familiar to participants. With the exception of new conferences, past programmes are normally available online and many conferences also post short video clips of past presentations or plenary sessions on their websites. Box 12.3 lists some relevant conferences for the field of research communication.

It's very important to be well prepared for a conference presentation and to bear in mind that some disciplines have different styles for presenting: readers may read verbatim from a script or essay, or formal presentations may be expected, while at other conferences the sessions will be more relaxed and interactive. Be prepared to adapt and reconsider materials for different conferences and their audiences.

Journal publication

There are opportunities to publish research and evaluation findings from research communication projects in a wide number of journals; Box 12.4 highlights some of the academic journals that you might consider. Before you select a journal it is important to have a detailed read of the advice it provides for authors. As well as academic journals, it is worth exploring whether there are professional association or organisational publications where your work could feature, including those focused on your own research discipline.

Journal publication can be very competitive and involve expectations that articles will have a theoretical and methodological underpinning. It

---

Box 12.3 **Research communication conferences**

Many national and regional organisations hold relevant annual or biannual conferences, including:

Asian Network of Science and Technology Centres

Australian Science Communication Network

Australia New Zealand Communication Conference

Ecsite Annual Conference

Engage International Conference

The European Communication Conference

ICA Annual Conference

ICOM General Conference

Museums Association

Museum iD

Network for Public Communication of Science and Technology (PCST) Conference

Redpop, Latin American and Caribbean Network for Science and Technology Popularisation

Science Communication Conference

---

might be the case that data from one research communication activity alone does not provide the depth required for a significant contribution to the literature; consider ways that you might link together research communication projects you are working on, or test a particular theory in the context of practice if you are looking to make a more substantial contribution. Some journals accept alternative types of submission; perhaps you could author a short research note, opinion piece or commentary, based on a particular research communication process. Alternatively, you could create a review article which brings together and critically examines the work of others. Regardless of the type of submission, be realistic about the time it will take. Writing of this type must be orientated to the journal in terms of its subject matter, aims, writing style and format for things like references. Journal publication of your work will often involve multiple drafts, and responses to peer reviewers and editors, as it is quite unusual for a paper to be accepted without at the very least some form of minor revision. This can require some resilience on your part, as it is important not to take this process personally, but if you are confident in the contribution your evidence

---

Box 12.4 **Selected academic journals of relevance to research communication**

Applied Environmental Education and Communication

British Journal of Educational Technology

Citizen Science: Theory and Practice

Communicating Astronomy with the Public

Communication Research

Communication Research and Practice

Continuum

Curator

Health Education

Information Communication and Society

International Citizen Science Journal

International Journal of Science Education (Part A and B)

Journal of Applied Communication Research

Journal of Health Communication

Journal of Science Communication

Leonardo

Media, Culture and Society

Museum and Society

Museums Journal

Museum Studies

New Media and Society

The Open Journal of Art and Communication

Online Journal of Media and Communication Technologies

Public Understanding of Science

Research in Drama Education

Science as Culture

Science Communication

Visitor Studies

could make it is worth persevering, as journal publication is certainly one way to share your work.

Non-traditional routes to dissemination

If reports, conferences and journal publications do not seem appropriate for your particular research communication adventure, there are a few other ways that you might consider disseminating your findings. Additionally, these might be things you do over and above a report. Rossi *et al.* (1999: 406) coin the term 'secondary dissemination' to describe the results of evaluations which might be designed to be secondary to a more formal report. This type of dissemination relies on the plethora of communication tools discussed already in this book. For example, if you maintain or contribute to a blog, consider reporting your findings there. Equally, there may be relevant professional magazines read by other research communicators to which you could contribute an article. Perhaps locally there is a network or social event organised for researchers (such as Bristol Sci-Com Social, www.facebook.com/events/1387525678205848/, in the United Kingdom), where you could discuss your findings with others interested in the field. It is also worth bearing in mind that many apparently subject-based groups, such as science communicator networks, are open to those communicating other types of research and should not be seen as exclusive to science. The label 'science' is sometimes a hangover from the origins of these groups, which increasingly recognise and value contributions from those engaged in research communication in other contexts. There is much to be learned by bringing the wider field of research communication together to share experiences, issues and practice.

General considerations

It is also worth stressing a point about novelty. It can be daunting to both disseminate work and explore work that has gone before, and some authors are concerned that someone will already have done something the same or very similar in terms of a research communication project or idea, or disseminating around it. We would argue that research communicators should not see this as a threat; rather, it is an excellent way to learn from others and to create depth and capacity across the field. In this book, whilst we are arguing for creative thinking where research communication is concerned, this should not be mistaken for an assumption that every research communication activity should be novel or unique. There is much that can be learned from the work of others, a further significant reason why disseminating your research communication experiences is important.

And finally, for any of the dissemination routes mentioned in this chapter it is important to establish any permissions you might need before sharing the information; this would include from project participants (see Chapter 11 for more information), other individuals or stakeholders with whom you might have been collaborating and funders who may have specific requirements. It's also important to discuss authorship with any collaborators.

Summing up

Communication has long had an important role in research. Since the establishment of professional research identities, the role of communication has had both practical and philosophical influences on the lives of researchers. At times communication has been seen to be devoid of any real benefits for research or researchers, at others it has been seen to be crucial to the development, character and application of knowledge. We are now in an era where research communication potentially has a role to play in both the impact of research and the monitoring of individual disciplines, but, as we have discussed throughout this book, the metrics for doing so can be unclear or even unsuitable, or lead to an instrumental perspective on the role of certain disciplines.

Approaches to research communication are many and varied, from face-to-face activities to artistic expressions, from policy-orientated communication to digital and social media contexts online. In all of these spaces we have demonstrated how you can incorporate interactivity and discussed the techniques, multiple benefits and constraints. Throughout the chapters a common theme has been the role that people – participants and audiences – have to play in different research communication settings, from the arts to the museums sectors, from policy engagement to research itself. Thus, whilst there is still a significant role for the communication of messages within research communication, it is impossible to ignore the increased influence of participation.

At the level of participants we find an enduring expectation that people will find benefits from involvement in research communication, be it on their knowledge, pleasure, creativity or awareness; both researchers and participants have a desire to 'play'. People now have complex relationships with information; thus, considering participants needs, aspirations and capacities to influence their own actions is important in considering groups with whom you may communicate, as well as those that are potentially under-served where research communication is concerned.

Research communication frequently involves tensions in terms of its role. This can be from the level of the individual researcher and the role that it should play within a research career, to the role of a research communication setting like a university, museum, gallery or science centre balancing educational, research and engagement agendas. Creativity is potentially one way to steer around some of these tensions; tensions of role, contribution and impact, fulfilling a desire to catalogue and record the influence of research within social settings, whilst at the same time driving quality and allowing researchers and participants to create their own interpretations of value in an ethical way. Creativity can involve taking risks, having failures, pushing beyond one's boundaries, and evaluation is one space in which to capture this, continuing to move the trajectory of research communication forwards without simply reducing research communication activities to those which might tick a box. Creative research communication is a recipe, concoction, a craft and a science, and it is up to each researcher to consider where their path lies on their own map of research communication.

References

Advertising Standards Authority (2014) 'Making ads clear: the challenge for advertisers and vloggers'. Retrieved 25 March 2015 at: http://asa. org.uk/News-resources/Media-Centre/2014/Making-ads-Clear-The-challenge-for-advertisers-and-vloggers.aspx#.VRKY104l8vZ.

Agar, J. (2012) *Science in the Twentieth Century and Beyond* (Cambridge: Polity Press).

Agsten, A. (2014) 'Five years of public engagement' (Los Angeles: Hammer Museum). Retrieved 20 March 2015 at: http://hammer.ucla.edu/blog/2014/06/five-years-of-public-engagement/.

AHRC (2015) 'Connected communities'. Retrieved 20 March 2015 at: www.ahrc.ac.uk/Funding-Opportunities/Research-funding/Connected-Communities/Pages/Connected-Communities.aspx.

Alsop, S. and Watts, M. (1997) 'Sources from a Somerset village: a model for informal learning about radiation and radioactivity', *Science Education*, 81:6 633–50.

Alston, A. (2013) 'Audience participation and neoliberal value: risk, agency and responsibility in immersive theatre', *Performance Research: A Journal of the Performing Arts*, 18:2 128–38.

Amabile, T.M. (1996) *Creativity in Context* (Oxford: Westview Press).

Anderson, D. (2003) 'Visitors' long-term memories of world expositions', *Curator*, 46:4 401–20.

Anker, S. and Nelkin, D. (2004) *The Molecular Gaze, Art in the Genetic Age* (Cold Spring Harbour, NY: Cold Spring Harbour Laboratory Press).

Anon (nd) *What is 'extreme citizen science?'* Retrieved 27 July 2015 at: www.ucl.ac.uk/excites/home-columns/full-what-is-extreme-citizen-science.

Anon (nd, b) 'Jack the Ripper 125'. Retrieved 1 December 2015 at: www.watershed.co.uk/dshed/jack-ripper-125-jtr125.

Anon (2012) *Life Online* (Brussels, European Commission).

Arends, B. and Slater, V. (2004) *Talking Back to Science: Art, Science and the Personal* (London: Wellcome Trust).

Arora, P. (2012) 'Typology of Web 2.0 spheres: understanding the cultural dimensions of social media spaces', *Current Sociology*, 60:5 599–618.

Arrasvuori, J., Boberq, M., Holopainen, J., Korhonen, H., Lucero, A. and Montola, M. (2011) 'Applying the PLEX Framework in designing for playfulness', *DPPI '11, Proceedings of the 2011 Conference on Designing Pleasurable Products and Interfaces, June 22–25, Milano, Italy*, Article 24. doi: 10.1145/2347504.2347531.

Attfield, R. (2012) *Ethics: An Overview* (London: Continuum).

Audience Agency (2014) *Audience Spectrum Overview* (London: The Audience Agency). Retrieved 15 January 2015 at: http://audiencefinder. org/audience/audience-spectrum-summary.

Australia Council for the Arts (2010) *More than Bums on Seats: Australian Participation in the Arts.* (Surrey Hills, NSW: Australian Council for the Arts). Retrieved 14 July 2014 at: www.austra liacouncil.gov.au/resources/reports_and_publications/subjects/audien ces_and_cultural_participation/arts_participation_research_more_than _bums_on_seats.

Australian Research Council (2014) *Research Impact Principles and Framework* (Canberra: Australian Government). Retrieved 3 December 2014 at: www.arc.gov.au/general/impact.htm.

Bakker, P. (2014) 'Mr. Gates returns: curation, community management and other new roles for journalists', *Journalism Studies*, 15:5 596–606.

Barbour, K. and Marshall, D. (2012) 'The academic online: constructing persona through the world wide web', *First Monday*, 17:9.

Barnett, C. and Mahony, N. (2011) *Segmenting Publics* (Swindon: ESRC/ NCCPE).

Bastow, S., Dunleavy, P. and Tinkler, J. (2014) *The Impact of the Social Sciences: How Academics and Their Research Make a Difference* (London: Sage).

Baym, N.K. (2009) 'A call for grounding in the face of blurred boundaries', *Journal of Computer-Mediated Communication*, 14:3 720–3.

Belfiore, E. and Bennett, O. (2008) *The Social Impact of the Arts: An Intellectual History* (Basingstoke: Palgrave Macmillan).

Belfiore, E. and Bennett, O. (2010) 'Beyond the "toolkit approach": arts impact evaluation research and the realities of cultural policy-making', *Journal for Cultural Research*, 14:2 121–42.

Bennett, T. (1995) *The Birth of the Museum: History, Theory, Politics* (Oxon: Routledge).

Bensaude-Vincent, B. and Blondel, C. (2008) 'Introduction', in Bensaude-Vincent, B. and Blondel, C. (eds) *Science and Spectacle in the European Enlightenment* (Aldershot: Ashgate) pp. 1–10.

Benyon, J. and David, M. (2008) *Developing Dialogue: Learned Societies in the Social Sciences: Developing Knowledge Transfer and Public Engagement* (London: Academy of Social Sciences and the ESRC).

Bernhardt, J.M., Mays, D. and Kreuter, M.W. (2011) 'Dissemination 2.0: closing the gap between knowledge and practice with new media and marketing', *Journal of Health Communication*, 16 32–44.

Bertucci, P. (2008) 'Domestic spectacles: electrical instruments between business and conversation', in Bensaude-Vincent, B. and Blondel, C. (eds) *Science and Spectacle in the European Enlightenment* (Aldershot: Ashgate) pp. 11–24.

Bienkowski, P. (2014) *Communities and Museums as Active Partners: Emerging Learning from the Our Museum Initiative* (London: Paul Hamlyn Foundation).

Bik, H.K. and Goldstein, M.C. (2013) 'An introduction to social media for scientists', *PLOS Biology*, 11:4 e1001535.

Birch, H. and Weitkamp, E. (2010) 'Podologues: conversations created by science podcasts', *New Media & Society*, 12:6 889–909.

Bjur, J., Christian Schrøder, K., Hasebrink, U., Courtois, C., Adoni, H. and Nossek, H. (2014) 'Cross-media use – unfolding complexities in contemporary audiencehood', in Carpentier, N., Christian Schrøder, K. and Hallett, L. (eds), *Audience Transformations: Shifting Audience Positions in Late Modernity* (New York: Routledge) pp. 15–29.

Blum, D., Knudson, M. and Henig, R.M. (2006) *A Field Guide for Science Writers*, second edition (Oxford: Oxford University Press).

Boden, M.A. (2004) *The Creative Mind: Myths and Mechanisms*, second edition (London: Routledge).

Bogenschneider, K. and Corbett, T. (2010) *Evidence-Based Policymaking: Insights from Policy-minded researchers and Research-minded policymakers* (New York: Routledge).

Bonney, R., Ballard, H., Jordan, R., McCallie, E., Phillips, T., Shirk, J. and Wilderman, C.C. (2009) *Public Participation in Scientific Research: Defining the Field and Assessing its Potential for Informal Science Education: A CAISE Inquiry Group Report* (Washington DC: CAISE) 1–58.

Borgonovi, F. (2004) 'Performing arts attendance: an economic approach', *Applied Economics*, 36:17 1871–85.

Bowater, L. and Yeoman, K. (2013) *Science Communication: A Practical Guide for Scientists* (Oxford: Wiley Blackwell).

Boyd Davies, S. (2009) 'Introduction to the special issue on creative evaluation', *Digital Creativity*, 20:3 133–9.

Braga, R., Gemignani Garcia, S. and Mello e Silva, L. (2008) 'Public sociology and public engagement', *Current Sociology*, 56:3 415–24.

Braun, K. and Schultz, S. (2010) '"… a certain amount of engineering involved": constructing the public in participatory governance arrangements', *Public Understanding of Science*, 19:4 403–19.

Brennan, L., Binney, W., Parker, L., Aleti, T. and Nguyen, D. (2014) 'Social marketing and behaviour change: where to from here?', in Brennan, L., Binney, W., Parker, L., Aleti, T. and Nguyen, D. (eds) *Social Marketing and Behaviour Change: Models, Theories and Applications* (Cheltenham: Edward Elgar Publishing Limited) pp. 331–5.

Bright Club (2014) 'Bright Club: researchers become comedians for just one night'. Retrieved 3 December 2014 at www.brightclub.org/.

Brock, C. (2006) 'The public worth of Mary Somerville', *The British Journal for the History of Science*, 39:2 255–72.

Brodzinski, E. (2010) *Theatre in Health and Care* (Basingstoke: Palgrave Macmillan).

Broks, P. (2006) *Understanding Popular Science* (Maidenhead: Open University Press).

Brook, O. (2011) *International Comparisons of Public Engagement in Culture and Sport* (London: Department for Culture, Media and Sport/ESRC).

Bruner, J. (2013) 'Tweets loud and quiet', *Radar*. Retrieved 3 March 2015 at: http://radar.oreilly.com/2013/12/tweets-loud-and-quiet.html.

Bruns, A. (2006) *Blogs, Wikipedia, Second Life and Beyond, From Production to Produsage* (Oxford: Peter Lang).

Bultitude, K. (2010) 'Presenting science', in Brake, M. and Weitkamp, E. (eds) *Introducing Science Communication* (Basingstoke: Palgrave Macmillan) pp. 128–53.

Bultitude, K., McDonald, D. and Custead, S. (2011) 'The rise and rise of science festivals: an international review of organised events to celebrate science', *International Journal of Science Education, Part B: Communication and Public Engagement*, 1:2 165–88.

Bultitude, K. and Sardo, A.M. (2012) 'Leisure and pleasure: science events in unusual locations', *International Journal of Science Education*, 34:18 2775–95.

Burall, S. and Shahrokh, T. (2010) *What the Public Say: Public Engagement in National Decision-Making* (London: Sciencewise-ERC).

Burawoy, M. (2005) 'For public sociology', *American Sociological Review*, 70:1 4–28.

Burgess, J. (2006) 'Hearing ordinary voices: cultural studies, vernacular creativity and digital storytelling', *Continuum*, 20:2 201–14.

Burningham, K., Barnett, J., Carr, A., Clift, R. and Wehrmeyer, W. (2007) 'Industrial constructions of publics and public knowledge: a qualitative investigation of practice in the UK chemicals industry', *Public Understanding of Science*, 16:1 23–43.

Bushell, G. (2015) 'Cascade – Science in games'. Retrieved 1 December 2015 at: www.fayju.com/blog/2015/04/cascade-science-in-games.

Cabinet Office (1999) *Modernising Government* (London: The Stationery Office).

Cahill, C. and Torre, M.E. (2007) 'Beyond the journal article: representations, audience and the presentation of Participatory Action Research', in Kindon, S., Pain, R. and Kesby, M. (eds), *Participatory Action Research Approaches and Methods: Connecting People, Participation and Place* (Abdingdon: Routledge) pp. 196–206.

Calhoun, C. (2009) 'Academic freedom: Public knowledge and the structural transformation of the university', *Social Research*, 76:2 561–98.

Cameron, D., Pope, S. and Clemence, M. (2014) *Dialogue on Data: Exploring the Publics View's on Using Administrative Data for Research Purposes* (London: IPSOS Mori).

Carpentier, N., Christian Schrøder, K. and Hallett, L. (2014a) 'Audience/ society transformations', in Carpentier, N., Christian Schrøder, K. and Hallett, L. (eds), *Audience Transformations: Shifting Audience Positions in Late Modernity* (New York: Routledge) pp. 1–12.

Carpentier, N., Dahlgren, P. and Pasquali, F. (2014b) 'The democratic (media) revolution: a parallel genealogy of political and media participation', in Carpentier, N., Christian Schrøder, K. and Hallett, L. (eds) *Audience Transformations: Shifting Audience Positions in Late Modernity* (New York: Routledge) pp. 123–41.

Carrozzino, M. and Bergamasco, M. (2010) 'Beyond virtual museums: experiencing immersive virtual reality in real museums', *Journal of Cultural Heritage*, 11:4 452–8.

Chalkstream Communications (2014) *Science Public Relations and Communication* (Tring: Chalkstream Communications).

Chalmers, M. (2009) 'Communicating physics in the information age', in Holliman, R., Thomas, J., Smidt, S., Scanlon, E. and Whitelegg, E. (eds.), *Practising Science Communication in the Information Age: Theorising Professional Practices* (Oxford: Oxford University Press) pp. 67–80.

Charter, M. and Keiller, S. (2014) 'Grassroots innovation and the circular economy: a global survey of repair cafes and hackerspaces'. Retrieved 20 July 2015 at: http://cfsd.org.uk/site-pdfs/circular-economy-and-grassroots-innovation/Survey-of-Repair-Cafes-and-Hackerspaces.pdf.

Chilvers, J. (2008) 'Deliberating competence: theoretical and practitioner perspectives on effective participatory appraisal practices', *Science, Technology and Human Values*, 33:2 421–51.

Collins, H. (2014) *Are We All Scientific Experts Now?* (Cambridge: Polity).

Collins, H.M. and Evans, R. (2002) 'The third wave of science studies: studies of expertise and experience', *Social Studies of Science*, 32:2 235–96.

Collins, H.M. and Evans, R. (2007) *Rethinking Expertise* (London: The University of Chicago Press).

Cook, G., Pieri, E. and Robbins, P.T. (2004) 'The scientists think and the public feels: expert perceptions of the discourse of GM food', *Discourse and Society*, 15:4 433–49.

Cortner, H.J. (2000) 'Making science relevant to environmental policy', *Environmental Science and Policy*, 3:1 21–30.

Craft, A. (2003) 'The limits to creativity in education: dilemmas for the educator', *British Journal of Educational Studies*, 51:2 113–27.

Cramb, A. (2014) 'Academic becomes instant hit on Twitter with Lego's female scientist figures', *Daily Telegraph*. Retrieved 13 March 2015 at: www.telegraph.co.uk/news/uknews/11031828/Academic-becomes-instant-hit-on-Twitter-with-Legos-female-scientist-figures.html.

Crest Network, The (2015) *Voice by Choice* (Crest Network, The University of York/University of Hull). Retrieved 20 March 2015 at: http://crestnetwork.org.uk/page/voice-by-choice.

Crick, T. and Winfield, A. (2013) 'Academic blogging – 10 top tips'. Retrieved 3 March 2015 at: www.theguardian.com/higher-education-network/blog/2013/dec/13/how-to-academic-blogging-tips.

Crosland, M. (2001) 'Popular science and the arts: challenges to cultural authority in France under the Second Empire', *The British Journal for the History of Science*, 34:3 301–22.

Csikszentmihalyi, M. (1996) *Creativity* (New York: HarperCollins).

Daft, R.L. and Lengel, R.H. (1986) 'Organizational information requirements, media richness, and structural design', *Management Science*, 32:5 554–71.

Dahlstron, M.F. and Ho, S.S. (2012) 'Ethical considerations of using narrative to communicate science,' *Science Communication*, 34:5 592–617.

Dallas, D. (2006) 'Café Scientifique – déjà vu', *Cell*, 126:2 227–9.

Davies, G. (2006) 'Mapping deliberation: calculation, articulation and intervention in the politics of organ transplantation', *Economy and Society*, 35:2 232–58.

Davies, S. and Hosein, G. (2006) 'Hang together – or we will hang separately', *Times Higher Education Supplement* (17 February). Retrieved 18 March 2015 at: www.timeshighereducation.co.uk/story.asp?section code=26&storycode=201402.

Davies, S.R. (2008) 'Constructing communication: talking to scientists about talking to the public', *Science Communication*, 29:4 413–34.

Davies, S.R., McCallie, E., Simonsson, E., Lehr, J.L. and Duensing, S. (2009) 'Discussing dialogue: perspectives on the value of science dialogue events that do not inform policy', *Public Understanding of Science*, 18:3 338–53.

Dawson, E. (2014a) 'Equity in informal science education: developing an access and equity framework for science museums and science centres', *Studies in Science Education*, 50:2 209–47.

Dawson, E. (2014b) '"Not designed for us": how science museums and science centres socially exclude low-income, minority ethnic groups', *Science Education*, 98:6 981–1008.

Dawson, M.M., Dawson, B.A. and Overfield, J.A. (2010) *Communication Skills for the Biosciences* (Chichester: John Wiley and Sons Ltd).

DeBoer, G.E. (2000) 'Scientific literacy: another look at its historical and contemporary meanings and its relationship to science education reform', *Journal of Research in Science Teaching*, 37:6 582–601.

DeBok, C. and Steinhaus, N. (2008) 'Breaking out of the local: international dimensions of science shops', *Gateways: International Journal of Community Research and Engagement*, 1, 165–78.

Déotte, J.L. (2004) 'Rome, the archetypal museum, and the Louvre, the negation of division', in Preziosi, D. and Farago, C. (eds), *Grasping the World: The Idea of the Museum* (Aldershot: Ashgate) pp. 51–64.

DePoy, E. and Gilson, S. (2008) *Evaluation Practice* (New York: Routledge).

Deterding, S., Dixon, D., Khaled, R. and Nacke, L. (2011) 'From game design elements to gamefulness: defining "gamification"', *ACM, Proceedings of the 15th International Academic MindTrek Conference: Envisioning Future Media Environments*, 9–15.

Dickert, N. and Sugarman, J. (2005) 'Ethical goals of community consultation in research', *American Journal of Public Health*, 95:7 1123–7.

Dietz, S. (2005) 'Fair assembly', in Latour, B. and Weibel, P. (eds), *Making Things Public: Atmospheres of Democracy* (Cambridge, MA: The MIT Press) pp. 910–15.

D'Ignazio, C., Warren, J. and Blair, D. (2014) 'Less is more: the role of small data for governance in the 21st Century', in Pimenta, M.S. and Canabarro, D.R., *Governancia Digital* (UFRGS Editoria). Retrieved 20 July 2015 at: www.ufrgs.br/cegov/files/livros/gtdigital.pdf.

Ding, Y., Du, Y., Hu, Y., Liu, Z., Wang, L., Ross, K. and Ghose, A. (2011) 'Broadcast yourself: understanding YouTube uploaders', *Internet Measurement Conference (IMC) 2011*, Berlin, 361–70.

Djorgovski, S.G., Hut, P., Knop, R., Longo, G., McMillan, S., Vesperini, E., Donalek, C., Graham, M., Mahabal, A., Sauer, F., White, C. and Lopes, C. (2012) 'The MICA experiment: astrophysics in virtual worlds', Proceedings of the SLACTIONS 2012 International Research Conference on Virtual Worlds. arXiv:1301.6808 [astro-ph.IM].

Donnelly, A., Crowe, O., Regan, E., Begley, S. and Caffarra, A. (2014) 'The role of citizen science in monitoring biodiversity in Ireland', *International Journal of Biometeorology*, 58:6 1237–49.

Doubleday, R. (2009) 'Ethical codes and scientific norms: the role of communication in maintaining the social contract for science', in Holliman, R., Thomas, J., Smidt, S., Scalon, E. and Whitelegg, E. (eds), *Practising Science Communication in the Information Age* (Oxford: Oxford University Press/The Open University) pp. 19–34.

Dougherty, D. (2014) 'An in depth study of makers at the forefront of hardware innovation'. Retrieved 21 July 2015 at: http://makerfairelisbon.com/assets/docs/makerstudy2014.pdf.

Dovey, J. and Kennedy, H.W. (2006) *Game Cultures* (Buckingham: Open University Press).

Dowell, E. and Weitkamp, E. (2010) 'An exploration of the collaborative processes of making theatre inspired by science', *Public Understanding of Science*, 21:7 891–901.

DuBois, J.M. (2006) 'Ethics in behavioural and social science research', in Smith Iltis, A. (ed.) *Research Ethics* (New York: Routledge) pp. 102–20.

Dufau, S., Dunabeitia, J.A., Moret-Tatay, C., McGonigal, A., Peeters, D., Alario, F., Balota, D.A., Brysbaert, M., Carreiras, M., Ferrand, L., Ktori, M., Perea, M., Rastle, K., Sasburg, O., Yap, M.J., Ziegler, J.C. and Grainger, J. (2011) 'Smart phone, smart science: how the use of smartphones can revolutionize research in cognitive science', *PLoS ONE*, 6:9 e24974.

Duncan, C. (2004) 'From the princely gallery to the public art museum: the Louvre museum and the National Gallery, London', in Preziosi, D. and Farago, C. (eds) *Grasping the World: The Idea of the Museum* (Aldershot: Ashgate) pp. 250–77.

Dunn, S. and Hedges, M. (2013) 'Crowd-sourcing as a component of humanities research infrastructures', *International Journal of Humanities and Arts Computing*, 7:1–2 147–69.

Durant, J. (2013) 'The role of science festivals', *Proceedings of the National Academy of Sciences*, 110:8 2681.

Eagle, L., Dahl, S., Hill, S., Bird, S., Spotswood, F. and Tapp, A. (2013) *Social Marketing* (Harlow: Pearson).

Ede, S. (2008) *Art and Science* (London: I.B. Tauris).

Edwards, D. (2008) *Artscience: Creativity in the post-Google generation* (Cambridge, MA: Harvard University Press).

Eisenbeiss, M., Blechenschmidt, B., Backhaus, B. and Freund, P.A. (2012) '"The (real) world is not enough:" motivational drivers and user behavior in virtual worlds', *Journal of Interactive Marketing*, 26:1 4–20.

Elamon, J., Franke, R.W. and Ekbal, B. (2004) 'Decentralization of health services: the Kerala people's campaign', *International Journal of Health Services*, 34:4 681–708.

Eliaeson, S. and Kalleberg, R. (2008) 'Academics as public intellectuals', in Eliaeson, S. and Kalleberg, R. (eds) *Academics as Public Intellectuals* (Newcastle: Cambridge Scholars Publishing) pp. 1–16.

EPSRC (2014) 'Framework for responsible innovation' (Swindon: EPSRC). Retrieved 20 March 2015 at www.epsrc.ac.uk/research/framework/.

European Commission (2008) *Scientific Evidence for Policy-Making* (Brussels: European Commission).

European Commission (2012) *Monitoring Policy and Research Activities on Science in Society in Europe (MASIS)* (Brussels: European Commission Directorate General for Research and Innovation).

European Commission (2013) *Responsible Research and Innovation (RRI), Science and Technology* (Brussels: European Commission).

European Commission (2014) 'European Researchers' Night: one night, several hundred cities all over Europe and beyond'. Retrieved 3 December 2014 at http://ec.europa.eu/research/researchersnight/index_en.htm.

European Commission (2015) 'Science Shops, knowledge for the community'. Retrieved 21 July 2015 at: https://ec.europa.eu/research/science-society/pdf/science_shop_en.pdf.

Ewins, R. (2005) 'Who are you? Weblogs and academic identity', *E-Learning and Digital Media*, 2:4 368–77.

Eyre, C. (2014) 'Teens flock to Movellas "immersive experience"', *The Bookseller*, 5632 12–13.

Falk, J.H. (2000) 'Assessing the impact of museums', *Curator*, 43:1 5–7.

Falk, J.H. (2011) 'Contextualizing Falk's identity-related visitor motivation model', *Visitor Studies*, 14:2 141–57.

Falk, J.H., Moussouri, T. and Coulson, D. (1998) 'The effect of visitors' agendas on museum learning', *Curator*, 41:2 107–20.

Falk, J.H., Storksdieck, M. and Dierking, L.D. (2007) 'Investigating public science interest and understanding: evidence for the importance of free-choice learning', *Public Understanding of Science*, 16:4 455–69.

Fauville, G., Dupont, S., von Thun, S. and Lundin, J. (2015) 'Can Facebook be used to increase scientific literacy? A case study of the Monterey Bay Aquarium Research Institute Facebook page and ocean literacy', *Computers & Education*, 82 60–73.

Featherstone, H., Wilkinson, C. and Bultitude, K. (2009) *Public Engagement Map: Report to the Science for All Expert Group* (Bristol: University of the West of England).

Featherstone, H. and Pope, H. (2011) *MS: The Big Knit, Evaluation Report*. Retrieved 26 June 2014 at: http://knitaneuron.blogspot.co.uk/.

Felt, U. and Fochler, M. (2008) 'The bottom-up meanings of the concept of public participation', *Science and Public Policy*, 35:7 489–99.

Festa Literária Internacional de Paraty (2015) 'Flip Paraty International Literary Festival' (Paraty: Festa Literária Internacional de Paraty). Retrieved 20 March 2015 at: www.flip.org.br/?idioma_new=I.

Findlen, P. (1994) *Possessing Nature: Museums, Collecting and Scientific Culture in Early Modern Italy* (Berkeley: University of California Press).

Fogg-Rogers, L., Bay, J., Burgess, H. and Purdy, S.C. (2015) '"Knowledge is power": a mixed methods study exploring adult audience preferences for engagement and learning formats over three years of a health science festival', *Science Communication*, 37:4 419–51.

Fox, S. and Madden, M. (2006) 'Riding the waves of "Web 2.0"'. Retrieved 13 March 2015 at: www.pewinternet.org/2006/10/05/riding-the-waves-of-web-2-0/.

Fox, S. and Rainie, L. (2014) 'The Web at 25 in the U.S.' (Washington:

Pew Research Centre). Retrieved 13 March 2015: www.pewinternet. org/2014/02/27/the-web-at-25-in-the-u-s/.

Frankel, F. and Whitesides, G.M. (2007) *On the Surface of Things, Images of the Extraordinary in Science* (Cambridge, MA: Harvard University Press).

Franklin, B. (2014) 'The future of journalism', *Journalism Studies,* 15:5 481–99.

Frost, C. (2010) *Reporting for Journalists* (Abingdon: Routledge).

Fuchs, C. (2014) *Social Media: A Critical Introduction* (London: Sage).

Fukushima, M. (2005) 'On small devices of thought: concepts, etymology and the problem of translation', in Latour, B. and Weibel, P. (eds), *Making Things Public: Atmospheres of Democracy* (Cambridge, MA: The MIT Press) pp. 58–63.

Furedi, F. (2004) *Where Have All the Intellectuals Gone?* second edition (London: Continuum).

Galison, P., Moss, R. and Students (2005) 'Wall of science', in Latour, B. and Weibel, P. (eds), *Making Things Public: Atmospheres of Democracy* (Cambridge, MA: The MIT Press) pp. 332–3.

Galloway, S. (2009) 'Theory-based evaluation and the social impact of the arts', *Cultural Trends,* 18:2 125–48.

Gammon, B. and Burch, A. (2006) 'A guide for successfully evaluating science engagement events', in Turney, J. (ed). *Engaging Science: Thoughts, Deeds, Analysis and Action* (London: Wellcome Trust) pp. 80–5.

Garrett, J.M. and Bird, S.J. (2000) 'Ethical issues in communicating science', *Science and Engineering Ethics,* 6:4 435–42.

Gastil, J. and Richards, R. (2013) 'Making direct democracy deliberative through random assemblies', *Politics & Society,* 41:2 253–81.

Gauntlett, D. (2011) *Making is Connecting: The Social Meaning of Creativity from DIY and Knitting to YouTube and Web 2.0.* (Cambridge: Polity).

Gaventa, J. and Barrett, G. (2010) 'So what difference does it make? Mapping the outcomes of citizen engagement', Research Summary of Working Paper 347 (Brighton: Institute of Development Studies).

Gay, P.L., Price, A. and Searle, T. (2006) 'Astronomy podcasting: a low-cost tool for affecting attitudes in diverse audiences', *Astronomy Education Review,* 5:1 36–52.

Glinkowski, P. and Bamford, A. (2009) *Insight and Exchange: An Evaluation of the Wellcome Trust's Sciart Programme* (London: Wellcome Trust). Retrieved 17 June 2014 at: www.wellcome.ac.uk/About-us/Publications/ Reports/Public-engagement/Sciart-evaluation-report/index.htm.

Goldacre, B. (2008) *Bad Science* (London: Fourth Estate).

Graham, E.A., Henderson, S. and Schloss, A. (2011) 'Using mobile phones to engage citizen scientists in research', *Eos, Transactions American Geophysical Union,* 92:38 313–15.

Grand, A. (2009) 'Engaging through dialogue: international experiences of Cafe Scientifique', in Holliman, R., Thomas, J., Smidt, S., Scanlon, E. and Whitelegg, E. (eds) *Practising Science Communication in the Information Age: Theorising Professional Practices* (Oxford University Press/Open University Press: Oxford) pp. 209–26.

Grand, A., Wilkinson, C., Bultitude, K. and Winfield, A. (2014) 'Mapping the hinterland: data issues in open science', *Public Understanding of Science*, online first, doi: 10.1177/0963662514530374.

Grant, J., Brutscher, P.B., Kirk, S.E., Butler, L. and Wooding, S. (2010) *Capturing Research Impacts: A review of international practice* (Santa Monica: RAND Corporation). Retrieved 3 December 2014 at: www.rand.org/content/dam/rand/pubs/documented_briefings/2010/RAND_DB578.pdf.

Grauerholz, L. and Baker-Sperry, L. (2007) 'Feminist research in the public domain: risks and recommendations,' *Gender and Society*, 21:2 272–94.

Gregory, J. (2009) 'Scientists communicating', in Holliman, R., Thomas, J., Smidt, S., Scanlon, E. and Whitelegg, E. (eds) *Practising Science Communication in the Information Age: Theorising Professional Practices* (Oxford: Oxford University Press) pp. 3–18.

Gregory, J. and Miller, S. (1998) *Science in Public: Communication, Culture and Credibility* (Cambridge: Basic Books).

Griffiths, A. (2008) *Shivers Down Your Spine: Cinema, Museums and the Immersive View* (New York: Columbia University Press).

Gustavsen, B. (1986) 'Social research as participative dialogue', in Heller, F. (ed), *The Use and Abuse of Social Science* (London: Sage Publications) pp. 143–56.

Gutmann, A. and Wagner, J. (2011) *'Ethically Impossible': STD Research in Guatemala from 1946 to 1948* (Washington D.C.: Presidential Commission for the Study of Bioethical Issues).

Hagendijk, R. and Irwin, A. (2006) 'Public deliberation and governance: engaging with science and technology in contemporary Europe', *Minerva*, 44:2 167–84.

Hammersley, M. (2004) 'A new political arithmetic to make sociology useful? Comments on a debate', *British Journal of Sociology*, 55:3 439–45.

Hara, N., Solomon, P., Kim, S.-L. and Sonnenwald, D.H. (2003) 'An emerging view of scientific collaboration: scientists' perspectives on collaboration and factors that impact collaboration', *Journal of the American Society for Information Science and Technology*, 54:10 952–65.

Haran, B. and Poliakoff, M. (2011) 'How to measure the impact of chemistry on the small screen', *Nature Chemistry*, 3 180–1.

Hassouneh, D. and Brengman, M. (2014) 'A motivation-based typology of social virtual world users', *Computers in Human Behaviour*, 33 330–8.

Hearn, A. (2008) '"Meat, mask, burden": probing the contours of the branded "self"', *Journal of Consumer Culture*, 8:2 197–217.

Heinelt, H. (2010) *Governing Modern Societies: Towards Participatory Governance* (London: Routledge).

Held, D. (2006) *Models of Democracy* (Cambridge: Polity Press).

Heller, F. (1986) 'Introduction and overview', in Heller, F. (ed.), *The Use and Abuse of Social Science* (London: Sage Publications) pp. 1–18.

Heller, P., Harilal, K.N. and Chaudhuri, S. (2007) 'Building local democracy: evaluating the impact of decentralization in Kerala, India', *World Development*, 35:4 626–48.

Henning, M. (2006) *Museums, Media and Cultural Theory* (Maidenhead: Open University Press).

Hewer, S. (2003) *Ask the Audience: Investigating the Impact of Science and Art Exhibitions on Their Audience. A Report for The Wellcome Trust.* Retrieved 11 July 2014 at: www.takingpartinthearts.com/content.php?content=1002.

Hilton, C. (2014) 'The immortalisation of Billy Apple: an art–science collaboration', *Leonardo*, 47:2 109–13.

Hitchcock, T. (2014) 'Twitter and blogs are not add-ons to academic research, but a simple reflection of the passion that underpins it'. Retrieved 3 March 2015 at: http://blogs.lse.ac.uk/impactofsocialsciences/2014/07/28/twitter-and-blogs-academic-public-sphere/.

Hoffmann, R. (2003) 'Thoughts on aesthetics and visualisation in chemistry', *Hyle – International Journal of Philosophy of Chemistry*, 9:1 7–10.

Hoggarth, L. and Comfort, H. (2010) *A Practical Guide to Outcome Evaluation* (London: Jessica Kingsley Publishers).

Holden, J. (2006) *Cultural Value and the Crisis of Legitimacy: Why Culture Needs a Democratic Mandate* (London: Demos). Retrieved 2 July 2014 at: www.demos.co.uk/publications/culturallegitimacy.

Holliman, R. and Jensen, E. (2009) '(In)authentic sciences and (im)partial publics: (re)constructing the science outreach and public engagement agenda', in Holliman, R., Whitelegg, E., Scanlon, E., Smidt, S. and Thomas, J. (eds), *Investigating Science Communication in the Information Age: Implications for Public Engagement and Popular Media* (Oxford: Oxford University Press) pp. 35–52.

Holmwood, J. (2014) 'This turbulent and challenging time', *Network*, 116, 20–1 (Durham: British Sociological Association).

Hooper-Greenhill, E. (1992) *Museums and the Shaping of Knowledge* (London: Routledge).

Horlick-Jones, T., Rowe, G. and Walls, J. (2007) 'Citizen engagement processes as information systems: the role of knowledge and the concept of translation quality', *Public Understanding of Science*, 16:3 259–78.

Hornig Priest, S. (2009) 'Reinterpreting the audiences of media messages about science', in Holliman, R., Whitelegg, E., Scanlon, E., Smidt, S. and Thomas, J. (eds) *Investigating Science Communication in the Information Age: Implications for Public Engagement and Popular Media* (Oxford: Oxford University Press) pp. 223–36.

Horst, M. (2008) 'In search of dialogue: staging science communication in consensus conferences', in Cheng, D., Claessens, M., Gascoigne, T., Metcalfe, J., Schiele, B. and Shi, S. (eds) *Communicating Science in Social Contexts: New models, New Practices* (New York: Springer) pp. 259–74.

Hourston Hanks, L., Hale, J. and MacLeod, S. (2012) 'Introduction: museum making, the place of narrative', in MacLeod, S., Hourston Hanks, L. and Hale, J. (eds) *Museum Making: Narratives, Architectures and Exhibitions* (London: Routledge) p. xix.

Hudson, K. (1975) *A Social History of Museums* (London: The Macmillan Press).

Huizinga, J. (2014) *Homo Ludens: A Study of the Play-Element in Culture* (Eastford, CT: Martino Fine Books).

Hüppauf, B. and Weingart, P. (2008) 'Images in and of science', in Hüppauf, B. and Weingart, P. (eds) *Science Images and Popular Images of Scientists* (New York: Routledge) pp. 3–32.

ICOM (2014) 'International Council of Museums, frequently asked questions'. Retrieved 3 December 2014 at: http://icom.museum/resources/frequently-asked-questions/.

InsightsNow (2012) *Seven Shades of Mobile*. Retrieved 8 October 2014 at: www.insightsnow.com/blog/DOWNLOAD-the-Award-Winning-AOL-Case-History.

International Association of Public Participation (2007) 'IAP2 spectrum of public participation'. Retrieved 18 March 2015 from http://c.ymcdn.com/sites/www.iap2.org/resource/resmgr/imported/IAP2 percent-20Spectrum_vertical.pdf.

Ipsos MORI (2014) *Public Attitudes to Science* (London: Ipsos MORI, Department for Business, Innovation and Skills and ESRC).

Irwin, A. (1995) *Citizen Science* (London: Routledge).

Irwin, A. (2001) 'Constructing the scientific citizen: science and democracy in biosciences', *Public Understanding of Science*, 10:1 1–18.

Irwin, A. (2006) 'The politics of talk: coming to terms with the "new" scientific governance', *Social Studies of Science*, 36:2 299–320.

Irwin, A. (2009) 'Moving forwards or in circles? Science communication and scientific governance in an age of innovation', in Holliman, R., Whitelegg, E., Scanlon, E., Smidt, S. and Thomas, J. (eds), *Investigating Science Communication in the Information Age: Implications for Public Engagement and Popular Media* (Oxford: Oxford University Press) pp. 3–17.

Irwin, A. and Michael, M. (2003) *Science, Social Theory and Public Knowledge* (Maidenhead: Open University Press).

Italian Presidency of the Council of the European Union (2014) *Rome Declaration on Responsible Research and Innovation in Europe* (Rome: Italian Presidency of the Council of the European Union). Retrieved 20 March 2015 at: www.sis-rri-conference.eu/wp-content/uploads/2014/07/RomeDeclaration.pdf.

ITU (2014a) 'ICT facts and figures'. Retrieved 8 October 2014 at: www.itu.int/en/ITU-D/Statistics/Documents/facts/ICTFactsFigures2014-e.pdf.

ITU (2014b) 'Measuring the Information Society'. Retrieved 13 March 2015 at: www.itu.int/ITU-D/ict/publications/idi/.

Jensen, E. (2013) 'Reconsidering *The Love of Art*: evaluating the potential of art museum outreach', *Visitor Studies*, 16:2 144–59.

Jensen, E. and Buckley, N. (2012) 'Why people attend science festivals: Interests, motivations and self-reported benefits of public engagement with research', *Public Understanding of Science*, 23:5 557–73.

John, P., Cotterill, S., Moseley, A., Richardson, L., Smith, G., Stocker, G. and Wales, C. (2011) *Nudge. Nudge, Think, Think: Using Experiments to Change Civic Behaviour* (London: Bloomsbury Academic).

Joppien, R. and Smith, B. (1998) *The Art of Captain Cook's Voyage, Vol 3, Text. The Voyage of the Resolution and Discovery 1776–1780* (New Haven, CT: Yale University Press).

Kac, E. (2007) *Signs of Life, BioArt and Beyond* (Boston: MIT Press).

Kaplan, A.M. and Haenlein, M. (2010) 'Users of the world, unite! The challenges and opportunities of social media', *Business Horizons*, 53 59–68.

Kappas, A. and Krämer, N.C. (2011) *Face-to-Face Communication over the Internet* (Cambridge: Cambridge University Press).

Keith, M. (2008) 'Public sociology? Between heroic immersion and critical distance: personal reflections on academic engagement with political life', *Critical Social Policy*, 28:3 320–34.

Kemp, M. (2006) *Seen/Unseen: Art, Science and Intuition from Leonardo to the Hubble Telescope* (Oxford: Oxford University Press).

Kera, D. (2012) 'NanoSmano Lab in Ljubljana: disruptive prototypes and experimental governance of nanotechnologies in hackerspaces.' *JCOM* 11:4 C03.

Kerr, A. (2003) 'Rights and responsibilities in the new genetics era', *Critical Social Policy*, 23:2 208–26.

Kerr, A., Cunningham-Burley, S. and Tutton, R. (2007) 'Shifting subject positions: experts and lay people in public dialogue', *Social Studies of Science*, 37:3 385–411.

Kidd, J. (2012) 'The museum as narrative witness: heritage performance and the production of narrative space', in Macleod, S., Hourston Hanks, L. and Hale, J. (eds) *Museum Making: narratives, architectures, exhibitions* (London: Routledge) pp. 74–82.

Kim, J. (2012) 'The institutionalization of YouTube: from user-generated content to professionally generated content', *Media, Culture and Society*, 34:1 53–67.

Kindon, S., Pain, R. and Kesby, M. (2007) 'Introduction: connecting people, participation and place', in Kindon, S., Pain, R. and Kesby, M. (eds) *Participatory Action Research Approaches and Methods: Connecting People, Participation and Place* (Abdingdon: Routledge) pp. 1–6.

Kitzinger, J. Chimba, M., Williams, A., Haran, J. and Boyce, T. (2008) *Gender, Stereotypes and Expertise in the Press: How Newspapers Represent Female and Male Scientists* (Bradford: UK Resource Centre for Women in Science, Engineering and Technology and Cardiff University).

Knight, D. (2006) *Public Understanding of Science: A History of Communicating Scientific Ideas* (Abingdon: Routledge).

Knight, D. (2009) *The Making of Modern Science: Science, Technology, Medicine and Modernity 1789–1914* (Cambridge: Polity Press).

Knight, J.F., Carley, S., Tregunna, B., Jarvis, S., Smithies, R., De Freitas, S., Dunwell, I. and Mackway-Jones, K. (2010) 'Serious gaming technology in major incident triage training: a pragmatic controlled trial', *Resuscitation*, 81:9 1175–9.

Korthals, M. (2013) 'Challenges to deliberations on genomics', in O'Doherty, K. and Einsiedel, E. (eds) *Public Engagement and Emerging Technologies* (Vancouver: UBC Press).

Krishna, V.V. (2014) 'Changing social relations between science and society: contemporary challenges', *Science, Technology & Society*, 19:2 133–59.

Kushner, S. (2000) *Personalizing Evaluation* (London: Sage).

Lafrenière, D. and Cox, S.M. (2012) 'Means of knowledge dissemination: are the *Café Scientifique* and the artistic performance equally effective?', *Sociology Mind*, 2:2 191–9.

Laub Hansen, G. (2012) 'Buffet serving – a nightmare of choices' (Kolding: International Design Camp 2012). Retrieved 4 March 2015 at: http://designcamp2012.dskd.dk/about/articles/buffet-serving-a-nightmare-of-choices/.

Lauder, H., Brown, P. and Halsey, A.H. (2004) 'Sociology and political arithmetic: some principles of a new policy science', *British Journal of Sociology*, 55:1 3–22.

Leão, M.J. and Castro, S. (2012) 'Science and rock: how music festivals can boost the progress of science', *EMBO Reports*, 13:11 954–8.

Lee-Wright, P., Phillips, A. and Witschge, T. (2012) *Changing Journalism* (London: Routledge).

Lefebvre, R.C. (2013) *Social Marketing and Social Change: Strategies and Tools for Health, Well-Being and the Environment* (San Francisco: Jossey-Bass).

Lehr, J.L., McCallie, E., Davies, S.R., Caron, B.R., Gammon, B. and Duensing, S. (2007) 'The value of "dialogue events" as sites of learning:

an exploration of research and evaluation frameworks', *International Journal of Science Education*, 29:12 1476–87.

Levy-Leboyer, C. (1986) 'Applying psychology or applied psychology', in Heller, F. (ed.) *The Use and Abuse of Social Science* (London: Sage Publications) pp. 24–35.

Lewis, J. (1990) *Art, Culture and Enterprise: The Politics of Art and the Cultural Industries* (London: Routledge).

Lightman, B. (2007) *Victorian Popularizers of Science: Designing Nature for New Audiences* (Chicago: The University of Chicago Press).

Loader, I. and Sparks, R. (2011) *Public Criminology?* (Abingdon: Routledge).

Lövbrand, E. (2007) 'Pure science or policy involvement? Ambiguous boundary-work for Swedish carbon cycle science', *Environmental Science and Policy*, 10:1 39–47.

Lukensmeyer, C.J. and Hasselblad Torres, L. (2006) *Public Deliberation: A Managers Guide to Citizen Engagement* (Washington, DC: IBM Center for the Business of Government).

Lynch, B. (2009) *Whose Cake Is It Anyway? A Collaborative Investigation into Engagement and Participation in 12 Museums and Galleries in the UK* (London: Paul Hamlyn Foundation).

Lynn, M.R. (2008) 'Experimental physics in enlightenment Paris: the practice of popularization in urban culture', in Bensaude-Vincent, B. and Blondel, C. (eds) *Science and Spectacle in the European Enlightenment* (Aldershot: Ashgate) pp. 65–74.

Maile, S. (2014) 'Social Science in the City™: reflections on public engagement', in Maile, S. and Griffiths, D. (eds) *Public Engagement and Social Science* (Bristol: Policy Press) pp. 29–46.

Maile, S. and Griffiths, D. (2014a) 'Cafe scientifique and the art of engaging publics', in Maile, S. and Griffiths, D. (eds) *Public Engagement and Social Science* (Bristol: Policy Press) pp. 7–28.

Maile, S. and Griffiths, D. (eds) (2014b) *Public Engagement and Social Science* (Bristol: Policy Press).

Malin, B.J. (2011) 'A very popular blog: the internet and the possibilities of publicity', *New Media & Society*, 13:2 187–202.

Markman, K.M. (2012) 'Doing radio, making friends, and having fun: Exploring the motivations of independent audio podcasters', *New Media & Society*, 14:4 547–65.

Marsh, O. (2013) 'A funny thing happened on the way to the laboratory: science and standup comedy' (12 July). Retrieved 3 December 2014 at: http://blogs.lse.ac.uk/impactofsocialsciences/2013/07/12/a-funny-thing-happened-on-the-way-tothe-laboratory/#author.

Marwick, A.E. and boyd, d. (2011) 'I tweet honestly, I tweet passionately: Twitter users, context collapse, and the imagined audience', *New Media & Society*, 13:1 114–33.

Maslow, A. (1970) *Motivation and Personality* (New York: Harper and Row).

Mayhew, M.A. and Hall, M.K. (2012) 'Science communication in a Café Scientifique for high school teens', *Science Communication*, 34:4 546–54.

McCormick, T. (2014) 'Social media for scientists – including the shy, over-committed and unconvinced', *Elsevier Connect*. Retrieved 3 March 2015 at: www.elsevier.com/connect/social-media-for-scientists-including-the-shy-overcommitted-and-unconvinced.

McLaughlin, N. and Turcotte, K. (2007) 'The trouble with Burawoy: an analytic, synthetic alternative', *Sociology*, 41:5 813–28.

McMaster, B. (2008) *Supporting Excellence in the Arts: From Measurement to Judgement* (London: Department for Culture, Media and Sport). Retrieved 3 December 2014 at: http://webarchive.nationalarchives.gov.uk/+/http:/www.culture.gov.uk/images/publications/supportingexcellenceinthearts.pdf.

McQuail, D. (1997) *Audience Analysis* (Thousand Oaks, CA: Sage Publications).

Mermikides, A., Van de Velde, A., Mermikides, M., Tanczos, A. and Weitkamp, E. (2015) 'Devised performance as a tool for public engagement in acute haematological cancers', in *30th General Meeting of the Belgian Haematological Society*, Belgium, 30–31 January.

Merriman, N. (2012) 'Transforming the university museum: the Manchester experience', in Jandl, S.S. and Gold, M.S. (eds), *A Handbook for Academic Museums: Beyond Exhibition and Education* (Edinburgh: MuseumsEtc) pp. 36–61.

Metzger, M.J. and Flanagin, A.J. (2011) 'Using Web 2.0 technologies to enhance evidence-based medical information', *Journal of Health Communication*, 16 45–58.

Mewburn, I. and Thomson, P. (2013) 'Why do academics blog? An analysis of audiences, purposes and challenges', *Studies in Higher Education*, 38:8 1105–19.

Meyer, G. and Sandøe, P. (2012) 'Going public: good scientific conduct', *Science and Engineering Ethics*, 18:2 173–97.

Meyer, M. (2010) 'The rise of the knowledge broker', *Science Communication*, 32:1 118–27.

Michael, M. (2009) 'Publics performing publics: of PiGs, PiPs and politics', *Public Understanding of Science*, 18:5 617–31.

Michael, M. and Brown, N. (2005) 'Scientific citizenships: self-representations of xenotransplantation's publics', *Science as Culture*, 14:1 39–57.

Miller, A.I. (2014) *Colliding Worlds: How Cutting-Edge Science Is Redefining Contemporary Art* (New York: W.W. Norton and Company).

Monro, S. (2009) 'The development of *Our Dynamic Earth*', in Holliman,

R., Thomas, J., Smidt, S., Scanlon, E. and Whitelegg, E. (eds) *Practising Science Communication in the Information Age: Theorising Professional Practices* (Oxford: Oxford University Press/Open University Press) pp. 195–208.

Moran, S. (2010) 'Roles of creativity in society', in Kaufman, J.C. and Sternberg, R.J. (eds) *The Handbook of Creativity* (Cambridge: Cambridge University Press) pp. 74–90.

Morrone, A. (2006) *Guidelines for Measuring Cultural Participation* (Montreal: UNESCO Institute for Statistics).

Nascimento, S., Guimaraes Pereira, A. and Ghezzi, A. (2014) 'From citizen science to do it yourself science: an annotated account of an ongoing movement' (Ispra, Italy: European Commission).

National Endowment for the Arts (2013) *How A Nation Engages with the Arts* (Washington, DC: National Endowment for the Arts). Retrieved 10 July 2014 at: http://arts.gov/publications/highlights-from-2012-sppa.

NCCPE (2014a) 'Communities of Practice'. Retrieved 3 December 2014 at www.publicengagement.ac.uk/.

NCCPE (2014b) 'Engaging the public as researchers'. Retrieved 3 December at www.publicengagement.ac.uk/.

Noguera Vivo, J.M., Villi, M., Nyiro, N., De Blasio, E. and Bourdaa, M. (2014) 'The role of the media industry when participation is a product', in Carpentier, N., Christian Schrøder, K. and Hallett, L. (eds), *Audience Transformations: Shifting Audience Positions in Late Modernity* (New York: Routledge) pp. 172–87.

O'Mahony, P. (2013) *The Contemporary Theory of the Public Sphere* (Oxford: Peter Lang).

O'Neill, O. (2009) 'Ethics for communication?' *European Journal of Philosophy*, 17:2 167–80.

Owl Re (2008) *Evaluating Communication Campaigns* (Commugny: Owl Re).

Ox, J. and Lowenberg, R. (2012) 'What is the challenge of art/science today and how do we address it?', *Leonardo*, 46:1 2.

Pawson, R. (2006) *Evidence-Based Policy: A Realist Perspective* (London: Sage).

Pearce, C., Diamond, S. and Bream, M. (2003) 'BRIDGES 1: Interdisciplinary collaboration as practice', *Leonardo*, 36:3 123–8.

Pearce, S.M. (1995) *On Collecting: An Investigation into Collecting in the European Tradition* (Abingdon: Routledge).

Peer, L. and Ksiazek, T.B. (2011) 'YouTube and the challenge to journalism: new standards for news videos online', *Journalism Studies*, 12:1 45–63.

Peers, L. and Brown, A.K. (2003) 'Introduction', in Peers, L. and Brown, A.K. (eds) *Museums and Source Communities: A Routledge Reader* (London: Routledge) pp. 1–16.

Percy-Smith, B. and Thomas, J. (2010) *A Handbook of Children and Young People's Participation* (London: Routledge).

Perez, L. (2008) 'Technology, curiosity and utility in France and in England in the eighteenth century', in Bensaude-Vincent, B. and Blondel, C. (eds) *Science and Spectacle in the European Enlightenment* (Aldershot: Ashgate) pp. 25–42.

Pew Research Centre (2010) 'Online activities' (Washington: Pew Research Centre).

Pew Research Centre (2012) 'Cell phone activities' (Washington: Pew Research Centre).

Pew Research Centre (2013) 'Online video report' (Washington: Pew Research Centre).

Pimple, K.D. (2002) 'Six domains of research ethics: a heuristic framework for the responsible conduct of research', *Science and Engineering Ethics*, 8:2 191–205.

Pitrelli, N. (2010) 'Road maps for the 21st century research in science communication', *Journal of Science* Communication, 9:3 1–3.

Posner, R.A. (2003) *Public Intellectuals: A Study of Decline* (Cambridge, MA: Harvard University Press).

Pouliot, C. (2011) 'Post-secondary students' relationship to people they consider to be scientific experts', *Research in Science Education*, 41:2 225–43.

Powell, M. and Colin, M. (2009) 'Participatory paradoxes: facilitating citizen engagement in science and technology from the top-down?', *Bulletin of Science, Technology and Society*, 29:4 325–42.

Presidential Commission for the Study of Bioethical Issues (2015) *A Study Guide to 'Ethically Impossible' STD Research in Guatemala from 1946 to 1948* (Presidential Commission *for the* Study of Bioethical Issues). Retrieved 20 March 2015 at: http://bioethics.gov/node/778.

Raddick, J.M., Bracey, G., Gay, P.L., Lintott, C.J., Murray, P., Schawinski, K., Szalay, A.S. and Vandenberg, J. (2010) 'Galaxy Zoo: exploring the motivations of citizen scientists', *Astronomy Education Review*, 9:1 010103.

Raddick, J.M., Bracey, G., Gay, P.L., Lintott, C.J., Cardamone, C., Murray, P., Schawinski, K., Szalay, A.S. and Vandenberg, J. (2013) 'Galaxy Zoo: motivations of citizen science volunteers', *Astronomy Education Review*, 12:1 010106.

RCUK (2009) 'What is public engagement?'. Retrieved 28 March 2014 at: www.rcuk.ac.uk/cmsweb/downloads/rcuk/scisoc/peupdate.pdf.

RCUK (2011) *Evaluation Practical Guidelines: A Guide for Evaluating Public Engagement Activities* (Swindon: RCUK).

Redfern, M. (2009) 'Speaking to the world: radio and other audio', in Holliman, R., Thomas, J., Smidt, S., Scanlon, E. and Whitelegg, E. (eds) *Practising Science Communication in the Information Age:*

Theorising Professional Practices (Oxford: Oxford University Press) pp. 178–92.

Reichle, I. (2009) *Art in the Age of Technoscience. Genetic Engineering, Robotics, and Artificial Life in Contemporary Art* (New York: Springer-Wien).

Rennie, L.J. and Williams, G.F. (2006) 'Adults learning about science in free-choice settings', *International Journal of Science Education*, 28:8 871–93.

Richards, R. (2007) *Everyday creativity and new views of human nature: psychological, social, and spiritual perspectives* (Washington, DC: American Psychological Association).

Riesch, H. (2015) 'Why did the proton cross the road? Humour and science communication', *Public Understanding of Science*, 24:7 768-75.

Riesch, H., Potter, C. and Davies, L. (2013) 'Combining citizen science and public engagement: the Open AirLaboratories Programme', *JCOM* 12:3 A03.

Riesch, H. and Potter, C. (2014) 'Citizen science as seen by scientists: methodological, epistemological and ethical dimensions', *Public Understanding of Science*, 23:1 107–20.

Riskin, J. (2008) 'Amusing physics', in Bensaude-Vincent, B. and Blondel, C. (eds) *Science and Spectacle in the European Enlightenment* (Aldershot: Ashgate) pp. 43–64.

Rosen, J. (2011) 'The people formerly known as the audience', *Huffington Post Media*. Retrieved 23 January 2015 at: http://huffingtonpost.com/jay-rosen/the-people-formerly-known_1_b_24113.html.

Rossi, P.H., Freeman, H.E. and Lipsey, M.W. (1999) *Evaluation: A Systematic Approach 6th Edition* (Thousand Oaks, CA: Sage).

Rowe, G. and Frewer, L.J. (2005) 'A typology of public engagement mechanisms,' *Science, Technology and Human Values*, 30:2 251–90.

Royal Society (2006) *Science Communication: Survey of Factors Affecting Science Communication by Scientists and Engineers* (London: Royal Society).

Runco, M.A. (1996) 'Personal creativity: definition and developmental issues', *New Directions for Child Development*, 72 3–30.

Sardo, A.M. and Weitkamp, E. (2012) 'Exploring the ways environmental science is used and valued by policy-makers in Portugal: a case study', *Journal of Science Communication*, 11:3 c05.

Schäfer, M.S. (2009) 'From public understanding to public engagement: an empirical assessment of changes in science coverage', *Science Communication*, 30:4 475–505.

Schaffer, S. (2005) 'Public experiments', in Latour, B. and Weibel, P. (eds), *Making Things Public: Atmospheres of Democracy* (Cambridge, MA: ZKM) pp. 298–307.

Schuster, J.M. (2007) 'Participation studies and cross-national comparison: proliferation, prudence and possibility', *Cultural Trends*, 16:2 99–196.

Science Foundation Ireland (2012) *Agenda 2020 Excellence and Impact* (Dublin: Science Foundation Ireland). Retrieved 3 December 2014 at: www.sfi.ie/assets/files/downloads/News percent20and percent20Events/ AGENDA percent202020.pdf.

Science Showoff (2014) 'What is Science Showoff?' Retrieved 3 December 2014 at: www.scienceshowoff.org/.

Scott, C. (2003) 'Museums and impact', *Curator*, 46:3 293–310.

Seeman, N.C. (2014) 'Art as a stimulus for structural DNA nanotechnology', *Leonardo*, 47:2 142–9.

Sharpe, L.J. (1975) 'The social scientist and policy-making: some cautionary thoughts and transatlantic reflections', *Policy and Politics*, 4:2 7–34.

Sheedy, A. (2008) *Handbook on Citizen Engagement: Beyond Consultation* (Ottawa: Canadian Policy Research Networks).

Shiner, L. (2001) *The Invention of Art* (Chicago: University of Chicago Press).

Short, J., Williams, E. and Christie, B. (1976) *The Social Psychology of Telecommunications* (Hoboken, NJ: John Wiley and Sons, Ltd).

Silvertown, J. (2009) 'A new dawn for citizen science', *Trends in Ecology & Evolution*, 24:9 467–71.

Singer, P. (1994) 'Introduction', in Singer, P. (ed.) *Ethics* (Oxford: Oxford University Press) pp. 3–13.

Smith Iltis, A. (2006) 'Human subjects research: ethics and compliance', in Smith Iltis, A. (ed.) *Research Ethics* (New York: Routledge) pp. 1–21.

Snow, C.P. (1993) *The Two Cultures* (Cambridge: Cambridge University Press).

Sonnenburg, S. (2004) 'Creativity in communication: a theoretical framework for collaborative product creation', *Creativity and Innovation Management*, 13:4 254–62.

Sprague, J. (2008) 'Sociology, the good, the bad and the public', *Gender and Society*, 22:6 697–704.

Stafford, B.M. (1994) *Artful Science: Enlightenment Entertainment and the Eclipse of Visual Education* (Cambridge, MA: The MIT Press).

Steele, D.R. (2012) *The Open-Source Everything Manifesto: Transparency, Truth and Trust* (Berkeley, CA: Evolver Editions).

Steel, B., List, P., Lach, D. and Shindler, B. (2004) 'The role of scientists in the environmental policy process: a case study from the American west', *Environmental Science and Policy*, 7:1 1–13.

Stewart, L. (2008) 'The laboratory, the workshop and the theatre of experiment', in Bensaude-Vincent, B. and Blondel, C. (eds) *Science and Spectacle in the European Enlightenment* (Aldershot: Ashgate) pp. 11–24.

Stilgoe, J., Owen, R. and Macnaghten, P. (2013) 'Developing a framework for responsible innovation', *Research Policy*, 42:3 1568–80.

Stryker, J.B. and Santoro, M.D. (2012) 'Facilitating face-to-face communication in high tech teams', *Research Technology Management*, 55:1 51–6.

Suda, E., Macer, D. and Matsuda, I. (2009) 'Challenges to public engagement in science and technology in Japan: experiences in the HapMap project', *Genomics, Society and Policy*, 5:1 114–33.

Sumner, D.E. and Miller, H.G. (2013) *Feature and Magazine Writing*, third edition (Chichester: Wiley-Blackwell).

Sumners, C., Reiff, P. and Weber, W. (2008) 'Learning in an immersive digital theatre', *Advances in Space Research*, 42:11 1848–54.

Sutcliffe, H. (2011) *A Report on Responsible Research and Innovation* (Brussels: Matter).

Sutcliffe, S. and Court, J. (2005) *Evidence-Based Policymaking: What Is It? How Does It Work? What Relevance for Developing Countries?* (London: Overseas Development Institute).

Sutcliffe, S. and Court, J. (2006) *A Toolkit for Progressive Policymakers in Developing Countries* (London: Overseas Development Institute). Retrieved 18 March 2015 at: www.odi.org.uk/sites/odi.org.uk/files/odi-assets/publications-opinion-files/190.pdf.

Sutton, G.V. (1995) *Science for a Polite Society: Gender, Culture and the Demonstration of Enlightenment* (Oxford: Westview Press).

Teacher, A.G.F., Griffiths, D.J., Hodgson, D.J. and Inger, R. (2013) 'Smartphones in ecology and evolution: a guide for the app-rehensive', *Ecology and Evolution*, 3:16 5268–78.

Terras, M. (2012) 'The verdict: is blogging or tweeting about research papers worth it?' Retrieved 1 December 2015 at: www.http://blogs.lse.ac.uk/impactofsocialsciences/2012/04/19/blog-tweeting-papers-worth-it/.

Thaler, R.H. and Sunstein, C.R. (2008) *Nudge: Improving Decisions about Health, Wealth, and Happiness* (New Haven, CT: Yale University Press).

The Royal Society (1985) *The Public Understanding of Science* (London: The Royal Society).

Thody, A. (2006) *Writing and Presenting Research* (London: Sage).

Thompson, P.B. (2012) 'Ethics and risk communication', *Science Communication*, 34:5 618–41.

Thorpe, C. and Gregory, J. (2010) 'Producing the post-Fordist public: the political economy of public engagement with science', *Science as Culture*, 19:3 273–301.

Thorpe, V. and Rogers, R. (2011) 'Women bloggers call for a stop to "hateful" trolling by misogynist men', *The Guardian Blogs*. Retrieved 25 March 2015 at: www.theguardian.com/world/2011/nov/05/women-bloggers-hateful-trolling.

TNS Opinion and Social (2013) *Special Eurobarometer 399: Cultural Access and Participation*. Retrieved 10 July 2014 at: http://ec.europa.eu/public_opinion/archives/ebs/ebs_399_en.pdf.

Torjesen, I. (2014) 'NHS England postpones roll-out of Care.data programme by six months', *British Medical Journal*, 348 g.1689.

Trench, B. (2008). 'Towards an analytical framework of science communication models', in Cheng, D., Claessens, M., Gascoigne, T., Metcalfe, J., Schiele, B. and Shi, S. (eds) *Communicating Science in Social Contexts: New Models, New Practices* (New York: Springer) pp. 119–35.

Tryon, E. and Ross, J.A. (2012) 'A Community–University Exchange Project Modeled after Europe's Science Shops', *Journal of Higher Education Outreach & Engagement*, 16:2 197–211.

TSO (2009) *Managing Successful Projects with Prince2®* (London: The Stationery Office).

Turner, S. (2007) 'Public sociology and democratic theory', *Sociology*, 41:5 785–98.

United Nations (2011) *Guidelines on Citizens' Engagement for Development Management and Public Governance* (New York: United Nations Department of Economic and Social Affairs).

United Nations (2013) *Citizen Engagement and the Post-2015 Development Agenda Report of the Expert Group Meeting* (New York: United Nations).

van Dijck, J. (2013a) *The Culture of Connectivity: A Critical History of Social Media* (Oxford: Oxford University Press).

van Dijck, J. (2013b) '"You have one identity": performing the self on Facebook and LinkedIn', *Media, Culture & Society*, 35:2 199–215.

van Noorden, R. (2014) 'Scientists and the social network', *Nature*, 512, 126–9.

Velarde, G. (2001) *Designing Exhibitions: Museums, Heritage Trade and World Fairs*, second edition (Aldershot: Ashgate).

Vitos, M., Stevens, M., Lewis, J. and Hakley, M. (2013) 'Making local knowledge matter: supporting non-literate people to monitor poaching in Congo', *Third Annual Symposium on Computing for Development* (ACM DEV 2013), doi: 0.1145/2442882.2442884.

Ward, B. (2008) 'Explaining controversial issues to the media and public', *SciDevNet*. Retrieved 2 March 2015 at: www.scidev.net/global/communication/practical-guide/explaining-controversial-issues-to-the-media-and-t.html.

Watchelder, J. (2003) 'Democratising science: various routes and visions of Dutch science shops', *Public Understanding of Science*, 28:2 244–73.

Weitkamp, E. (2012) 'Researchers need help to speak the language of policy', *Research Europe*. Retrieved 18 March 2015 at: http://eprints.uwe.ac.uk/17089/2/Research_php.mht.

Weitkamp, E. and Mermikides, A. (in preparation) 'Audience engagement with Bloodlines'.

Wenger, E. (1998) *Communities of Practice: Learning, Meaning, and Identity* (Cambridge: Cambridge University Press).

Wheeler, S. (2012) 'Digital literacies for engagement in emerging online cultures', *eLC Research Paper Series*, 5 14–25.

White, G. (2012) 'On immersive theatre', *Theatre Research International*, 37:3 221–35.

Wiggins, A. and Crowston, K. (2015) 'Surveying the citizen science landscape', *First Monday*, 20:1. Retrieved 23 July 2015 at: http://firstmonday. org/ojs/index.php/fm/article/view/5520.

Wiles, R. (2013) *What Are Qualitative Research Ethics?* (London: Bloomsbury Academic).

Wilkinson, C. (2010) 'Science and the citizen', in Brake, M. and Weitkamp, E. (eds) *Introducing Science Communication* (Basingstoke: Palgrave Macmillan) pp. 52–76.

Wilkinson, C. (2012) *The ESRC Festival of Social Science: Learning and Success* (Swindon: ESRC).

Wilkinson, C. (2013) *Community Engagement and Mobilisation: Critique of a Public Dialogue Day* (Swindon: ESRC).

Wilkinson, C. and Weitkamp, E. (2013) 'A case study in serendipity? Environmental researchers' use of traditional and social media for dissemination'. *PLoS ONE*, 8:12 e84339.

Wilkinson, C., Bultitude, K. and Dawson, E. (2011b) '"Oh yes, robots! People like robots; the robot people should do something": perspectives and prospects in public engagement with robotics', *Science Communication*, 33:3 367–97.

Wilkinson, C., Dawson, E. and Bultitude, K. (2011a) '"Younger people have like more of an imagination, no offence": participant perspectives on public engagement', *International Journal of Science Education, Part B: Communication and Public Engagement*, 2 (1) 43–61.

Wilkinson, H. (2014) 'Sharing worlds: managing complex community relationships in challenging times', in Maile, S. and Griffiths, D. (eds) *Public Engagement and Social Science* (Bristol: Policy Press) pp. 201–14.

Wilsdon, J. and Willis, J. (2004) *See-Through Science: Why Public Engagement Needs to Move Upstream* (London: Demos).

Wilson, S. (2010) *Art + Science Now: How Scientific Research and Technological Innovation Are Becoming Key to 21st-Century Aesthetics* (London: Thames and Hudson).

Wolinsky, H. (2010) 'Of guerrillas and cafés: scientists are experimenting with new initiatives to talk to the people', *EMBO Reports*, 11:4 263–6.

Woolf, F. (2004) *Partnerships for Learning: A Guide to Evaluating Art Education Projects* (London: Arts Council for England).

World Bank (2015) 'Internet users (per 100 people)'. Retrieved 13 March 2015 at: http://data.worldbank.org/indicator/IT.NET.USER.P2.

Worpole, K. (1991) 'The age of leisure', in Corner, J. and Harvey, S. (eds)

Enterprise and Heritage: Cross-currents of National Culture (London: Routledge) pp. 137–50.

Zhou, Z., Jin, X.-L., Vogel, D.R., Fang, Y. and Chen, X. (2011) 'Individual motivations and demographic differences in social virtual world uses: an exploratory investigation in Second Life', *International Journal of Information Management*, 31:3 261–71.

Zwijnenberg, R. (2009) 'Art, the life sciences and the humanities: in search of a relationship', preface to Reichle, I., *Art in the Age of Technoscience. Genetic Engineering, Robotics and Artificial Life in Contemporary Art* (New York: Springer-Wien), pp. xiii–xxix.

Index